Disinventing and Reconstituting Languages

BILINGUAL EDUCATION AND BILINGUALISM
Series Editors: Professor Nancy H. Hornberger, *University of Pennsylvania, Philadelphia, USA* and Professor Colin Baker, *University of Wales, Bangor, Wales, Great Britain*

Recent Books in the Series
Trilingualism in Family, School and Community
Charlotte Hoffmann and Jehannes Ytsma (eds)
Multilingual Classroom Ecologies
Angela Creese and Peter Martin (eds)
Negotiation of Identities in Multilingual Contexts
Aneta Pavlenko and Adrian Blackledge (eds)
Beyond the Beginnings: Literacy Interventions for Upper Elementary English Language Learners
Angela Carrasquillo, Stephen B. Kucer and Ruth Abrams
Bilingualism and Language Pedagogy
Janina Brutt-Griffler and Manka Varghese (eds)
Language Learning and Teacher Education: A Sociocultural Approach
Margaret R. Hawkins (ed.)
The English Vernacular Divide: Postcolonial Language Politics and Practice
Vaidehi Ramanathan
Bilingual Education in South America
Anne-Marie de Mejía (ed.)
Teacher Collaboration and Talk in Multilingual Classrooms
Angela Creese
Words and Worlds: World Languages Review
F. Martí, P. Ortega, I. Idiazabal, A. Barreña, P. Juaristi, C. Junyent, B. Uranga and E. Amorrortu
Language and Aging in Multilingual Contexts
Kees de Bot and Sinfree Makoni
Foundations of Bilingual Education and Bilingualism (4th edn)
Colin Baker
Bilingual Minds: Emotional Experience, Expression and Representation
Aneta Pavlenko (ed.)
Raising Bilingual-Biliterate Children in Monolingual Cultures
Stephen J. Caldas
Language, Space and Power: A Critical Look at Bilingual Education
Samina Hadi-Tabassum
Developing Minority Language Resources
Guadalupe Valdés, Joshua A. Fishman, Rebecca Chávez and William Pérez
Language Loyalty, Language Planning and Language Revitalization: Recent Writings and Reflections from Joshua A. Fishman
Nancy H. Hornberger and Martin Pütz (eds)
Language Loyalty, Continuity and Change: Joshua A. Fishman's Contributions to International Sociolinguistics
Ofelia Garcia, Rakhmiel Peltz and Harold Schiffman
Bilingual Education: An Introductory Reader
Ofelia García and Colin Baker (eds)

For more details of these or any other of our publications, please contact:
**Multilingual Matters, Frankfurt Lodge, Clevedon Hall,
Victoria Road, Clevedon, BS21 7HH, England
http://www.multilingual-matters.com**

BILINGUAL EDUCATION AND BILINGUALISM 62
Series Editors: Nancy H. Hornberger and Colin Baker

Disinventing and Reconstituting Languages

Edited by
Sinfree Makoni and Alastair Pennycook

MULTILINGUAL MATTERS LTD
Clevedon • Buffalo • Toronto

Dedicated to
Sibusisiwe Dube-Makoni,
my life-long partner

Library of Congress Cataloging in Publication Data
Disinventing and Reconstituting Languages/Edited by Sinfree Makoni and Alastair Pennycook.
Bilingual Education and Bilingualism: 62
1. Language and languages. I. Makoni, Sinfree. II. Pennycook, Alastair. III. Series.
P107.D57 2006
400–dc22   2006014472

British Library Cataloguing in Publication Data
A catalogue entry for this book is available from the British Library.

ISBN 1-85359-924-7 / EAN 978-1-85359-924-8 (hbk)
ISBN 1-85359-923-9 / EAN 978-1-85359-923-1 (pbk)

Multilingual Matters Ltd
UK: Frankfurt Lodge, Clevedon Hall, Victoria Road, Clevedon BS21 7HH.
USA: UTP, 2250 Military Road, Tonawanda, NY 14150, USA.
Canada: UTP, 5201 Dufferin Street, North York, Ontario M3H 5T8, Canada.

Copyright © 2007 Sinfree Makoni, Alastair Pennycook and the authors of individual chapters.

All rights reserved. No part of this work may be reproduced in any form or by any means without permission in writing from the publisher.

The policy of Multilingual Matters/Channel View Publications is to use papers that are natural, renewable and recyclable products, made from wood grown in sustainable forests. In the manufacturing process of our books, and to further support our policy, preference is given to printers that have FSC and PEFC Chain of Custody accreditation. The FSC and/or PEFC logos will appear on those books where full accreditation has been granted to the printer concerned.

Typeset by Wordworks Ltd.

Contents

The Contributors vii

Foreword
Ofelia García xi

1 Disinventing and Reconstituting Languages
  Sinfree Makoni and Alastair Pennycook. 1

2 Then There were Languages: Bahasa Indonesia was One Among Many
  Ariel Heryanto 42

3 Critical Historiography: Does Language Planning in Africa Need a Construct of Language as Part of its Theoretical Apparatus?
  Sinfree Makoni and Pedzisai Mashiri 62

4 The Myth of English as an International Language
  Alastair Pennycook. 90

5 Beyond 'Language': Linguistic Imperialism, Sign Languages and Linguistic Anthropology
  Jan Branson and Don Miller 116

6 Entering a Culture Quietly: Writing and Cultural Survival in Indigenous Education in Brazil
  Lynn Mario T. Menezes de Souza. 135

7 A Linguistics of Communicative Activity
  Steven L. Thorne and James P. Lantolf 170

8 (Dis)inventing Discourse: Examples from Black Culture and Hiphop Rap/Discourse
  Elaine Richardson 196

9 Educational Materials Reflecting Heteroglossia: Disinventing Ethnolinguistic Differences in Bosnia-Herzegovina
   Brigitta Busch and Jürgen Schick 216

10 After Disinvention: Possibilities for Communication, Community and Competence
   Suresh Canagarajah 233

Index 240

The Contributors

Jan Branson is Professor of Education and Director of the National Institute for Deaf Studies and Sign Language Research at La Trobe University in Melbourne, Australia. Her research has focused on the comparative understanding of processes of social and cultural discrimination and oppression. Jan pioneered Women's Studies in Australia, researched comparative studies of the role of women in Australia and Indonesia and then moved to the study of the cultural construction of 'the disabled' leading to the intensive study of the language and culture of Deaf communities in Australia, Indonesia and Thailand.

Brigitta Busch is a Senior Research Fellow at the Department of Applied Linguistics, University of Vienna. Between 1999 and 2003 she was the head of the Centre for Intercultural Studies at the University of Klagenfurt. During her work as an expert for the Council of Europe's Confidence-Building Measures Programme, she was involved in a number of projects in Eastern and South-Eastern Europe. Her main research interests focus on: sociolinguistics, discourse analysis, media policies and intercultural communication. Recent publications include *Sprachen im Disput. Medien und Öffentlichkeit in multilingualen Gesellschaften* (Klagenfurt: Drava, 2004) and *Language, Discourse and Borders* (co-edited with Helen Kelly-Holmes), Current Issues in Language and Society series (Clevedon: Multilingual Matters, 2004).

Suresh Canagarajah is Professor of English at Baruch College and the Graduate Center of the City University of New York. His book *Resisting Linguistic Imperialism in English Teaching* (Oxford University Press, 1999) won the Mina P. Shaughnessy Award by the Modern Language Association for the best 'research publication in the field of teaching English language, literature, rhetoric and composition.' His subsequent book *Geopolitics of Academic Writing* (University of Pittsburgh Press, 2002) won the Gary Olson Award by the Association of the Teachers of Advanced Composition for the best book in social and rhetorical theory. Suresh edits the *TESOL Quarterly*.

Ariel Heryanto is Senior Lecturer, and Convener of the Indonesian Program, Asia Institute at The University of Melbourne. His main interest has revolved around issues of cultural signifying practices, especially the everyday politics of identity and representation. Thus, he is interested in the study of semantic history, discourse analysis, media, popular culture, ethnicity, nationality, hybridity and diasporas. His recent books are *State Terrorism and Political Identity in Indonesia; Fatally Belonging* (Routledge, 2006) and *Challenging Authoritarianism in South-East Asia: Comparing Indonesia and Malaysia* (co-edited with Sumit Mandal) (Routledge Curzon, 2003).

James P. Lantolf is the Greer Professor in Language Acquisition and Applied Linguistics in the Department of Linguistics and Applied Language Studies at Penn State University. He is also Director of the Center for Language Acquisition and co-Director of CALPER (Center for Advanced Language Proficiency Education and Research). He was President of the American Association for Applied Linguistics (2004–05) and Program Chair for AAAL's Annual Conference (Portland, Oregon, May 2004). He served as co-editor of *Applied Linguistics* (1995–2000). He has been a visiting scholar at the universities of Auckland, Melbourne, Nottingham, Rome and Kassel. His research focuses on Sociocultural theory and second language learning and he has published numerous articles and book chapters in this area. He has also published a co-edited volume (with G. Appel) *Vygotskian Approaches to Second Language Research* (Ablex, 1994), an edited volume, *Sociocultural Theory and Second Language Learning* (Oxford University Press, 2000), and a co-authored book (with S.T. Thorne), *Sociocultural Theory and the Genesis of Second Language Development* (Oxford University Press, 2006).

Sinfree Makoni is a Pan Africanist. He has held professional appointments in southern Africa and currently teaches at Pennyslvania State University in the US. He is the co-author of *Language and Aging in Multilingual Contexts* (2005), co-editor of *Black Linguistics: Language, Society and Politics in Africa and the Americas* (2003), *Ageing in Africa: Sociolinguistic and Anthropological Approaches* ((2002), *Freedom and Discipline: Essays in Applied Linguistics from Southern Africa* (2001) and *Language and Institutions in Africa* (1999). His main research interests are in language in urban contexts, language and health and language planning.

Lynn Mario T. Menezes de Souza is Associate Professor of the Department of Modern Languages at the University of São Paulo, Brazil. With a background in linguistics, applied linguistics, semiotics and post-colonial theory, he has published widely in these areas in Brazil and abroad. His recent research has focused on indigenous education and literacies.

The Contributors

Pedzisai Mashiri is the Executive Dean of the Faculty of Arts at the University of Zimbabwe (2006–2009). He is also a senior lecturer in sociolinguistics and onomastics at the same institution, and a former visiting Professor of Folklore at the University of California Santa Cruz (2003).

Don Miller is Adjunct Associate Professor in the National Institute for Deaf Studies and Sign Language Research at La Trobe University in Melbourne, Australia. An anthropologist, Don has focused on the relationship between religion and the reproduction of structured social inequalities in India, Indonesia and Thailand and has worked jointly with Jan Branson on the cultural construction of 'the disabled' and the language and culture of deaf communities in Australia, Indonesia and Thailand.

Alastair Pennycook is concerned with how we understand language in relation to globalization, colonial history, identity, popular culture and pedagogy. Publications have therefore focused on topics such as *The Cultural Politics of English as an International Language* (Longman, 1994), *English and the Discourses of Colonialism* (Routledge, 1998), *Critical Applied Linguistics: A Critical Introduction* (Lawrence Erlbaum, 2001) and *Global Englishes and Transcultural Flows* (Routledge, in press). This current book on disinvention is the result of a sustained dialogue with Sinfree Makoni on language, politics and the world. Alastair is Professor of Language in Education at the University of Technology Sydney.

Elaine Richardson is interested in language and literacy studies. Her book *African American Literacies* (Routledge, 2003) explores the use of African American language and literacy traditions in the teaching of literacy and composition. This point of view begins with the premise that African Americans have language and literacy traditions that are intellectually worthy and that represent particular ways of being in the world. Students are taught to analyse, contextualize, historicize and write the languages they speak/write and to do the same for the written and spoken languages of the dominant society. Another book-length project, *Hip Hop Literacies* (Routledge, in press) focuses on the knowledge and meaning making systems represented in hip hop language usage (broadly defined) as an extension of Black folk cultural traditions. She is Associate Professor of English and Applied Linguistics at Penn State.

Jürgen Schick (MA), born in 1968, has a law degree of the University of Graz in Austria, where he graduated in 1992. He continued his education and research at the European Peace University in Stadtschlaining in Austria, and attended several other courses and training programmes thereafter. From 1994 until 1997 he worked for the NGO World University

Service in support of universities in Bosnia. Since 1997 he has been the Austrian Education Coordinator for Bosnia and Herzegovina on behalf of the Austrian Federal Ministry of Education, Science and Culture as well as the NGO KulturKontakt. He currently lives with his wife and son in Sarajevo.

Steve Thorne is the Associate Director of the Center for Language Acquisition and Assistant Professor in the department of Linguistics and Applied Language Studies at the Pennsylvania State University. His research areas include cultural-historical activity theory, additional language learning and mediated communication, with developing interests in cognitive linguistics and neuroscience. Recent publications include articles in *The Modern Language Journal, Language Learning & Technology, The CALICO Journal* and *Intelligence*. Books include a co-edited volume on *Internet-mediated Intercultural Foreign Language Education* (Thomson/Heinle, 2006) and the co-authored monograph *Sociocultural Theory and the Genesis of Second Language Development* (Oxford University Press, 2006).

Foreword
Intervening Discourses, Representations and Conceptualizations of Language

OFELIA GARCÍA

Rarely does one pick up a book that decenters epistemological knowledge and simultaneously expands understandings in dynamic ways, as it presents an inter-related perspective. Makoni and Pennycook's *Disinventing and Reconstituting Languages* is such a book. For the reader, and particularly for those of us who work on language scholarship, the image of the *banyan tree*, referred to in Makoni and Mashiri's chapter, comes to mind. Our understandings grow up, out and down at the same time. Although the book *disinvents* language, asking us to question languages, conceptions of language and metalanguages, it also *reconstitutes* it, warning us that the results of the invention are *real*, but that we must rethink what the social, political and economic consequences would be if we no longer posited the existence of separate languages. In other words, this book argues that the invention of languages has implications that are situated in very material language effects. Rooted firmly on the communication that takes place among people and not on language as 'a thing that leads a life of its own outside and above human beings' (Yngve, 1996: 28), the book takes a step beyond the allegations of language as imagined or invented and yet roots itself firmly in the discursive field that constitutes acts of *languaging*.

The book achieves its original dynamism by presenting the ideology of Dis/Invention posited by the two editors and the content of the individual chapters in ways that are inter-related and mutually implicated and that juxtapose different historical and philosophical scholarly traditions, spatializing time. Drawing from the scholarship on the invention of Africa (Makoni) and the invention of English (Pennycook), the editors refer to a dialectic process in which language and nation were constructed together. But Makoni and Pennycook's disinvention of language is also rooted in Hopper's concept of 'emergent grammar' and his claim that the systematicity of language is just an illusion, a regulated process of repetition in discourse, a product of performative acts. Signification is produced by the partial settling or 'sedimentation' of frequently used forms. And so language itself has been mediated by and constrained by, historically sedimented patterns of usage.

The process of disinvention of languages that the book proposes calls into question many of the significant issues that surrounded the study of language in the 20th century and that form the basis of our present understandings of sociolinguistics and applied linguistics in the 21st century. Drawing on different situations of language dis/invention – the inventing of Bahasa Indonesian, language planning in southern Africa, English as an international language, sign language, Hiphop Rap/Discourse, language education in different contexts – the book challenges basic assumptions. For me, who has spent a lifetime studying language in schools and particularly bilingual education, this book has engaged me in further reflection about questions that I thought I had settled long ago.

Since I started teaching in 1970, I have defended the use of the students' mother tongue in their education and particularly the use of Spanish in teaching US Latinos. But in demonstrating how the indigenous languages of Africa were constructed, Makoni and Pennycook remind me that Spanish was also 'administratively assigned' to the colonized population and continues to be so in many parts of Latin America. In fact, Spanish has been shown to create and accentuate many of the social differences in Latin America. Although in 1970, most of my students in New York City were Spanish-speaking Puerto Ricans, leading us to 'forget' the genocide of the Taíno indians and their language, today New York City Latino students are increasingly users of other languages, besides Spanish, confronting all of us with the complexity of identifying the students' mother tongue, or what it means to be a 'Spanish-speaker.'

Makoni contends that, instead of focusing on the invented indigenous languages, African language policy should be looking at urban vernaculars that are not 'hermetically sealed'. This also reminds me that my New York Puerto Rican students in the 1970s were not simply users of Spanish. Living side by side with urban African Americans and increasingly in contact with speakers of other contact-Spanishes, my students' vernacular often had little to do with either the 'standard English' of the autonomous texts used in schools, or the 'standard Spanish' that was purported to be their link to a better education in the bilingual education programs.

The bilingual education models that I have worked with throughout my professional career have always been founded on notions of difference, ideas that in the United States are still considered inappropriate and maybe even 'dangerous.' But Makoni and Pennycook remind us that, if language is an invention, then there is no reason to separate students into ESL classes or to advocate for bilingual education that simply is 'monolingual pluralization.' This book has engaged me in a key question that must surround the ways in which we think about bilingual education in the future: What would language education look like if we no longer posited the existence of separate languages? How would we teach bilingually in ways that reflect people's use of language and not simply people as language users?

This book proposes an innovative model of language education based on what the authors call 'translingual language practices'. Cen Williams coined the Welsh term *trawysieithu* (translanguaging) to refer to a language education pedagogy where students heard or read a lesson in one language and developed their work in the other. Baker (2003) clarifies that translanguaging is not about code-switching, but rather about an arrangement that normalizes bilingualism without diglossic functional separation. But in disinventing language, Makoni and Pennycook go way beyond William's pedagogical innovation. Language classification has been a construct to control variety and difference and thus it excludes mixed language practices, creoles and other ways of using languages in multilingual networks. Language teaching then, as Canagarajah tells us in his chapter, should aim not at mastery of an invented 'target language', but at developing negotiation strategies and a repertoire of codes. Students should, Canagarajah tells us, 'shuttle between' repertoires. And so the notion of 'Spanglish' which has been so controversial in the United States, is as invented as is the notion of Spanish or English. And the question that we should be asking is not whether code-switching is an appropriate responsible pedagogy, or whether 'translanguaging' is valuable in itself or whether 'Spanglish' should be accepted in the classroom. If language is an invention, then we must observe closely the way in which people use language and base our pedagogical practices on that use, and not on what the school system says are valuable practices.

Throughout my professional life I have defended multilingualism and linguistic diversity and have supported language policy that enables peoples to use their languages in public. I have often used language census data to show the strength of language diversity in the United States, but Makoni and Pennycook remind me that the enumerability of languages is an invention and acts as a measure to contain and control. With Phillipson I have argued against the linguistic imperialism of the United States, especially with regards to their language minorities. But Makoni and Pennycook critique linguistic imperialism by pointing out that the imposition is not of English as a language, but of the ways in which speech forms are constructed into languages. Multilingualism and linguistic human rights, this book tells us, may indeed romanticize plurality rather than question the language inventions and critique the damage it has caused. What the world needs, Makoni and Mashiri propose, is not linguistic human rights, but 'linguistic citizenship' (Stroud, 2001), interaction 'governed by stylistic and strategic deployment of numerous styles and a range of languages'. This is a novel idea, one that challenges, expands and builds on linguistic human rights. It is people themselves that have rights to use their styles and ranges of languages in whichever way they do. And our work is to support people, enhance communication between them and create 'communicative contexts which would enhance people's abilities to carry out their activities to improve their social welfare.'

This book, especially through the position of Pennycook, also argues against what I had believed to be accurate ideas about English in the 21st century – the fact that there are many Englishes, and that English is a world or global language. Pennycook reminds us that English is not a language per se, but could be considered a discursive field – neoliberalism, globalization, human capital. What is important is to study what people do with English, their Englishing, that is, their investments, desires and performances in English.

When I was asked to write this Foreword, I had no idea that I would find myself questioning some of my 'venerable' assumptions about language and education or language and minority rights. What is most valuable about this book is that it disinvents language without dismissing the effects that it has had in our scholarship, in our teaching, in our societies, in our schools. It links pre-modern discursive and communicative use with the present-day desires and performances that technology juxtaposes as people engage in the act of *languaging*. It offers then, not just a criticism of the invention of language, an intervention at the level of discourse, representations and conceptualization, but a way of reconstituting these to facilitate people's ability to carry out their activities to improve their social welfare.

Nowhere is this proposition more problematic than in school. And yet, as the children's linguistic heterogeneity is brought closer together through the communication enabled by technology in the 21st century, the distance between the invented languages that schools have chosen to teach and assess in and the children's practices only grows larger. Translation of instructional material, offering the tests in the child's language, bilingual teachers, bilingual pedagogy is not enough, for it is based on an invention and it rarely reflects the ways in which children communicate. The value of Makoni and Pennycook's proposition is precisely that it makes evident, at least to me, that schooling is not about improving children's social welfare. The Dis/Invention paradigm facilitates for all of us who take it seriously, the ability to become aware and move beyond the ways in which language has been thought about in the real world and in particularly in sociolinguistic and applied linguistic scholarship.

References

Baker, C. (2003) Biliteracy and transliteracy in Wales: Language planning and the Welsh National Curriculum. In N. Hornberger (ed.) *Continua of Biliteracy* (pp. 71–90). Clevedon: Multilingual Matters.

Stroud, P. (2001) African mother tongues and the politics of language: Linguistic citizenship versus linguistic human rights. *Journal of Multilingual and Multicultural Development* 22 (4), 339–353.

Yngve, V. (1996) *From Grammar to Science: New Foundations for General Linguistics*. Amsterdam: John Benjamins.

Chapter 1
Disinventing and Reconstituting Languages

SINFREE MAKONI and ALASTAIR PENNYCOOK

This book starts with the premise that *languages, conceptions of languageness* and the *metalanguages* used to describe them are inventions. By making this claim we are pointing to several interrelated concerns. First, languages were, in the most literal sense, invented, particularly as part of the Christian/colonial and nationalistic projects in different parts of the globe. From Tsonga, Shona, Afrikaans, Runyakitara, chiNyanja in Africa (Harries, 1987; Chimhundu, 1992) or Fijian in the Pacific and Bahasa Malay in Indonesia (Heryanto, 1995) to Inkha in Latin America (Mannheim, 1991) and Hebrew (Kuzar, 2001) in Israel, the history of language inventions is long and well documented. Our interest here is in the naming and development of these languages, not so much as part of a diachronic linguistic focus on the invention of languages but rather as an attempt to propose an alternative, more 'useful notion of history' (Inoue, 2004: 1), a critical historiography that allows for multiple temporalities rather than a linear progression of change and development.

Second, a related interest here is not only in the invention and naming of specific languages but also in the broader processes and contexts of linguistic construction. From this point of view, all languages are social constructions, artifacts analogous to other constructions such as time: The rotation of the earth on its axis is a natural phenomenon, but the measurement of time is an artifact, a convention. When we argue that languages are constructed, we seek to go beyond the obvious point that linguistic criteria are not sufficient to establish the existence of a language (the old language/ dialect boundary debates), in order to identify the important social and semiotic processes that lead to their construction. Social processes include, for example, the development of colonial and nationalist ideologies through literacy programs. Semiotic processes, following Irvine and Gal (2000) include the ways in which various language practices are made invisible (*erasure*), the projection of one level of differentiation onto another (*fractal recursivity*) and the transformation of the sign relationship between linguistic features and the social images with which they are linked (*iconization*). These different social and semiotic processes interact in complex ways, so that nationalism, for example, generates iconization and fractal recursivity, which in turn generate more nationalism as part of an ideological process of homogenization. As Irvine and Gal (2000: 47) describe the process of 'linguistic description' of Senegalese languages by 19th century European linguists, 'The ways these languages were identified, delimited, and mapped, the ways their relationships were interpreted, and even the ways they were described in grammars and dictionaries were all heavily influenced by an ideology of racial and national essences'.

Third, in a parallel process, a linguistic metalanguage – or as we prefer, given its broader coverage, a *metadiscursive regime* (Bauman & Briggs, 2003: 299) – was also invented. Metadiscursive regimes are representations of language which, together with material instantiations of actual occurring language, constitute forms of 'social action, social facts and can function as agents in the exercise of social and political power' (Jaffe, 1999: 15). Alongside or, rather, in direct relation with the invention of languages, therefore, an ideology of languages as separate and enumerable categories was also created. In one of its extreme manifestations, this nominalist view becomes a biological essentialist one in which languages are posited as having identities that correspond to species (Jaffe, 1999: 121; Pennycook, 2004). In its most common guise, this metadiscursive regime treats languages as countable institutions, a view reinforced by the existence of grammars and dictionaries (Joseph, 2004). The enumerability of language has to be understood as part of a broader project of 'governmentality', part of a Eurocentric culture which 'relentlessly codified and observed everything about the non-European ... in so thorough and detailed a manner as to leave no item untouched, no culture unstudied' (Said, 1989: 6; cited in Thomas, 1994: 38). In addition to the enumerability of languages, other aspects of these metadiscursive regimes include the widespread view of language in terms of what Grace (1981; 2005) calls *autonomous texts*. Autonomous texts are those which the speakers would require very limited amounts of contextual information to process, the prototypical mode being the written.

Fourth, these inventions have had very real and material effects. On the one hand, by advocating a view of languages as constructions, our position may be seen as a non-materialist view of language: languages do not exist as real entities in the world and neither do they emerge from or represent real environments; they are, by contrast, the inventions of social, cultural and political movements. On the other hand, we would argue for the very real material effects of linguistic inventions since they influence how languages have been understood, how language policies have been constructed, how education has been pursued, how language tests have been developed and administered, and how people have come to identify with particular labels and at times even to die for them, as the violent nature of ethnic rivalry in Africa, South Asia and elsewhere amply demonstrates. Thus, while the entities around which battles are fought, tests are constructed and language policies are written are inventions, the effects are very real.

Finally, as part of any critical linguistic project, we need a project not only of critique but also one of reconstruction. We need therefore to reconstitute languages, a process that may involve both becoming aware of the history of the construction of languages, and rethinking the ways we look at languages and their relation to identity and geographical location, so that we move beyond notions of linguistic territorialization in which language is linked to a geographical space. Given the real and contemporary effects of these constructions, our intention is not to return to some Edenic pre-colonial era (although we are willing to look to the past to seek inspiration; see Canagarajah, this volume). Rather, our intention is to find ways of rethinking language in the contemporary world, a need arising from an acute awareness that there is all too often a lack of fit between ostensible language problems and the languages promoted as part of the solution (Povinelli, 2002: 26). The broad discursive field of indigeneity and language maintenance, for example, has emerged from a set of particular constructions of the indigenous and of languages that frequently cannot address the current problems faced by disadvantaged people in the contemporary world (Povinelli, 2002).We need to rethink language in order to provide alternative ways forward.

We are not, of course, the first to draw attention to some of these concerns. The invention of languages is reasonably well documented, the problematic assumptions underlying the metalanguage of linguistics have not escaped the attention of some linguists (e.g. Harris, 1980, 1981; Mühlhäusler, 1996; Yngve, 1996) and anthropological linguists have drawn our attention to the ways in which local language ideologies construct languages in particular ways (e.g. Blommaert, 1999b; Kroskrity, 2000). It is our contention, however, that the interrelationship between these elements, the implications for domains of applied linguistics, and the development of strategies for moving forward have not been adequately considered. It is one of the objectives of this book to outline how such strategies can take us beyond a framework only of critique. A central part of our argument, therefore, is that it is not enough to acknowledge that languages have been invented, or that linguistic metalanguage constructs the world in particular ways. Rather, we need to understand the interrelationships among metadiscursive regimes, language inventions, colonial history, language effects, alternative ways of understanding language and strategies of disinvention and reconstitution.

Invention, Imagination, Co-Construction

Our use of the concept of invention locates this work within a particular tradition of historical and philosophical scholarship. In *The Invention of Africa*, Mudimbe (1988) critically examines the different Eurocentric categories that have been used to analyse Africa, dramatizing the distinction between an invented Europe and an invented Africa. Zeleza & Makoni (2006) enumerate seven origins of the name Africa, all of which are non-African in origin. The foreign nature of the origins of the term prompted African Nobel laureate Wole Soyinka (1976/87) to propose alternative names rooted in African languages, *Abibirim* and *Abibiman* from Akan, a language widely spoken in Ghana in West Africa. The term Africa was initially used in Roman times to refer exclusively to North Africa, an area roughly equivalent to modern Libya. Subsequently, Africa was then used to refer to the entire continent; more recently it tends to be restricted to sub-Saharan Africa and is divorced from its original usage.

The key issue is that the ways in which notions about Africa are understood have changed over the years, and that, in a very real sense, the idea of Africa is a European construct. The argument that Africa is a European idea is effectively articulated by Nyerere, as quoted by Mazrui (1967):

> Thus, to use Nyerere's rhetoric 'Africans, all over the continent, without a word being spoken either from one individual to another or from one country to another, looked at the European, looked at one another, and knew that in relation to the European they were one. In relation to another continent, this continent was one: this was the logic of the situation'. (Mazrui, 1967: 47)

A similar point can be made for Aboriginal Australians' identification with each other as Indigenous, or for the possibility of identifying as Indian (Krishnaswamy & Burde, 1998).

Crucially, however, it is not only the geographical and political space of Africa that was constructed through European eyes, but also African history, languages and traditions. As Terence Ranger (1983) argued in his influential essay, *The Invention of Tradition in Colonial Africa*, what came to count as tradition was often a retrospective image constructed in colonial interests. There are at least four distinct ways in which Africa is constructed: Africa as biology, as image, as space, as memory. The invention of Africa and African tradition, furthermore, was part of the massive 19th century project of invention, with Europeans inventing both their own histories and those of the people they colonized (Hobsbawm & Ranger, 1983; and see Pennycook, this volume).

The concept of invention is relevant to both colonial and contemporary post-colonial metropolitan contexts. Hobsbawm and Ranger (1983: 1) use the term to describe those traditions which on the one hand appear to be relatively old, but which 'in reality are quite recent in origin': 'Novelty is no less novel for being able to dress easily as antiquity' (Hobsbawm & Ranger, 1983: 3). The Scottish kilt, for example, which, as well as the Highland culture of which it is supposed to be an integral part, is often presented as if it has been part of Scots culture since time immemorial, is a relatively recent creation. In the 18th century, Gaelic, which is thought of as one of the defining features of Highland Scots, was referred to as Irish. The 19th Century Gothic style used for buildings such as the British Houses of Parliament was also part of the creation of an illusion of a long 'factitious' tradition: 'A striking example is the deliberate choice of a Gothic style for the 19th century rebuilding of the British Parliament, and the equally deliberate decision after World War II to rebuild the parliamentary chamber on exactly the same plan' (Hobsbawm & Ranger, 1983: 1–2)

A great deal of historical work has drawn attention to the common project of the invention of history (the processes by which we establish legitimacy, lineage and linkage by reference to a constructed past (see Hobsbawm, 1983, Ranger 1983, Wallerstein, 2000)). As Cohn (1996) and Wallerstein (2000) argue, a major aspect of the British colonial project in India was to turn Indian languages, culture and knowledge into objects of European knowledge, to invent an India not in Britain's image, but in Britain's ideal of what India should look like. This project of invention needs, therefore, to be seen not merely as part of European attempts to design the world in their own image, but rather as part of the process of constructing the history of others for them, which was a cornerstone of European governance and surveillance of the world. Although this process was perhaps most self-evident in the late 19th century and early 20th centuries in colonial times, it developed as a form of national-imaginary whose original focus was the European nation state.

It is this European national imagination that Ranger has in mind when he writes:

> The 1870s, 1880s and 1890s were a time of a great flowering of European traditions – ecclesiastical, educational, military, republican and monar-

chical. They were also the time of the European rush into Africa. There were many complex connections between the two processes. (Ranger, 1983: 211)

As Ranger suggests for Africa, and Cohn (1983) for India, the invention of traditions became a crucial part of colonial rule as Europeans sought to justify their presence and redefine the colonized societies in new terms. According to Hardt and Negri:

> British administrators had to write their own 'Indian history' to sustain and further the interests of colonial rule. The British had to historicize the Indian past in order to have access to it and to put it to work. The British creation of an Indian history, however, like the formation of the colonial state, could be achieved only by imposing European colonial logics and models of Indian reality. (Hardt & Negri, 2000: 126)

Invented traditions derive their strength from compulsory repetition, such as the wearing of wigs by British judges. It is important in this discussion of invented tradition to keep the notions of tradition and custom separate: 'The object and characteristic of traditions, including invented ones, is invariance. Custom cannot afford to be invariant because even in traditional societies life is not so' (Hobsbawm, 1983: 2). While custom is therefore a changing and dynamic space, tradition is all too often a retrospective construction of stasis, an invention of a prior way of being that is used to justify supposed historical continuity. Similarly, when we talk of the invention of languages, we are looking at the construction of linear histories that imply particular origins; we are not suggesting that language use itself is anything but dynamic and changing.

In questioning the invention of tradition, we should of course also be wary of casting notions of tradition aside. In African historiography it is not so much modernity that has been a source of controversy as the notion of tradition itself (Spear, 2003). Traditions have endured because (while creating the impression of timelessness) they have survived owing to an ongoing dialogical tension between social and historical realities. According to Vansina (1990), 'tradition is a robust and enduring endogenous process which represents, contrary to ahistorical expectations, fundamental continuities which shape the futures of those who hold them'. In African historiography, it is not language per se that is of central importance, but discourse. Tradition is one type of discourse, with different traditions having different discourses through which their individual histories are articulated.

Our understanding of invention links closely with what Blommaert (1999a: 104) calls the 'discovery attitude', the defining aspect of which is that, prior to colonization, the colonial territories were a blank slate on which Europeans had to map their categories. The categories that were created included names of ethnic groups, languages, and how they were to be described. The categories are of interest not only theoretically, but because of their impact on social life. Another concept related to invention is Said's 'being there' (Said, 1985: 156–7). The very fact of having been present in Africa, in the Middle East, India or South-East Asia, irrespective of length of stay or nature of association, is deemed adequate to claim knowledge of the native languages and cultures. Everyone who had some knowledge could present this knowledge as 'discovery'.

Missionaries, administrators and other colonial functionaries who wrote grammars and textbooks learnt their own versions of indigenous languages. The local languages that the missionaries and colonial administrators learnt were at times given special names by the colonized persons themselves. For example, in Zimbabwe, the variety of Shona spoken by the priests was referred to as *chibaba* – the language of the priest. These invented indigenous languages arose throughout the European empires and central to the claims being made is that the languages as they were described were products of the inadequate language skills of the missionary linguists. In other words, linguistic descriptions were what we might call *interlinguistic descriptions* based on European interlanguages (Fenton, 2004: 7).

There are substantial similarities between the notion of 'invention' and Anderson's (1991) 'imagined communities': Both point to the ways in which nations are imagined and narrated into being, and both stress the role of language, literacy and social institutions in that process. While Ranger (2004) has suggested that Anderson's use of 'imagined' may be preferable to his own use of 'invented', since it effectively captures the multidimensionality of the process of construction, we prefer to use what we see as the more dynamic, intentional and complex concerns that underlie the notion of invention. Thus, while Spear's (2003) point is well made that the notion of invention runs the danger of downplaying the agency of the colonized, leaving us with an impression of a gullible and malleable populace, it is also equally (if not more) dangerous to exaggerate the agency of the colonized. Arguments about the agency of the colonized need to foreground the severe constraints within which that agency might have been exercised.

Unlike Anderson, furthermore, we regard both languages and nations as dialectically co-constructed, and thus concur with Joseph (2004) in his critique of the one-sidedness of Anderson's formulation:

Anderson's constructionist approach to nationalism is purchased at the price of an essentialist outlook on languages. It seems a bargain to the sociologist or political scientist, to whom it brings explanatory simplicity not to mention ease. But ... it is a false simplicity. National languages and identities arise in tandem, dialectically, if you like, in a complex process that ought to be our focus of interest and study. (Joseph, 2004: 124)

Important here too is Woolard's argument that

'the historicization of language ... had such profound political reverberations, specifically in relation to consciousness of nation and national belonging, at least two centuries earlier than the conventional dates given for the phenomena of historicism and nationalism on which Anderson depends. (Woolard, 2004: 58)

Thus, while Anderson's notion of imagined community remains important here, it needs to be seen as both a dialectic process, with language and nation constructed together, and as located in a different time frame, with ways of thinking about time and language reframed in relation to nation.

Several important issues emerge here. First, the invention of tradition is about the creation of a past into which the present is inserted. Thus, these constructed histories are also about the constructed present. Secondly, a particular type of relationship between past and present is implied here, one characterized by linear development. Such a developmental view of history, which sees a continuous line of progress between the past and the present constitutes a very particular way of understanding time and change. We shall return later to discuss alternative and competing views of time and history that are equally plausible. Third, the process of invention was always one of co-construction. That is to say, the position from which others' languages and histories were invented was not a preformed set of extant ideologies, but rather was produced in the process. Thus:

Even if the European national imaginary of colonial states were derived from European imagination of itself, European colonialists were more a work in progress than fully formed, multiple rather than singular, diverse rather than uniform, contradictory rather than consistent, and at times a reflection of the despotism which was produced under colonial rule. (Mamdani, 1996: 39)

European colonizers invented themselves and others in a reciprocal process.

Finally, then, it was not just colonized languages that were invented but also the languages of the colonizers. The invention of languages such as French entailed forging relations between language, citizenship and patriotism, and the military and national service were crucial in that respect. A French Army manual in the late 1800s, for example, made these associations explicit by insisting that recruits be taught that:

> (1) we call our mother tongue the tongue that is spoken by our parents, and in part, by our mothers (that which is) spoken also by our fellow citizens and by the persons who inhabit the same place as we do; (2) our mother tongue is French. (quoted in Weber, 1976: 311 cited from Jaffe, 1999: 84).

The First World War (1914–1918), with its large numbers of recruits and deaths, continued to reinforce these European associations between language and citizenship.

An important starting point for understanding the invention of and specific ways of imagining language is, therefore, within the broader context of colonial invention. Our position that languages are inventions is consistent with observations that many structures, systems and constructs such as tradition, history or ethnicity, which are often thought of as natural parts of society, are inventions of a very specific ideological apparatus. To claim authenticity for such constructs, therefore, is to become subject to very particular discourses of identity. That is to say, while lived contemporary practices may create an authenticity of being and identification with certain traditions, languages and ethnicities, the history behind both their construction and maintenance needs to be understood in terms of its contingent constructedness.

Inventing Languages and Constructing Ways of Thinking about Language

It was the metadiscursive regimes of European thought that produced the histories and the languages of the empire from the materials they found in the field. One of the great projects of European invention was Sir George Abraham Grierson's massive linguistic *Survey of India*, completed in 1928. A central problem for Grierson, as with many other linguists, was to decide on the boundaries between languages and dialects. Dialects tended to be considered spoken forms, while languages were accorded their special status according to other criteria such as regional similarities, family trees or literary forms. One of the problems with this, however, was that while people had terms for their dialects – or at least terms for other people's dialects (their own being considered the way one speaks) – they did not have terms for these larger constructions, 'languages'. As Grierson explained:

> Few natives at the present day are able to comprehend the idea connoted by the words of a language. Dialects they know and understand. They separate them and distinguish them with a meticulous, hair-splitting subtlety, which to us seems unnecessary and absurd, but their minds are not trained to grasp the conception so familiar to us, of a general term embracing a number of interconnected dialects. (Grierson, 1907: 350)

Grierson makes several important moves here. He positions himself as able to perceive the reality of languages while local knowledge is dismissed as on the one hand an irrelevantly hair-splitting obsession with difference and on the other an inability to grasp the broader concept of languages. Having thus opened up a position in favour of a European understanding of superordinate languages, he is then able to explain why:

> ... nearly all the language-names have had to be invented by Europeans. Some of them, such as Bengali, Assamese, and the like, are founded on words which have received English citizenship, and are not real Indian words at all, while others, like 'Hindostani', 'Bihari', and so forth, are based on already existing Indian names of countries and nationalities. (Grierson, 1907: 350)

While it is interesting at one level to observe simply that the names for these new entities were invented, the point of greater significance is that these were not just new names for extant objects (languages pre-existed the naming), but rather the invention and naming of new objects. The naming performatively called the languages into being. As suggested above, this invention of Indian languages has to be seen in the context of the larger colonial archive of knowledge. The British, as Lelyveld (1993: 194) points out, 'developed from their study of Indian languages not only practical advantage but an ideology of languages as separate, autonomous objects in the world, things that could be classified, arranged, and deployed as media of exchange'. This whole project was of course a cornerstone of the Orientalist construction of the colonial subject. Orientalism, suggests Ludden (1993: 261), 'began with the acquisition of the languages needed to gain reliable information about India. Indian languages became a foundation for scientific knowledge of Indian tradition built from data transmitted to Europeans by native experts'.

At the heart of the problem here is the underlying ideology of countability and singularity, reinforced by assumptions of a singular, essentialized language-object situated and physically located in concepts of space founded on a notion of territorialization. The idea of linguistic enumerability and singularity is based on the dual notions of both languages and speakers of those languages being amenable to counting. It has been widely attested that there is a massive disparity between the number of languages that linguists believe exist and the number of languages people report themselves as speaking. Ethnologue, the Christian language preservation society, for example, notes the disparity between the close to 7000 languages that exist in the world according to their 'approach to listing and counting languages as though they were discrete, countable units', and the 40,000 or so names for different languages that are in use. As they point out, 'the definition of language one chooses depends on the purpose one has in identifying a language' (*Ethnologue*, 2005: np).

Nevertheless, many linguists interested in preservation are content to deal in terms of enumerative strategies that on the one hand reduce significant sociolinguistic concerns to the level of arithmetic, and on the other overlook both the problematic history of the construction of such languages and the contemporary interests behind their enumeration:

> Over 95% of the world's spoken languages have fewer than one million native users, some 5000 have less than 100000 speakers and more than 3000 languages have fewer than 10000 speakers. A quarter of the world's spoken languages have fewer than 1000 users, and at least some 500 languages had in 1999 under a hundred speakers. (Skutnabb-Kangas, 2003: 32)

Mühlhäusler (2000: 358) views this position as a continuation of the tradition of segregational linguistics, which insists that 'languages can be distinguished and named'. To abstract languages, to count them as discrete objects, and to count the speakers of such languages, is to reproduce a very particular enumerative strategy. Yet the enumeration of speakers of a language is founded on a 'monolingual norm of speakerhood' (Hill, 2002: 128), a paradoxical state of affairs given that many language counters are also proponents of multilingualism. At the heart of such language enumeration is the same census ideology that has been such a cornerstone of the colonial imaginary (Anderson, 1991; Appadurai, 1993; Leeman, 2004).

Discussing language use in Papua New Guinea, Romaine (1994) asks how we come to terms with the problem that speakers may claim to speak a different language when linguistically it may appear identical. She goes on to point out that the:

> ... very concept of discrete languages is probably a European cultural artifact fostered by procedures such as literacy and standardization.

Any attempt to count distinct languages will be an artifact of classificatory procedures rather than a reflection of communicative practices. (Romaine, 1994: 12)

If the notions of language that form the basis of language planning are artifacts of European thinking, language policies are therefore (albeit unintentionally) agents of the very values which they are seeking to challenge:

Like hygiene (the control of diseases often introduced or spread by colonization), 'vagabondage' and alcoholism, the language question belonged to those problems of largely European making whose relative importance lay in the fact that they legitimatized regulation from above. (Fabian, 1991: 82)

A census ideology founded on the enumerability of languages masks the differences in the way the objects have been conceptualized. For example, although there has been a language question focusing on mother tongues in the Indian census since 1881, the conceptualization of what was being counted has changed radically as the following illustrates (see Pattanayak, 2000: 40):

1881 the language spoken by the child from the cradle;
1891 the language spoken by the parents;
1901 the language of general use;
1921 the language spoken by the parents;
1961 the language spoken by the mother. If the mother is dead, then write the name of the language used in the household.

Although the notion of mother tongue has also been used in other parts of the world it has been conceptualized radically differently as the following census categories from Slovenia show.

1923 the language of thought;
1934 the language of the cultural circle;
1951 the language of day to day;
1961 the language of the household.

The advantage of the term 'invention' is that it points to specific contexts – as well as the specific agendas and conceptual beliefs – in which institutions, structures, language and languages are produced, regulated and constituted. One aspect of colonial governance, as Cohn (1996) points out, was relating the language of command and the command of language. Assuming on the one hand that European languages were identifiable, separable and countable entities, European colonial administrators sought, on the other, to map this same belief onto the contexts they governed. This belief was later extended to include other languages such as sign languages (Branson & Miller, this volume).

The invention of other languages ties in closely with mythologies of origin. Thus an important dimension of understanding invention is to trace the 'harmonies' in the linguistic description of language – in particular, the ways in which the historiographies of speakers of those languages are written. Thus, there are connections between, for example, the various ways in which the linguistic descriptions of Hebrew are written and the histories of Jewish people are written (Kuzar, 2001). In southern Africa, '

> ... the shying away from pidgin and Creole linguistics in discussing the genesis of Afrikaans has been an essential component of the invented community of Afrikaner culture and neo-social Darwinist explanations of the origins of Afrikaans which have dominated Afrikaans historical linguistics. (Brown, 1992: 78)

The linguistic analysis of the origins of Afrikaans corresponded with the social and political theories about the origins of the Afrikaners that they encouraged.

In Africa, after languages were decreed into existence, the first generation of linguists spent their energies writing grammars for their 'own' languages and dialects, a process that provided opportunities for turning 'tribalized' material into describable objects and granting them social and intellectual legitimacy (Chimhundu, 1992). The process of converting the 'tribalized material' also took place in other disciplines, such as ethnography, history, literatures. From the muddled mass of speech styles they saw around them, languages needed identification, codification and control: they needed to be invented: African languages were thus historically European scripts (Makoni, 1998a). The legacy of African languages as European scripts is still felt in the general tendency to regard the representations of languages as synonymous with the languages themselves.

Once the success of the European project of invention was established, other empires sought to emulate it: As Heryanto (1995; this volume) suggests in his discussion of the imposition of Bahasa Indonesia:

> The newly acquired meanings of bahasa were derived from one or more European languages ... At least in the two most widely spoken and influential languages in Indonesia (Malay and Javanese) there was no word for 'language' and no way of, and no need for, expressing its idea until the later part of the past century. (Heryanto, 1995: 28)

As he goes on to argue, the process of making bahasa 'a generic, abstract, and universal category strips off people's vernacular world views' (Heryanto, 1995: 30). Indeed Heryanto argues that Bahasa Indonesia was introduced into *language free communities*.

Samarin (1996) makes a similar point when he suggests that Africa was 'a continent without languages.' This is not of course to suggest that Africans or Indonesians did not use language, but rather that languages as they came to be invented were not part of the linguascape:

> Africans used language in a linguistic sense to communicate with each other, and we have learned that these are beautifully complex and awesomely elegant means of verbal expression, not the primitive jabberings that they were first taken to be. But they were not languages in the socio-cultural sense. There is little in our knowledge of Africa to suggest ethnolinguistic self consciousness. Thus we can say before literacy there were no languages. (Samarin: 1996: 390)

In speaking of 'language free communities' or a 'continent without languages' the point, to be sure, is not that these contexts involved any less language use, but rather that these language users did not speak 'languages'. We need instead to view this through a different lens, not in terms of discrete items but rather in terms of stylistic inventories, stylistic commons, where people ostensibly from different 'language backgrounds' use language.

While many of these invented languages were projected onto their putative speakers as indigenous languages, they were often experienced as mixtures of local and foreign discourses. These constructed languages were administratively assigned to colonized populations as mother tongues and went on to form the basis of so-called *mother tongue education* and *vernacular literacy*. The constructed languages in such cases might have inhibited rather than facilitated literacy. When the constructed languages were introduced into local communities they had the effects of creating, and at times accentuating, social differences. Since the constructed languages could be acquired only through formal education, frequently coupled with Christianity, those who had acquired them tended to have a higher social status than those who were not exposed to them.

Many of the constructed languages were not only based on external norms like Fijian, but more importantly were written in terms of metalinguistic categories derived from other languages, a process that had consequences for the valuation of those languages (Rafael, 1988: 26). That analytical categories are translated from English into Yoruba, for example, does not change the nature of the problem since the translated terms have their origins in a language other than Yoruba (in most cases Latin). If anything, the translation masks the analytical dependency of Yoruba on Latin via English, leading to a misguided conclusion that Yoruba as a linguistic system is equivalent to English. If the objective, as is the case in many language planning projects, is to make Yoruba as a language equivalent to English, then the intervention has to take place at an analytical level and must not be restricted to shifting the sociolinguistic status of Yoruba only, while retaining the use of analytical categories derived from languages other than Yoruba.

Rafael's (1988) study of the Spanish descriptions of Tagalog in the later 16th and early 17th centuries is another good example of this. Latin, as Anderson (1991) also notes, became a language bound up with notions of truth, legitimizing these language descriptions while also acting as both a means and ends for propagating faith.

> As the paradigm of written language, Latin was a descriptive resource: an ideal icon, template, and source of analytical categories for written (mis)representations of Tagalog speech. Castillian mediated this theo-linguistic hierarchy as the language of secular authority, used to frame discursively the 'reduction' of Tagalog to writing. (Errington, 2001: 22)

Within this hierarchy of languages, a written version of Tagalog based on Latin categories was then used for the propagation of religious materials. 'Latin texts licensed descriptive deployment of Latin categories, grounding the division of linguistic descriptive labor in which written European vernaculars mediated between pagan tongues and sacred writ' (Errington, 2001: 23).

Epistemologically, one of the key rhetorical moves of colonialism was to foster, then to mask, the artificiality of indigenous languages and so-called customary laws, presenting them as if they were a natural part of local contexts (Mamdani, 1996; Thomas, 1994). An analysis of the ways the indigenous languages were represented reflects a shift in understanding language from one predicated upon a belief that languages exist in and of themselves outside relations of power, to one in which languages and their descriptions are seen as 'suffused with power relations' (Thomas, 1994: 44). Lest this focus on colonial and Christian contexts suggests that our argument pertains only to colonial epochs, we extend it to postcolonial eras when we focus on the work of the Summer Institute of Linguistics (SIL) (Pennycook & Makoni, 2005; Makoni & Meinhof, 2004), which can be regarded as a 'postcolonial American successor to colonial era missionizing' (Errington, 2001: 21). For the SIL there is a clear connection between linguistics and Christianity: Christian phonetician Pike, for example, saw phonemics as 'a control system blessed of God to preserve tribes from chaos' (quoted in Hvalkof & Aaby, 1981: 37).

The 'writability' (Errington, 2001: 19) or conversion of speech forms into writing and representations of languages such as Tagalog or Yoruba in metalinguistic terms more familiar to Europeans was conducted by Europeans as part of their diverse, and at times conflicting, colonial and Christian interests. By reformulating indigenous languages in terms consistent with their own beliefs and underwritten by comparative philology, the colonial regimes were able to interact through indigenous languages with the colonized in terms not of the choosing of the colonized, but that of the colonizers (Comaroff & Comaroff, 1991). Applying disinvention, by situating language within the total Christian and colonial contexts in a manner partially reminiscent of Fabian (1991), we aim to shed light on how these intellectual and political contexts contributed towards the emergence of specific conceptualizations of language, and how these in turn have shaped our understandings of diverse areas of sociolinguistics, from language planning and language rights to language loss and language maintenance.

Part of our argument, then, is that current approaches to diversity, multilingualism and so forth, all too often start with the enumerative strategy of counting languages and romanticizing a plurality based on these putative language counts. It is our contention that, while opening up questions of diversity with one hand, at the same time such strategies are also reproducing the tropes of colonial invention, overlooking the contested history of language inventions, and ignoring the 'collateral damage' (Grace, 2005: np) that their embedded notions of language may be perpetrating. By rendering diversity a quantitative question of language enumeration, such approaches continue to employ the census strategies of colonialism while missing the qualitative question of where diversity lies.

Metadiscursive Regimes and Epistemic Violence

The construction of metadiscursive regimes to describe language and languages has implications for both language (as a general capacity) and languages as entities. That is to say, although we acknowledge that all humans have language, the way in which both senses of language are understood is constructed through a particular ideological lens dependent in a large measure on specific metadiscursive regimes and the analysts' cultural and historical 'locus of enunciation' (Mignolo, 2000: 116). These metadiscursive regimes are significant because linguists, perhaps more than any other scientists, create the objects of their analysis through the nature and type of metadiscursive regimes that they deploy in their analysis. As Yngve argues, language and grammar:

> ... are theories of theories in the logical domain representing imaginary objects introduced by assumption. Being fictions, they are not the sorts of things that could be innate. To argue otherwise is to confuse fiction with reality, to confuse the logical domain and the physical, to confuse philosophy with science. One cannot have a science that invents its own objects of study and introduces them by assumption. (Yngve: 2004b: 34)

Disinvention here is tied to a question of rethinking understandings of language (such as language as a medium of communication, language as system, language as a describable entity, or language as competence) that tend to be predicated upon notions of uniformity and homogeneity (Canagarajah this volume; Kyeyune, 2004). Drawing attention to new and alternative metaphors is an important strategy aimed at finding a way in which linguists and applied linguists can avoid being imprisoned by their own semiotic categories. In order to understand the development of these regimes, we need to return (as with the invention of languages reviewed above) to the historical origins of particular modes of thought, and the history of linguistic ideologies.

In their discussion of the work of Latour (1993) and Michel Foucault (1970), both of whom, in their different ways, sought to understand how it is that we came to be modern, Bauman & Briggs (2003: 8) suggest that Latour 'misses language, that is, the role of its construction as autonomous and the work of purification and hybridization this entails in making modernity'. By viewing language as only a mode of mediation between the primary domains of science and society, Latour remains 'simply modern here, having succumbed to the definition of language as real and its relegation to the role of carrying out particular modernist functions, such as conveying information' (Bauman & Briggs, 2003: 8). They argue, therefore, for 'the full recognition of language as a domain coequal in this enterprise with Latour's society and nature' (Bauman & Briggs, 2003: 10).

While Foucault (1970) acknowledged the significance for modernity of the construction of language as a separate realm in the 17th century, Bauman and Briggs contend that he constructs too unified a view of language. They demonstrate the struggles over the construction of language by comparing contemporary folk and institutional perceptions of language and the role these competing constructions of language have on impacting the production of modernity:

While Foucault's account of language thus provides an excellent starting point for discerning how *reimagining language was crucial for imagining modernity*, we suggest that the story needs to be retold if its broader significance – particularly for understanding how modernity produces and structures inequality – is to become more intellectually and politically accessible. (Bauman & Briggs. 2003: 10; emphasis added).

For Bauman and Briggs (2003: 7), the key question is how modernism (through the work of philosophers such as Locke) created language as a separate domain, how language 'came into being' and the 'process involved in creating language and rendering it a powerful means of creating social inequality' (2003: 9). This, then, is a crucial step prior to the rise of the European nation state's production of languages as separate and distinct, national entities. This latter point has been widely discussed and observed, from Anderson's discussion of the role of language in the construction of the nation state (though, as suggested above, he fails to observe that this was a bidirectional construction, involving both language construction and nation constructing language) to observations such as Mühlhäusler's (2000: 358) that the notion of a 'language' 'is a recent culture-specific notion associated with the rise of European nation states and the Enlightenment. The notion of "a language" makes little sense in most traditional societies'. Bauman and Briggs, however, are pointing to the period that precedes this, when language itself was constructed, philosophically as well as politically, as an entity separable from the social world. Crucial to this project was Locke's 'positioning of language as one of the three "great provinces of the intellectual world" that are "wholly separate and distinct"' (Bauman & Briggs, 2003: 299). As they go on to explain, 'separating language from both nature/science and society/politics, Locke could place practices for purifying language of any explicit connections with either society or nature at the center of his vision of modern linguistic and textual practices' (Bauman & Briggs, 2003: 299–300).

This construction of language, either as an autonomous object or a linguistic system, has been challenged both from the inside by the *integrational linguistics* of Harris (1981) and the *hard-science linguistics* of Yngve (1996, 2004a, 2000b), and from the outside by *critical localism* (Geertz, 1983; Canagarajah, 2002) and studies of *language ideologies* (Blommaert, 1999b; Kroskrity, 2000), which aim to understand how language may be understood differently in different contexts. Harris has argued that linguistics (or segregational linguistics as he calls orthodox linguistics) has profoundly misconstrued language through its myths about autonomy, systematicity and the rule-bound nature of language, privileging supposedly expert, scientific linguistic knowledge over everyday understandings of language, which, following Geertz, we are referring to as 'local knowledge.'

An integrationalist redefinition of linguistics, Harris (1990: 45) suggests, can dispense with at least the following assumptions: '(1) the linguistic sign is arbitrary; (2) the linguistic sign is linear: (3) words have meanings; (4) grammar has rules; and (5) there are languages'. As both Mühlhäusler (2000) and Toolan (2003) argue, an integrational view of language suggests not merely that language is integrated with its environment, but rather that languages themselves cannot be viewed as discrete items, rejecting as a 'powerful and misleading myth, any assumption that a language is essentially an autonomous system which humans can harness to meet their communicational needs' (Toolan, 2003: 123). Thus, drawing on Harris' work, this version of linguistic ecology takes seriously Harris' (1990: 45) claim that 'linguistics does not need to postulate the existence of languages as part of its theoretical apparatus'. As Harris goes on to argue, the question here is whether 'the concept of a language, as defined by orthodox modern linguistics, corresponds to any determinate or determinable object of analysis at all, whether social or individual, whether institutional or psychological. If there is no such object, it would be difficult to evade the conclusion that modern linguistics has been based upon a myth' (Harris, 1990: 45).

An alternative perspective is provided by Yngve, who argues for a 'hard' scientific approach to language study rather than the 'soft' science offered by linguistics:

> Accepting language as an object of study leads to accepting the scientifically unjustified special assumptions involved in continuing a philosophically-based program of grammatical and semiotic research that can be traced back to the ancients ... If we give priority to studying language we cannot have true science. If we give priority to science, we must give up the goal of studying language. Giving up language in favour of science would be victory for linguistics, not a defeat. (Yngve, 2004a: 16)

For Yngve, in a parallel move to Harris' integrational linguistics and our arguments here for ways of reconstituting language, linguistics needs to become the 'study of how people communicate rather than the scientific study of language, which is impossible. It becomes a human linguistics rather than a linguistics of language' (Yngve: 2004b: 28)

From the perspective of linguistic anthropology, with a particular interest in the notion of language ideologies, or regimes of language (Kroskrity, 2000), the question becomes one of asking how it is that languages are understood locally. As Woolard (2004: 58) notes, such work has shown that 'linguistic ideologies are never just about language, but rather also concern such fundamental social notions as community, nation, and humanity itself'. For linguistic anthropologists, the problem was that the 'surgical removal of language from context produced an amputated 'language' that was the preferred object of the language sciences for most of the 20th century' (Kroskrity, 2000: 5). By studying language ideologies as contextual sets of belief about languages, or as Irvine (1989: 255) puts it, 'the cultural system of ideas about social and linguistic relationships, together with their loading of moral and political interests,' this line of work has shown the significance of local knowledge about language. Put together, the internal and external challenges to notions of language embedded in the language sciences suggest on the one hand that there are no grounds to postulate the existence of languages as separate entities and on the other that in order to understand language use, we need to incorporate local knowledge.

Branson and Miller (2000: 32) argue that we 'must not only revel in linguistic difference but cope with that difference analytically. Let us recognize the culturally specific nature of our own schemes and search for new modes of analysis that do not fit other languages into a mould but celebrate and build on their epistemological differences'. While pluralist (socio)linguistics and applied linguistics focus on linguistic differences, they fail to address the metadiscursive concern of how we understand linguistic difference, avoiding thereby an engagement with the ways in which languages and differences have been constructed. As Branson and Miller (2000; this volume) argue, the problem for many languages previously dismissed as non-languages (dialects, sign languages, creoles) is that they have had to submit to the regulatory apparatus of linguistics in order to achieve the status of 'real languages.' The possibility of understanding language differently, from the local perspective of the users of those sign languages, dialects and creoles, is thereby dismissed as languages are brought into the universalist paradigm in which similarity and difference have already been assigned.

From a creolist perspective, Degraff (2005: 534) berates linguists for perpetuating the 'most dangerous myth' of what he calls *creole exceptionalism*: 'the postulation of exceptional and abnormal characteristics in the diachrony and/or synchrony of creole languages as a class.' Degraff argues that creole exceptionalism was posited in order to resolve the contradiction of how, on the one hand, slaves could be regarded as speaking fully-fledged languages whilst on the other hand they were not regarded as fully-fledged human beings. While we are sympathetic to the overall objectives of Degraff's critique of creole exceptionalism, we want to push this insight further. Since we are skeptical of the notion of language itself, the solution is not to normalize creole languages by seeing them as similar to other languages, but to destabilize languages by seeing them as similar to creoles.

Similarly, the critique of the myth of sign language exceptionalism should not then render sign languages just like any other language, but should start to undermine the ways in which languages are understood. If anything we would like to argue that all languages are creoles, and that the slave and colonial history of creoles should serve as a model on which other languages are assessed. In other words, it is what is seen as marginal or exceptional that should be used to frame our understandings of language. Furthermore, since most communities have been affected by colonialism and slavery at one time or other, languages without a colonial history are an exception From such a perspective, creoles therefore should provide a prism through which we can view other languages, hence our argument that all languages are creoles rather than all creoles are languages.

Our overall argument, then, is that the metadiscursive regimes that emerged to describe languages are part of a process of epistemic violence visited on the speakers of those languages as they were called into existence. Unless we actively engage with the history of invention of languages, with the processes by which these inventions are maintained, with the political imperative to work towards their disinvention and with the reformulation of basic concepts in linguistics and applied linguistics, we will continue to do damage to speech communities and deny those people educational opportunities. Languages were posited as separate entities at a particular moment in European philosophical and political thought. After so much harm has been done to communities through this epistemic violence, it is time to put languages back into the world.

The Material Effects of Inventions

While it is useful to understand languages as inventions, it is also crucial to recognize that the effects of language inventions are very real. As we suggested above, this is where we generally part company with those fighting for language rights and multilingualism, since the struggle is all too often conducted on a terrain on which the existence of languages as real entities is left unquestioned. While we may support some aspects of these struggles as political movements, we would argue that the battle also has to be an epistemological one, and that unless this issue is adequately addressed, the very real effects of language inventions will continue to be felt by different communities.

Having stressed the epistemological nature of the problem, we also need to emphasize that our position does not take up some supposed idealist side of a realist/idealist dichotomy. While we are indeed arguing that languages are invented, we locate the implications of such inventions not only in the abstract domain of language definitions but also in the very material domain of language effects. Thus, while our argument is not one that could be described as materialist in the sense that languages are nothing but the product of real social and economic relations, it may be seen as materialist in that it is a way of conceptualizing language that focuses on the real and situated linguistic forms deployed as part of the communicative resources by speakers to serve their social and political goals (see Blommaert, 1999b; Baumann & Briggs, 2003, for related views). Thus, we focus not only on the real and situated forms of language, but on what the speakers believe they should and ought to talk about, and how they analyse their talk as well. We are arguing therefore for an understanding of the relationships between what people believe about their language (or other people's languages), the situated forms of talk that they deploy, and the material effects – social, economic, environmental – of such views and uses.

The view of language we are suggesting here has serious implications for many of the treasured icons of liberal-linguistic thought. Not only do the notions of language become highly suspect, but so do many related concepts that are premised on a notion of discrete languages, such as language rights, mother tongues, multilingualism or code-switching. It is common in both liberal and more critical approaches to issues in sociolinguistics to insist on plurality, sometimes strengthened by a concept of rights. Thus, there are strong arguments for mother tongue education, for an understanding of multilingualism as the global norm, for understanding the prevalence of code-switching in bilingual and multilingual communities, and for the importance of language rights to provide a moral and legal framework for language policies. Our position, however, is that although such arguments may be preferable to blinkered views that posit a bizarre and rare state of monolingualism as the norm, they nevertheless remain caught within the same paradigm. They operate with a strategy of pluralization rather than questioning those inventions at the core of the discussion. Without strategies of disinvention, most discussions of language rights, mother tongue education, or code-switching reproduce the same concept of language that underpins all mainstream linguistic thought; multilingualism may, therefore, become a pluralization of monolingualism.

Sonntag (2003: 25) makes a singular point when she argues that the rights-based approach to support for linguistic diversity and opposition to the English-Only movement 'has not fundamentally altered the American projection of its vision of global English ... because a rights based approach to promoting linguistic diversity reinforces the dominant liberal democratic project rather than dismantling it'. The point here, then, is that while on the one hand seeming to promote a progressive, liberal cause for diversity, rights and multilingualism, such arguments, by employing the same epistemologies on which monolingualism and the denial of rights have been constructed, may simultaneously do more to reproduce than oppose the conditions to which they object. In a similar vein, Rajagopalan suggests that:

> the very charges being pressed against the hegemony of the English language and its putative imperialist pretensions themselves bear the imprint of a way of thinking about language moulded in an intellectual climate of excessive nationalistic fervor and organized marauding of the wealth of alien nations, an intellectual climate where identities were invariably thought of in all or nothing terms. (Rajagopalan, 1999: 20)

Thus as Sonntag (2003: 25) goes on to argue, 'the willingness to use the language of human rights on the global level to frame local linguistic demands vis-à-vis global English may merely be affirming the global vision projected by American liberal democracy'.

The invention of languages has had particularly insidious consequences for indigenous people, since the invention of the construct of indigenous peoples, particularly in contexts such as multicultural Australia, produces for Aboriginal Australians a need for identification with their prenational selves during some 'mythological dreamtime' in which they ostensibly cared for their relatives, lived in harmonious accord with the land in a mode consistent with the ideals propagated by the environmentalist movement, reflecting the extent to which the thinking of the environmentalist movement has permeated even the ways in which indigenousness is construed (Thomas, 1994: 28). This construction of indigenousness is bought at a social price; it fixes their identity, consequently disqualifying socially embedded urbanized indigenous peoples.

A complete identification of indigenous people with their prenational selves is not possible, for two reasons. First, it is not be possible to retrieve prenational selves because of the impossibility of overriding colonialism's traumatic effects on indigenous social life (Povinelli, 2002: 36). Second, retrieving the indigenous forms from prenational selves is a 'back-projection' which assumes as a given the existence of the prenational selves (Kuzar, 2001: 281). In some cases the nature, or indeed even the existence, of these prenational selves may be open to serious debate. Even if the form and nature of the cultural artifacts in the prenational era had not been subjected to strong colonial influence, the key question is, as Catherine Coquerty-Vidrovitch queries (in Mamdani, 1996: 39), how far back do we have to go? In Africa, for instance, when we seek to appeal to prenational forms, do we have to go as far back as pre-Portuguese, colonial Islamic expansion, or Bantu expansion (Mamdani, 1996: 39)? The central point here is that while indigenous people are caught between impossible pressures to identify on the one hand with prenational selves and on the other with their colonizers (Fanon, 1952/1967), any solution needs to avoid both those discourses that construct an essential character to indigeneity and insist on the integrity of indigenous languages, and those that insist the only solution is to adopt wholesale the dominant languages of modernity, such as English. Our argument is that only a disinvention and reconstitution of language can open up ways out of these cycles of discourse.

The invention of some African languages, such as Tswana, Shona, Tsonga and Yoruba was based upon the Herderian view that was a significant part of the German Intellectual Movement in which language, race, and geographical location were constructed as indivisible. These conceptual insights have encouraged us to explore the essential contradictions in colonial rhetoric between preserving the past, promoting economic development and protecting Africans and other colonized people from the traumas of modernity. These contradictions were eloquently captured in colonial disdain for the 'detribalized' or 'trousered' Africans who responded most enthusiastically to the 'colonial civilizing mission' (Spear, 2003: 4). Trousered Africans, who were more likely than not to be educated, were held in disdain because they were treated as 'mimics' or 'hybrids' parodying white discourse (Jeater, 2002). The discomfort that colonial and postcoloniality has with 'trousered' Africans is not peculiar to the ways Africans are treated. It is common to contemporary celebrations of indigenous life that:

> denigrate and marginalize urbanized or apparently acculturated members of these populations who speak English, lack ethnic dress, do not obviously conduct ceremonies and do not count as real natives to the same extent as those who continue to live in the bush and practice something closer to traditional subsistence. (Thomas, 1994: 30)

The term 'hybrid' was being used negatively to refer to the appropriation which took place in moments of encounter between Africans and Whites (see Makoni & Meinhof, 2004). When colonizers appropriated material from encounters, they were not regarded as hybrids. The term hybrid was thus restricted to appropriation by the colonized 'trousered'

Africans. The term hybrid is a metaphor that is derived from biology, so can be read as a biological construal of cultural practices. That something or someone is a hybrid presupposes that the individuals and social practices are pure but, as Bauman and Briggs (2003) point out, every pure form can be regarded as a hybrid by a different measure; so the notion of hybridity may be misleading unless one seriously challenges the underlying biological metaphor. Of central concern here for our argument are the ways in which the romanticization of tradition, the use of biological metaphors (Pennycook, 2004), the denigration of the trousered and the hybrid, have very real material effects for language users in the contemporary world.

Even if it were possible to strip the past of the traumatic effects of colonialism, the nature of that past is still open to serious contestation – a contestation that may occur even at a national level. For example, the politically and economically beleaguered Zimbabwean state is engaged in an ongoing struggle to seize control over the various ways in which it can represent and create the past. It is doing so by propagating 'patriotic history', a much more acutely narrowed-down version of nationalistic history (Ranger, 2004: 215). Of course, appeals to tradition have always been made in order to justify the present:

> Elders tended to appeal to tradition in order to defend their dominance of the rural means of production challenged by the young. Men tended to appeal to tradition in order to ensure that the increasing role which women played in production in rural areas did not result in any diminution of male control over women as economic assets. Paramount chiefs and ruling aristocracies in polities which included numbers of ethnic and social groupings appealed to tradition in order to maintain or extend their control over their subjects. Indigenous populations appealed to tradition in order to ensure that the migrants who settled amongst them did not achieve political or economic rights. (Ranger, 1983: 254)

Yet claims to tradition take on a very different role when made by the State. Patriotic history focuses on three 'revolutions': the 1896 African colonial encounters, the guerilla war and the third *chimurenga* of land distribution, dividing the nation into patriots and 'sell outs'. With its doctrine of permanent revolution, patriotic history glorifies violence and omits other forms of popular action, marginalizing the cities and trade unions. Patriotic history is an example of the invention of the past, and an attempt to use the past to serve contemporary political goals. Today, authenticity is the watchword and the Zimbabwean state claims to be a repository of indigenous knowledge, seeking support among indigenous peoples across the world. Such claims should always lead us to be wary of the discourses of indigeneity; the waters are muddied by such attempts to own indigenous knowledge. It is the past that is a product of the present, and not vice versa.

The invention of languages in the context of Christian missionary work had significant effects on social and cultural relations. In the Philippine context Rafael describes how the categories introduced through conversion refashioned social life, particularly the relationships between masters (*maginoo* – principles) and slaves (*alipin*). Conversion not only constituted the introduction of a new category, but it radically altered the relationship between life and death, affecting the social meanings people may have of fear itself (Rafael, 1988: xi). Looking at the introduction of literacy into the Kaluli community in Papua New Guinea by Australian missionaries, Schieffelin (2000: 294) notes how this 'challenged and changed Kaluli notions of truth, knowledge, and authority, thereby affecting Kaluli linguistic as well as social structures'.

Schieffelin (2000: 296) argues that 'everyday language practices, local metalinguistics, and language ideologies that are embedded in complex cultural and historical moments intersect in ongoing processes of social reproduction and rapid cultural change'. Thus, from the initial grammar of Kaluli, in which Christian and Western practices 'were simply slipped into the linguistic materials and treated as if they had always been there,' so that it was impossible to distinguish between Kaluli ways of saying things and 'what an Australian missionary linguist thought were good sentences illustrating linguistic structures' (Schieffelin, 2000: 302), to literacy practices, which emphasized, in true Christian fashion, reading over writing, and truth as inherent in the text itself, the colonial missionary work on and through Kaluli was aimed at 'domination, control and conversion to a particular point of view' (2000: 321) and wrought profound changes on the social, cultural and linguistic practices of the Kaluli. As Schieffelin suggests, 'every language choice is a social choice that has critical links to the active construction of culture' (2000: 323).

The insights from disinvention can serve as a critique of some aspects of language 'endangerment' as articulated by Nettle and Romaine (2000), Crystal (2000), and Skutnabb-Kangas (2003), amongst others. Currently, there is a discernible shift from indigenous languages towards urban vernaculars in Africa. While some linguists may regard the shift as regrettable because it constitutes a form of enlargement, from an invention perspective, promoting the continued use of indigenous languages constitutes a retrospective justification of colonial structures. While the shift from indigenous languages to urban vernaculars may also be read as catastrophic from the perspective of some linguists, those who shift from indigenous languages to urban vernaculars may construe the shift as a reflection of a creative adaptation to new contexts (Makoni & Meinhof, 2004). The advantage of the notion of 'invention' is that it provides opportunities for social intervention and counter-practices through disinvention and reconstitution. For example, the widespread use of urban speech forms that are ontologically inconsistent with notions of language as 'hermetically sealed units' (Makoni, 1998b) challenges existing dominant ideologies that constrain official policies, particularly in South Africa.

Towards Disinvention and Reconstitution

In the disinvention project we are, therefore, not merely reiterating the generally accepted notions that languages have fuzzy boundaries, and that the distinction between language and dialect is arbitrary, as is frequently stated in conventional sociolinguistics. Rather, we want to argue that the concept of language, and indeed the 'metadiscursive regimes' used to describe languages are firmly located in Western linguistic and cultural suppositions. They do not describe any real state of affairs in the world, i.e. they are not natural kinds (Danzinger, 1997): they are convenient fictions only to the extent that they provide a useful way of understanding the world and shaping language users, and they are very inconvenient fictions to the extent that they produce particular and limiting views on how language operates in the world. In response, we want to propose neither a view that we need better descriptions, nor mere acknowledgement of fuzziness, but instead strategies of disinvention and reconstruction.

The perspective that languages are socially and politically constructed is necessary not only for an understanding of languages, but also for situations in which there are reasons either to change them or to change the way we think about them. We are focusing on language because definitions of language have material consequences on people and because such definitions are always implicitly or explicitly statements about human beings in the world (Yngve, 1996). It is, therefore, necessary to overcome ideas about language if we are to imagine alternative ways of conceptualizing the role and status of individuals in the world. For example, a world in which plurality is preferred over singularity requires rethinking concepts founded on notions of uniformity over those predicated on diversity (Blommaert, 2005: 187; Bauman & Briggs, 2003: 9; Canagarajah, Chapter 10, this volume).

Part of the process of rethinking language involves questioning the broader assumptions that have been linked to languages. One crucial element here is time and history, particularly as it has been constructed in relation to diachronic linguistics. As Blommaert (1999b: 1) puts it, 'The socioculturally motivated ideas, perceptions and expectations of language, manifested in all sorts of language use and in themselves objects of discursive elaboration in metapragmatic discourse, seem to have no history'. Our interest here is to locate language inventions, disinventions and reconstructions within a broader project in critical historiography, in which there is latitude for multiple temporalities. Contrary to historical linguistics, we are arguing here for the possibilities of 'a discontinuous history – one in which no state of affairs can be derived simply from a preceding one' (Fabian, 1991). A discontinuous notion of history is different from the conventional notions of history in historical linguistics that are predicated upon linguistic continuity as understood in terms of mutations through successive stages (Ehret, 2002). If we can allow for 'multiple, heterogeneous and uneven temporalities and histories that the dominant historical narrative, often presenting itself as singular and linear, suppresses' (Inoue, 2004: 2), it becomes possible conceptually to question the linearity at the heart of much historical linguistics and to see that time, like language, presents far more diverse ways of thinking about overlapping, translingual language uses.

Any critical applied linguistic project that aims to deal with language in the contemporary world, however good its political intent may be, must incorporate ways of understanding the detrimental effects it may engender unless it confronts the need for linguistic reconstitution. For example, in North America and Australia, there have been strong movements towards the teaching of heritage languages (Hornberger, 2005), but the concept of heritage languages may resonate differently in different contexts because of its emphasis on the roots of the speakers, on their 'ancestral language'. In situations characterized by massive migration, the promotion of heritage languages might easily be appropriated and harnessed and fuel xenophobic tendencies in which some people end up being defined as permanent outsiders and others as insiders (Brutt-Griffler & Makoni, 2005).

Our argument, then, is that just as languages were invented, so too were related concepts such as multilingualism, additive bilingualism, or codeswitching. Language planning policies seeking to promote additive bilingualism are founded upon a very specific view of language, a view that takes languages to be 'entities' which, when accessed, will then be beneficial to the speakers. Thus although they tend to be projected as if they were goals that language-planning policies must seek to achieve, additive bilingualism or multilingualism must also be understood as particular ways of thinking about language. Language planning research therefore needs to focus not only on the political contexts in which it operates, but also on the nature of the concepts of language that underpin the different policy options, to question not only the *realpolitik* but also the *reallinguistik* of the 20th century.

In our view there is a disconcerting similarity between monolingualism and additive bilingualism in so far as both are founded on notions of language as 'objects'. By talking of monolingualism, we are referring to a single entity, while in additive bilingualism and multilingualism the number of 'language-things' has increased. Yet the underlying concept remains unchanged because additive bilingualism and multilingualism are at best a pluralization of monolingualism. In the context of South African language policy Makoni (1998a: 244–5) argues that 'emerging discourses about multilingualism derive their strength through a deliberate refusal to recollect that in the past multilingualism has always been used to facilitate the exploitation of Africans'. Proponents of multilingualism seem to suffer from a process of 'historical amnesia' (Stuart Hall, 1997: 20), in which they believe that just because they have started thinking about the idea, so the idea has just begun. Furthermore, proponents of multilingualism are the ideological captives of the very system that they are seeking to challenge. Makoni suggests that

> The battle for independence is simply not won by opting for vernaculars over English as normally articulated in the decolonization literature ... From UNESCO to the multicultural lobby the potential negative effects of learning through vernaculars assigned to speakers is not addressed as it is assumed that it is cognitively and emotionally advantageous that a child learns through such a medium as it does the colonized images encoded in such versions of African vernaculars. (Makoni, 1998b: 162–3)

More importantly, in disinvention we are seeking to provide alternative ways of understanding some of the frequently reported problems about language planning. For example, it is frequently suggested that in a lot of cases, particularly in Africa, parents may object to their children being taught in their mother tongues. The refusal to be taught in their mother tongue is treated as the legacy of colonialism. We would like to adopt a different perspective. Some indigenous communities object to being taught in 'their mother tongue' because schooling is perceived not as the place were knowledge is transmitted, but as a point of contact between the 'indigenous world and the white-man's world'. Non-indigenous languages (i.e. European languages) are regarded as central to that contact. Education and the transmission of knowledge from the perspective of indigenous communities take place in the oral tradition in the home. While indigenous communities regard schools as sites of contact between indigenous communities and the 'white-man's world,' education being understood as taking place at home, Western scholarship takes the opposite view, defining what indigenous communities regard as education to the relegated status of socialization (Reagan, 1996).

The conceptual orientations that we adopt in disinvention and reconstruction may also vary depending upon the problems we are seeking to address. Language planning debates have tended to think and articulate their positions in terms of solutions. Through disinvention we prefer to argue that it is more realistic to think in terms of viable alternatives than solutions. The conceptual alternatives that we propose vary between situations. For example, in some situations the viable solution may lie in essentializing mother tongues, in other cases, in problematizing them (Pennycook, 2002). The ideology of invention serves as a critique of language imposition or linguistic imperialism, not in the sense that dominant languages are imposed on minority groups, but rather in the sense that the imposition lies in the ways in which speech forms are constructed into languages, and particular definitions of what constitutes language expertise are construed and imposed.

Instead of the often static notions of language implied by concepts of multilingualism, we need to start to move towards concepts such as Jacquemet's (2005) *transidiomatic practices*: ' the communicative practices of transnational groups that interact using different languages and communicative codes simultaneously present in a range of communicative channels, both local and distant.' Jacquemet explains that:

> Transidiomatic practices are the results of the co-presence of multilingual talk (exercised by de/reterritorialized speakers) and electronic media, in contexts heavily structured by social indexicalities and semiotic codes. Anyone present in transnational environments, whose talk is mediated by deterritorialized technologies, and who interacts with both present and distant people, will find herself producing transidiomatic practices. (Jacquemet, 2005: 265)

And yet, we would also argue that such practices are not so much the product of contemporary linguistic contexts mediated by deterritorialized technologies, as they are the common ways in which languages have been and still are used throughout the world.

It is instructive to note that plurality was the pervasive state of affairs in most pre-colonial communities and it was not regarded as problematic. Indeed, as Fabian (1991) stated, the idea of a monolingual Shaba-speaking person was unusual, so, paradoxically, communication models that derive their inspiration from pre-colonial periods might aid us in addressing some of the conceptual problems which face contemporary sociolinguistics as it tries to address issues about plurality and diversity. This is not to say we are arguing for a wholesale return to pre-colonial conditions in order to address postcolonial problems, because an unselective return to pre-colonial conceptual artifacts is not feasible owing to the inescapable effects of colonialism on many social and analytical artifacts (Povinelli, 2002).

Rather, we are interested in a project akin to Degraff's (2005) *radical postcolonial creolistics* that illuminates the epistemological continuity between slavery, colonialism and 'scientific notions' of creole exceptionalism while also turning the tables on contemporary linguistics by emphasizing *language exceptionalism*: all claims to know, count, name and define languages need to justify themselves against the normality of creoles. If we frame our contemporary problems using prisms derived from pre-colonial eras, we may be able to radically alter the role and status of language within applied linguistics. The analytical categories drawn from pre-colonial eras were not language categories per se, but categories designed to deal with communication and other social activities. So, an applied linguistics that seeks to draw its inspiration from a deployment of pre-colonial era categories has to deal with the paradox that it will be an applied linguistics in which language is of secondary importance.

Overview of the Book

This book is divided into three sections. The first section deals with analyses of socio-political contexts within which ways of thinking about language emerged. The second section is an examination of how these ways of thinking about sign languages, indigenous literacies, or African American Vernacular may militate against the development of radically different and perhaps more nuanced understandings of language. Our contention throughout the book is that ways of thinking about language are not only a conceptual issue: they have potentially negative effects on language users – what Grace (2005) has termed 'collateral damage.' If ways of conceptualizing language might result in 'collateral damage', in the final section of the book we show how revising how we think about language affects the nature of the language teaching materials we develop, and our language-teaching goals.

' ... And then there were languages'

In the first section of the book we examine the historical contexts in which languages and notions about language were constructed. Ariel Heryanto (Chapter 2) analyses the historical circumstances in which Bahasa Indonesia emerged as a language. He analyses how the meanings of bahasa, which in vernacular Malay and Javanese communities referred to socially-bound practices, shifted to refer to rule-governed systems. The term referred not so much to something abstract and neutral as to a social activity. But with the introduction of Bahasa Indonesia – as part of the universalizing discourse of development – came particular notions of languageness. Consequently, formerly 'language-free' communities now had language. This does not of course imply that prior to the invention of Bahasa Indonesia, there were no languages in Indonesia; rather it suggests that the construction of Bahasa Indonesia required a radical shift in the conceptualization of what constitutes 'language'. In a similar vein, but focusing on a different part of the world, Sinfree Makoni and Pedizasi Mashiri (Chapter 3) focus on the constructions of Shona and Tsonga in southern Africa. They argue that the construction and crystallization of these speech forms into languages were shaped by a complex interplay between literacy, writing and European views of language.

From a perspective that differs from these, which look at the construction of languages from within complex multilingual matrices, Pennycook (Chapter 4) argues that the notion of English as an International Language is also a myth. Looking at how myths about English (English as a language of development, opportunity and equality) are constantly put into discourse, he argues that such myths simultaneously contribute to the larger construction of English itself. For Pennycook there are therefore two pertinent questions to ask. First, what is the nature of the political and discursive interests that lead scholars to regard English to be a real entity that can be described as an international language, and secondly, perhaps even more importantly, what are the real-life consequences arising from the tendency to treat this 'thing' as an international language? Pennycook's concerns about the effects of constructing English as an international language are the converse of the critique that Sinfree Makoni and Mashiri are making about the claims of indigenous African languages as authentic repositories of African cultures, which in turn are a product of African nationalistic historiography. All the papers in this section insist that we should take our descriptions seriously, not only because the descriptions are linguistically important, but because any language description implies an intervention into people's lives, and the intervention might have unexpected adverse effects on exactly those same people whose interests we think we are promoting or safeguarding.

Language epistemologies and local knowledge

Through a critical historiography of the development of the epistemology of thinking about sign linguistics, Branson and Miller (Chapter 5) trace some of the changes that have taken place in the ways sign languages are understood. They draw our attention to a key paradox: while the linguistic argument that sign languages were like any other languages challenged denigratory views of such languages, the continued use of linguistics as the dominant (and in many cases exclusive) lens through which to understand sign languages has also limited our understanding of the complexity of sign languages because of pressure to fit sign languages into conventional models of linguistic analysis. This is a central argument for a number of concerns we are trying to address in this book: it has often been an important move to use the academic status of linguistics to support denigrated semiotic systems. Thus, sign languages, creole languages, dialects of languages, indigenous languages and other stigmatized codes have often benefited from careful description and the argument that they are complex linguistic systems like any other. Yet, at the same time, by confining such diverse domains to the straitjacket of linguistic description, their complexity, variety and locatedness in social and cultural worlds has often been lost

Focusing his analysis on the Kashinawa people in Brazil, Lynn Mario de Souza (Chapter 6) argues for a more locally grounded perspective about the nature of language, writing and literacy. Writing, its necessity and its forms of dissemination in indigenous education, he argues, tend to be anchored in a non-indigenous locus of enunciation. De Souza shows how concepts of language and writing in indigenous education in Brazil have been deeply implicated in colonial ideologies of conversion and civilization, where they became instruments of a politics of inequality and the negation of difference. This collusion, in Brazil as elsewhere, has historically permeated much of the work done in linguistics in the field of indigenous education. Basing his analysis on his ongoing project in Brazil he demonstrates the sharp differences between Euro-Brazilian ways of understanding language, writing and literacy and language learning from that of the Kashinawa people, arguing that a lack of awareness of these local modes of understanding the nature of language, learning and literacy renders it difficult for language teaching to achieve its goals.

From a very different perspective, Steven Thorne and James Lantolf (Chapter 7) examine the implications for language learning of constructing languages as 'nouns', 'objects', 'things'. Examining Saussure's astute rhetorical and philosophical move which contributed significantly towards a construction of language as a 'thing' and linguistics as a science, they show how he downgraded the role and impact of human activity in language, thus unintentionally preserving and reinforcing Cartesian dualisms of mind/body, langue/parole, competence/performance. In a move analogous to Hopper (1998) and the arguments we made earlier about dealing with interactions rather than languages, Thorne and Lantolf argue for an approach that places significance on human communication, and treats grammar not as a precondition for communication but a product of communication.

In the fourth article in this section, Elaine Richardson (Chapter 8) examines how the identities of African Americans that can be gleaned from a linguistic description of African American Vernaculars is inadequate. Looking at how rappers exploit linguistic stereotypes to upset and redefine social reality from meanings rooted in their everyday experience, she suggests that they thereby (dis)invent relationships between identity and language. Where conventional Anglo-American discourses attempt to ascribe certain language forms to certain identities, or particular identities to language forms, Hiphop discourses recall African language histories from before the European invention of languages and imposition of metadiscursive regimes, drawing on language possibilities that can cross, challenge and unravel hostile conditions.

Applied disinvention

The final section of the book is made up of two chapters (by Brigitta Busch and Jürgen Schick, and Suresh Canagarajah) that examine the educational implications of revising some of the assumptions we make about language. Busch and Schick (Chapter 9) report on a project that sought to experiment with novel ways of designing language teaching materials amid the intense language wars of the former Yugoslavia. They demonstrate how in such contexts language teaching materials that draw on diverse registers, styles and different languages might reduce possibilities of language-based political conflict because the diversity crafted in the materials may approximate the heteroglossic nature of language. By accommodating differences, heteroglossic materials may reduce pressures that arise from attempts to approximate a monolithic standard.

Finally, in Chapter 10, Suresh Canagarajah argues for a model of language learning and teaching that is founded on notions of differences. He cites examples of frameworks such as accommodation or crossing that have tried to demonstrate how differences may be negotiated. He also argues paradoxically, that in pre-colonial times differences were not seen as constituting an impediment to successful communication. Drawing inspiration from the ways communication was structured in pre-colonial times might assist in addressing modern problems.

Conclusion

Where then does this leave us? When Heryanto speaks of 'language free zones', when Branson and Miller show how the move to constitute sign languages as 'real languages' was also an act of epistemic violence, or what Grace calls the 'collateral damage' of linguistics, when, from an integrational linguistic perspective, Harris tells us that linguistics does not need to posit the existence of languages as separate and autonomous objects, and when linguistic anthropology draws our attention to the imperative of understanding local ideologies of language, we have clearly embarked on a different trajectory from much of applied and unapplied linguistics, with their belief in the existence and describability of discrete languages, their positing of languages as systems that exist outside and beyond communicative acts, their location of language within the heads of people, and their use of disembodied texts to represent language use.

The position we have been trying to establish here, however, goes much further than challenging narrow linguistic and applied linguistic orthodoxies. The old issues of description versus prescription, linguistics applied versus applied linguistics simply fade from view as irrelevant. For some this might still imply little more than a turn towards sociolinguistics or pragmatics. Yet from a disinvention perspective, many of the assumptions of more socially oriented approaches to language study also come under critical scrutiny. The givens of sociolinguistics, such as bilingualism and multilingualism, notions such as language rights, or the idea of language pragmatics, are also questionable from the perspective we are developing here since they are in a sense the by-products of the invented languages and metadiscursive regimes we are questioning. If languages hadn't been invented as isolated, enumerable objects separated from their environment in the first place, we wouldn't need these add-on frameworks, and thus to talk of sociolinguistics or pragmatics is to uphold metalinguistic inventions.

This view has many implications for applied linguistic domains. Let us take an area such as language testing (for a critical exploration, see Shohamy, 2001). Why is it, we might ask, that a language test such as the TOEFL (Test of English as a Foreign Language) remains so desperately monolingual? At first glance, this question may seem bizarre: it is a test of English, after all. Yet the cultural psychology developed by Thorne and Lantolf (in Chapter 7), which opens up ways for us to see how languages may be mediational tools to develop each other, as well as the broader questioning of language inventions across this volume, suggest that a multilingual TOEFL may be a far more appropriate test (to the extent that testing can be appropriate). What we mean by this is not, of course, that TOEFL should be offered in separate but discrete languages (test of French, German, Japanese, Tsonga or Tagalog as foreign languages) but rather that to test language users in one narrow element of their linguistic repertoire while admitting of no leakage across the tight linguistic boundaries echoes a history of strange linguistic inventions. When we talk of 'washback' in testing, it is more common to think of this in terms of the curricular effects of evaluation. More broadly, however, it is interesting to note the 'collateral damage' for language users, policy makers, citizens and educators of the strange notion that languages exist in separation from the world and each other and can be tested in isolation.

Language education suffers similarly from such peculiar linguistic inventions. For a start, the enumerative strategies based on the notions of *second* language acquisition, or English as a *second* language become highly questionable. From our point of view, there is no good reason to separate and count languages in this way. And while some useful work has sought to break down these divides by talking more in terms of bilingual education, we are still left here with a monolingual pluralization. The question we would like to ask (and see Busch and Schick in Chapter 9) is what would language education look like if we no longer posited the existence of separate languages? Once again an answer might lie in starting to understand language and language education in terms of majority world local knowledge, in starting to relocate language learning from an additional to a transidiomatic practice.

Further questions need to be addressed to other domains of linguistics and applied linguistics. What does translation look like within disinvented and reconstituted languages? The position we have been developing suggests that this boundary we set up between languages, making translation an issue when we speak 'different languages' but not when we speak the 'same language' is yet again a distinction that is hard to maintain. This does not dissolve translation into a meaningless activity; rather it suggests that all communication involves translation. The twin effects of metadiscursive regimes that divided languages into separable entities and pedagogical dictates that eschewed translation have had sadly detrimental effects on language education. If language learning could be seen as a form of translingual activism or transidiomatic practice far more dynamic effects might be achieved.

Language policy, meanwhile, becomes a very different project from its current orientation towards choosing between languages to be used in particular domains, or debating whether one language threatens another. If language policy could focus on translingual language practices rather than language entities, far more progress might be made in domains such as language education. Applied linguistics more generally needs to address the question of what it might look like if we took seriously the implications of no longer positing the existence of separate languages, of acknowledging that if a science of language is an impossibility, so too is an applied science of language. But as a domain of work more readily able to lead the way towards understanding the transidiomatic practices of speakers, applied linguistics may be able to help linguistics get over its unfortunate long-term obsession with the impossible study of languages.

References

Anderson, B. (1991) *Imagined Communities: Reflections on the Origin and Spread of Nationalism*. London: Verso.
Appadurai, A. (1993) Number in the colonial imagination. In C.A. Breckenridge and P. van der Veer (eds) *Orientalism and the Postcolonial Predicament: Perspectives on South Asia* (pp. 314–339). Philadelphia: University of Pennsylvania Press.
Bauman, R. and Briggs, C. (2003) *Voices of Modernity: Language Ideologies and the Politics of Inequality*. Cambridge: Cambridge University Press.
Blommaert, J. (1999a) Reconstructing the sociolinguistic image of Africa: Grassroots writing in Shaba (Congo). *Text* 19 (2), 175–200.
Blommaert, J. (1999b) The debate is open. In J. Blommaert (ed.) *Language Ideological Debates* (pp. 1–38). Berlin: Mouton.
Blommaert, J. (2005) Situating linguistic rights: English and Swahili in Tanzania revisited. *Journal of Sociolinguistics* 9 (3), 390–417.
Branson, J. and Miller, D. (2000) Maintaining, developing and sharing the knowledge and potential embedded in all our languages and cultures: On linguists as agents of epistemic violence. In R. Phillipson (ed.) *Rights to Language: Equity, Power and Education* (pp. 28–32). Mahwah, NJ: Lawrence Erlbaum.
Brutt-Griffler, J. and Makoni, S. (2005) The use of heritage language: An African perspective. *The Modern Language Journal* 89 (4), 609–612.
Canagarajah, A.S. (2002) Celebrating local knowledge on language and education. *Journal of Language, Identity and Education* 1 (4), 243–261.
Chimhundu, H. (1992) Early missionaries and the ethnolinguistic factor during the invention of tribalism in Zimbabwe. *Journal of African History* 33, 87–109.
Cohn, B. (1983) Representing authority in Victorian England. In E. Hobsbawm and T. Ranger (eds) *The Invention of Tradition*. Cambridge: Cambridge University Press.
Cohn, B. (1996) *Colonialism and its Forms of Knowledge*. Princeton, NJ: Princeton University Press.
Comaroff, J. and Comaroff, J. (1991) *Of Revelation and Revolution* (Vol 1.): *Christianity, Colonialism and Consciousness in South Africa*. Chicago: Chicago University Press.
Crystal, D. (2000) *Language Death*. Cambridge: Cambridge University Press.
Danzinger, K. (1997) *Naming the Mind: How Psychology Found its Language*. London: Sage.
Degraff, M. (2005) Linguists' most dangerous myth: The fallacy of Creole exceptionalism. *Language in Society* 34, 533–591.
Ehret, C. (2002) *The Civilizations of Africa: A History to 1800*. Charlottesville, VA: University Press of Virginia.

Errington, J. (2001) Colonial linguistics. *Annual Review of Anthropology* 30, 19–39.
Ethnologue (2005). On WWW at http://www.ethnologue.com/ethno_docs/introduction.asp#language_id. Accessed 19.11.05.
Fabian, J. (1991) *Language and Colonial Power: The Appropriation of Swahili in the Former Congo 1880–1938*. Cambridge: Cambridge University Press.
Fanon, F. (1952/1967) *Black Skin, White Masks* (translation of *Peau Noire Masques Blancs*). New York: Grove Publishing.
Fenton, S. (ed.) (2004) *For Better or Worse: Translation as a Tool for Change in the South Pacific*. Manchester: St Jerome Publishing.
Foucault, M. (1970) *The Order of Things: An Archaeology of the Human Sciences*. New York: Vintage.
Geertz, C. (1983) *Local Knowledge: Further Essays in Interpretive Anthropology*. New York: Basic Books.
Grace, G.W. (1981) *An Essay on Language*. Columbia, SC: Hornbeam Press.
Grace, G. (2005) Ethnolinguistic notes 4 (2). On WWW at http: www2.hawaii.edu / ~grace. Accessed 19.11.2005.
Grierson, G. (1907) Languages. In W.W. Hunter (ed.) *The Imperial Gazetteer of India* (Vol. 1): *The Indian Empire: Descriptive* (new edn; pp. 349–401). Oxford: Clarendon Press.
Hall, S. (1997) The local and the global: Globalization and ethnicity. In A.D. King (ed.) *Culture, Globalization, and the World System* (pp. 19–40). Minneapolis: University of Minnesota Press.
Hardt, M. and Negri, A. (2000) *Empire*. Cambridge, MA: Harvard University Press.
Harris, R. (1980) *The Language-makers*. Ithaca, NY: Cornell University Press.
Harris, R. (1981) *The Language Myth*. London: Duckworth.
Harris, R. (1990) On redefining linguistics. In H. Davis and T. Taylor (eds) *Redefining Linguistics* (pp. 18–52). London: Routledge.
Harries, P. (1987) The roots of ethnicity: Discourse and the politics of language construction in South Africa. *African Affairs*, 25–52.
Heryanto, A. (1995) *Language of Development and Development of Language: The Case of Indonesia*. Pacific Linguistics Series D-86. Canberra: Department of Linguistics, Australia National University.
Hill, J. (2002) Expert rhetorics in advocacy for endangered languages: Who is listening, and what do they hear? *Journal of Linguistic Anthropology* 12 (2), 119–133.
Hobsbawm, E. (1983) Introduction: Inventing traditions. In E. Hobsbawm and T. Ranger (eds) *The Invention of Tradition*. Cambridge: Cambridge University Press.
Hobsbawm, E. and Ranger, T. (eds) *The Invention of Tradition*. Cambridge: Cambridge University Press.
Hopper, P. (1998) Emergent grammar. In M. Tomasello (ed.) *The New Psychology of Language* (pp. 155–175). Mahwah, NJ: Lawrence Erlbaum.
Hornberger, N.H. (2005) Opening and filling up implementational and ideological spaces in heritage language education. *The Modern Language Journal* 89 (4), 605–609.
Hvalkof, S. and Aaaby, P. (1981) *Is God an American? Anthropological Perspectives on Missionary Work of the Summer Institute of Linguistics*. Copenhagen: IWSIA and Survival International.

Inoue, M. (2004) Introduction: Temporality and historicity in and through linguistic ideology. In M. Inoue (ed.) *The History of Ideology and the Ideology of History. Journal of Linguistic Anthropology (Special Issue)* 14 (1), 1–5.
Irvine, J. and Gal S. (2000) Language ideology and linguistic differentiation. In P.V. Kroskrity (ed.) *Regimes of Language: Ideologies, Politics and Identities* (pp. 35–85). Santa Fe, NM: School of American Research Press.
Jacquemet, M. (2005) Transidiomatic practices: Language and power in the age of globalization. *Language and Communication* 25, 257–277.
Jaffe, A. (1999) *Ideologies in Action: Language Politics on Corsica*. Berlin: Mouton de Gruyter.
Jeater, D. (2002) Speaking like a native. *Journal of African History* 43, 449–468.
Joseph, J. (2004) *Language and Identity, National, Ethnic, Religious*. Palgrave: Macmillan.
Krishnaswamy, N. and Burde, A. (1998) *The Politics of Indians' English: Linguistic Colonialism and the Expanding English Empire*. Delhi: Oxford University Press.
Kroskrity (2000) Regimenting languages: Language ideological perspectives. In P.V. Kroskrity (ed.) *Regimes of Language: Ideologies, Politics and Identities* (pp. 1–34). Santa Fe, NM: School of American Research Press.
Kuzar, R. (2001) *Hebrew and Zionism*. Berlin: Mouton de Gruyter.
Kyeyune R. (2004) Challenges of using English as a medium of instruction in the multilingual contexts: A view from Ugandan classrooms. In M. Jepkirui and A. Nduku Kioko (eds) *New Language Bearings in Africa* (pp. 77–89). Clevedon: Multilingual Matters.
Latour, B. (1993) *We Have Never Been Modern* (C. Porter, trans.). Cambridge, MA: Harvard University Press.
Leeman, J. (2004) Racializing language: A history of linguistic ideologies in the US census. *The Journal of Language and Politics* 3 (3), 507–534.
Lelyveld, D. (1993) The fate of Hindustani: Colonial knowledge and the project of a national language. In C.A. Breckenridge and P. van der Veer (eds) *Orientalism and the Postcolonial Predicament: Perspectives on South Asia* (pp. 189–214). Philadelphia: University of Pennsylvania Press.
Ludden, D. (1993) Orientalist empiricism: Transformations of colonial knowledge. In C.A. Breckenridge and P. van der Veer (eds) *Orientalism and the Postcolonial Predicament: Perspectives on South Asia* (pp. 250–278). Philadelphia: University of Pennsylvania Press.
Makoni, S. (1998a) African languages as European scripts: The shaping of communal memory. In S. Nuttall and C. Coetzee (eds) *Negotiating the Past: The Making of Memory in South Africa* (pp. 242–248). Oxford: Oxford University Press.
Makoni, S. (1998b) In the beginning was the missionaries' word: The European invention of an African language: The case of Shona in Zimbabwe. In K.K. Prah (ed.) *Between Distinction and Extinction: The Harmonisation and Standardisation of African Languages* (pp. 157–164). Johannesburg: University of Witwatersrand Press.
Makoni, S. and Meinhof, U. (2004) Western perspectives on applied linguistics in Africa. *AILA Review* 17, 77–105.
Mamdani, M. (1996) *Citizen and Subject: Contemporary Africa and the Legacy of Late Colonialism*. Princeton, NJ: Princeton University Press.
Mannheim, B. (1991) *The Language of the Inkha since the European Invasion*, Austin, TX: University of Texas Press.

Mazrui, A. (1967) *Towards a Pax Africana: A Study of Ideology and Ambition*. London: University of Chicago Press.

Mignolo, W. (2000) *Coloniality, Subaltern Knowledges, and Border Thinking: Local Histories/Global Designs*. Princeton, NJ: Princeton University Press,

Mudimbe, V.Y. (1988) *The Invention of Africa: Gnosis, Philosophy, and the Order of knowledge*. Bloomington: Indiana University Press.

Mühlhäusler, P. (1996) *Linguistic Ecology: Language Change and Linguistic Imperialism in the Pacific Region*. London: Routledge.

Mühlhäusler, P. (2000) Language planning and language ecology. *Current Issues in Language Planning* 1 (3), 306–367.

Nettle, D. and Romaine, S. (2000) *Vanishing Voices. The Extinction of the World's Languages*. Oxford University Press.

Pattanayak, D.P. (2000) Multilingual contexts and their ethos In A. Ouame (ed.) *Towards a Multilingual Culture of Education* (pp. 37–47). Hamburg: UNESCO Institute of Education.

Pennycook, A. (2002) Mother tongues, literacy and colonial governmentality. *International Journal of the Sociology of Language* 154, 11–28.

Pennycook A. (2004) Language policy and the ecological turn. *Language Policy* 3, 213–239.

Pennycook, A. and Makoni. S. (2005) The modern mission: The language effects of Christianity. *Journal of Language, Identity and Education* 4 (2), 137–156.

Povinelli, E. (2002) *The Cunning of Recognition*. Durham: Duke University Press.

Rafael, V. (1988) *Contracting Colonialism.Translation and the Christian Conversion in Tagalog Society under Early Spanish Rule*. Ithaca: Cornell University Press.

Rajagopolan, K. (1999) Of EFL teachers, conscience and cowardice. *ELT Journal* 53, 200–206.

Ranger, T. (1983) The invention of tradition in colonial Africa. In E. Hobsbawm and T. Ranger (eds) *The Invention of Tradition*. Cambridge: Cambridge University Press.

Ranger, T. (2004) Nationalist historiography, patriotic history and the history of the nation: The struggle over the past in Zimbabwe. *Journal of Southern African Studies* 30 (2), 215–234.

Reagan, T.G. (1996) *Non-Western Educational Traditions: Alternative Approaches to Educational Thought and Practice*. Mahwah, NJ: Erlbaum Associates

Romaine, S. (1994) *Language in Society: An Introduction to Sociolinguistics*. Oxford: Oxford University Press.

Said, E. (1985). An ideology of difference. *Critical Inquiry* 12 (1), 38–58.

Said, E. (1989) Representing the colonized: Anthropology's interlocutors. *Critical Enquiry* 15 (2), 205–225.

Samarin, W. (1996) Review of Adegbija Efurosibina: Language attitudes in Sub-Saharan Africa: A sociolinguistic overview. *Anthropological Linguistics* 38 (2), 389–395.

Schieffelin, B. (2000) Introducing Kaluli literacy: A chronology of influences. In P. Kroskrity (ed.) *Regimes of Language: Ideologies, Politics and Identities* (pp. 293–327). Santa Fe, NM: School of American Research Press.

Shohamy, E. (2001) *The Power of Tests: A Critical Perspective on the Uses of Language Tests*. London: Longman.

Skutnabb-Kangas, T. (2003) Linguistic diversity and biodiversity: The threat from killer languages. In C. Mair (ed.) *The Politics of English as a World Language: New Horizons in Postcolonial Cultural Studies* (pp. 31–52). Amsterdam: Rodopi.
Soyinka, W. (1976/87) In Ogun Abibiman. In W. Odelberg (ed.) *Les Prix Nobel: The Nobel Prizes 1986*. Stockholm: Nobel Foundation.
Spear, T. (2003) Neo-traditionalism and the limits of invention in British Colonial Africa. *Journal of African History* 44, 3–27.
Thomas, N. (1994) *Colonialism's Culture: Anthropology, Travel and Government*. Oxford: Polity.
Vansina, J. (1990) *Paths in the Rain forests: Toward a History of Political Tradition in Equatorial Africa*. Madison: University of Winsconsin Press.
Wallerstein, I. (2000) *The Essential Wallerstein*. New York: The New Press.
Woolard, K. (2004) Is the past a foreign country? Time, language origins, and the nation in early modern Spain. *Journal of Linguistic Anthropology* 14 (1), 57–80.
Yngve, V. (1996) *From Grammar to Science: New Foundations for General Linguistics*. Amsterdam, PA: John Benjamins.
Yngve, V. (2004a) Issues in hard-science linguistics. In V. Yngve and Z. Wasik (eds) *Hard-Science Linguistics* (pp. 14–27). New York: Continuum.
Yngve, V. (2004b) An Introduction to Hard-Science Linguistics. In V. Yngve and Z. Wasik (eds) *Hard-Science Linguistics* (pp. 27–35). New York: Continuum.
Zeleza, P. and Makoni, S. (2006) Rethinking African languages. *Journal of Language Policy* (in press).

Chapter 2
Then There were Languages: Bahasa Indonesia was One Among Many

ARIEL HERYANTO

Having lost its naive objectivism, universalism has been unfashionable among many in the humanities. One consequence of this is illustrated in the discourses on the concept of 'culture'. In the last 50 years or so, culture has been severely deconstructed, demystified and pluralised. One culmination of such awareness finds articulation in the work of Joel S. Kahn, who argues that, despite its inclusive claims and pretensions, 'universalism always has its others and this is unavoidable ... universalism is a culture like any other, differing only in that it always fails to recognise itself as such' (Kahn, 2001: 23). Having seen this we must, nonetheless, admit that the legacies of universalism survive in various areas and often in implicit ways. A case in point is the idea of 'language;' 'human' is another.

This chapter looks at one such universalist legacy in the invention of 'bahasa' (now commonly translated as 'language') in post-colonial Indonesia, the world's fourth most populous nation, and more specifically during the authoritarian government of New Order (1966–98). It will examine the historical circumstances under which such invention could take place the way it did. In order to highlight the radical social transformation that the invention has required, a brief reconstruction of the situation before invention will be attempted. This is a story of an irreversible, though incomplete, restructuring of pre-existing vernacular world-views and social activities of non-Western and non-industrialised communities. I will proceed with an introductory note of the major features of vernacular Javanese and Malay communities, where 'language' was neither existent, nor imaginable. For contrast, salient characteristics of contemporary Bahasa Indonesia will then be examined. Finally, I will suggest some preliminary interpretation of how developmentalism as one form of universalism and practice came to the fore in this historical process. I will also note some of the resistance that the process has provoked.

A World with No Language

Theorists of the incipience of nations have commonly given serious attention to the role of language in the global construction of nations. Not many among them, however, perceive the relationship between nation and language as dialectical and mutually constitutive. Instead they see languages largely as a property of changing communities that facilitated the transformation of these communities from older forms of affinity into nations. In what follows we will examine how the historical construction of Bahasa Indonesia as a *bahasa*, 'language', was both similar and integral to the process of constructing Indonesia as a *bangsa*, 'nation' – as well as her national *Pembangunan*, 'Development'.[1] Once a prevailing and highly ideological term in many parts of the world, Development has started to appear obsolete. The logic that gave it its earlier power, however, and the material interests of those who benefited from its past hegemony survive well under different names ('globalisation' is one of the most popular) with various forms of adjustment to contemporary contexts.

The word *bahasa* has a long history, with Sanskrit origin, that spread well in several communities of what is now South-East Asia, including Indonesia. It did not mean 'language', and not many contemporary Indonesians recognise this. It took European colonialism to introduce the idea of 'language' before the old word *bahasa* came to articulate this newly-acquired concept. The adoption of a pre-existing word in East Asia to articulate a new concept from modern Western Europe helped make the concept appear universal. Language was – as it is today – believed to be a universal property of human species, in all its variations, existing in a separate sphere from, but universally referring to, more or less one and the same objective world.

My preliminary survey suggests that at least in the two most widely spoken and influential languages in Indonesia, Malay and Javanese, there was no word for 'language'. More importantly, there was neither a way nor a need to express the idea until the latter part of the 19th century. Here I am not concerned with semantic or morphological precision. Obviously, the modern words *'bahasa'* and 'language' have more than one variant of meanings and definitions, and each variant has undergone a long history of changes. Taken together, however, they belong to a commonly shared history and particular worldview radically different from that of the old Malay or Javanese *ba(ha)sa*, as we will soon see. For this reason, the discussion below is inevitably problematic. Neither contemporary English nor Bahasa Indonesia can express and represent the vernacular worlds of Javanese and Malay 'as they actually were' so to speak.

The oldest case that I have been able to find where *'bahasa'* makes an entry into a dictionary is in R.O. Windstedt's *The English–Malay Dictionary* (1939: 100). Even as late as that it was used to translate the English word 'culture', presumably because 'language' would mean a very different thing at that time. Now we have some idea of how long and complicated the semantic history of the word 'culture' is in English is (see Williams, 1977: 11–20, 1983: 87–93; Kahn, 1989), but this should not complicate the issue at hand. Apparently there was no word for 'culture' in what is now Indonesia, until the early decades of the 20th century when a few privileged natives in the Dutch East Indies colony began to read what their colonial masters wrote (in admiration, disgust or pity) about 'their own' native cultures. From the third decade of the century, a new term, *kebudayaan*, entered with authority into the public consciousness to translate the various notions of 'culture' as prevailed in Europe.

The very late birth of *kebudayaan* may also explain why Windstedt translated *bahasa* as 'culture' in his dictionary. His rendering of 'culture' as *bahasa* was presumably the best anyone could do at that point. In any case, to equate the old word *bahasa* with 'culture' was then and is now still problematic. Anthropologist Errington tried to exhaust modern English categories to embrace the old idea of *bahasa* in Malay communities: 'religion, culture, manners, norms and speech are equated in the term *bahasa*' (Errington, 1974: 7), and yet with no satisfactory success. She admits that 'it is a falsification even to say that ... these "aspects" are "equated". *Bahasa is unitary* ...' The meanings of *bhāsa* in Old Javanese always include some reference to mighty, highly respected, respectful, or respectable persons, activities, or things (see Zoetmulder, 1974: 146–7, 1982: 220). In contrast to the neutral meanings of the tool-like 'language', both *bahasa* in old Malay and *bhāsa* in Old Javanese did not belong to ordinary persons. They occupy a domain that was confined to persons and activities of high status. This is not something that deserves our celebration, but as we shall soon see, neither does what has come to colonise it in a later period.

The old sense of *bhāsa* survives in modern Javanese in the 20th century as *'basa'* (see Wolff & Poedjosoedarmo, 1982: 5). *Basa* is not an abstract and generic category as 'language' is. It strictly refers to the Javanese speech act, and more specifically to *Krama* (high-level Javanese). Thus, when Indonesians of ethnic Javanese speak in Bahasa Indonesia to each other, they are engaged in a social interaction very similar to their speaking to non-Javanese who speak it. From a vernacular Javanese viewpoint, this is an interaction between 'neutrally' individual interlocutors with disturbingly 'ambiguous' social positions and relationships to each other and to the world. When the same Javanese switch to *basa*, they find themselves in a radically different world. For better or worse, it is unequivocally Javanese, where persons and the whole cosmos have been hierarchically defined and categorised. A Javanese who fails to speak *basa* in any situation where it is called for is described as *during nJawani* ('not yet Javanese'), implying immaturity or being less than human. Anthropologist James T. Siegel (1986) offers a rather cynical account of the nature and complexity of the Javanese *basa* (see more below), and indiscriminately calls it 'language'.

When beginning to study Malay or Indonesian, foreigners often unselfconsciously speak of 'Bahasa' to refer to what the Malaysians and Indonesians invariably call *Bahasa Malaysia* or *Bahasa Indonesia*, the standard names of their respective twin national languages. Most likely, these foreigners want to shorten the proper name, but such utterance sounds odd to the contemporary Indonesian ear. To the latter, *bahasa* is a generic term, 'language', quite distinct from the proper name of a specific language. True, there was a time when *bahasa* meant specifically Malay. However, that was the time in Malay vernacular communities where *bahasa* meant a great deal more than linguistic skills or exchange. One's integrity and stature was to a significant degree measured by it. The expression *budi bahasa* implies stature. Richard J. Wilkinson translates the phrase as 'good taste and courtesy; tact and breeding' (1901: 136). In the old Malay world not every adult necessarily 'knew language'. The popular expression *orang yang tak tahu bahasa* (literally 'a person who does not know language') was commonly used to refer to those who 'know no manners'.[2] In this light, Windstedt's 1939 dictionary rendering of *bahasa* as 'culture' can be better appreciated.

Another indicator of the great shift from the old to the new meanings of *bahasa* is available in the contemporary appropriation of the proverb *bahasa menunjukkan bangsa*, ('manners reveal descent') (Wilkinson, 1901: 136). To many contemporary Indonesians, that old proverb translates as 'language reflects nationality,' a symptomatically modern way of saying 'each community has its own way of life'. The appropriation is mostly unconscious, and the motivation can be understood by examining semantic changes of the words *bahasa* and *bangsa*.

For most of the 19th century, the idea of 'nation' was non-existent in this region, and it remained alien to many indigenous intellectuals at the turn of the century. Pramoedya Ananta Toer's *Anak Semua Bangsa* (*The Child of All Nations*) depicts how absurd the idea of 'nation' was for the late 19th century protagonist personifying Tirto Adhi Soerjo, supposedly the first Indonesian nationalist figure, upon hearing it for the first time from a Dutch acquaintance. It was also extremely difficult for this acquaintance to formulate an explanation (Toer, 1980: 274–5). Even as late as 1921, when writing the now-famous sonnet, *'Bahasa Bangsa'* (see Teeuw, 1979: 10),

Mohammad Yamin (another notable figure in the nationalist movement) did not have the notion of Indonesian nationhood in mind. Rather he was referring to Sumatera island as his homeland, and Minang his mother tongue. Formerly, *bangsa* did not exactly or exclusively mean 'descent'; it could be broadly rendered as 'kind' or 'sort.' Even today in Java one still speaks of *bangsa* as denoting 'groups' or 'type.' Descent is one of several indicators or attributes of one's *bangsa*. Many royal families were called *bangsawan*. In today's Bahasa Indonesia, *bangsa* is an important word meaning 'nation,' one where there is less and less place and privileges for any *bangsawan*, although a new type of aristocrat with global credentials and outlook (the middle class and the bourgeoisie) appears on the horizon (see Wallerstein, 1988).

Ivan Illich (1982), whose insight has been a source of inspiration to this discussion, revitalises the old word 'vernacular' in reference to anything home-made, homespun, home-grown, 'not destined for the market place'. For our present purpose, important features of vernacular worlds include a relatively large degree of autonomy, considerable self-sufficiency and minimal standardisation of human and social practices. The Javanese musical instrument set, the *gamelan*, illustrates this point. To outsiders, a remarkable characteristic of *gamelan* is the fact that each set constitutes not only a complete, coherent and harmonious range of tunes, but it has its own structure and range of sounds. There are no standard tones for different sets and no standard scales for each instrument within a set.[3] Members of a *gamelan* set belong exclusively to each other; each is not always exchangeable with those belonging to other sets. The important implication is that there is no objective and standardised criterion for 'false notes' in this tradition. In other words, there is no one hegemonic set of values providing meanings for a range of concrete entities and activities. Just as is the case with sounds, neither are persons, activities, tools, properties, space, time, words or meaning neutral and standardised units.[4] They are mutually and deeply embedded. They are signified within the particular community's immediate memory and concern. In the words of Illich, they are 'vernacular'. Thus, even if we accept the common ethnocentric and tempocentric biases in the view of 'traditional' rural communities as more static, more rigid and less participatory than their modern counterparts, this judgemental view is seriously flawed in its own terms.

The inseparable re-definitions of *bahasa* and the people to whom it belongs signify a complex chain of historical events. For the moment, let me proceed with two major developments: the idea that *bahasa* (as 'language') and human beings are essentially universal and inseparable entities; and the triumph of industrialised Western definitions of humanity and the world over various non-Western vernacular conceptions and values. It must be said from the outset, this process has not been entirely a coercive imposition. Segments of the vernacular communities welcome it, with different degrees of enthusiasm, and for various reasons.

New Wine in Old Bottles

In vernacular Malay and Javanese communities, the term *bahasa* (or *bhāsa; basa*) did not refer to something abstract and neutral. It was neither a handy tool of communication nor a system of codes or symbols that arbitrarily signified something else (a reality) as 'language' has come to be most commonly understood. It was overtly – more so than today's 'languages' – a social activity. It was explicitly a socially bound practice, rather than secularly and logically rule-governed.

The contrast between that vernacular activity and the meanings of *bahasa* should now be obvious. The prestigious *Ensiklopedi Indonesia* describes *bahasa* as,

Kumpulan kata dan aturannya yang tetap di dalam menggabungkannya berupa kalimat. Merupakan sistem bunyi yang melambangkan pengertian-pengertian tertentu ... Secara umum bahasa tak tergantung kepada susunan masyarakat. Perubahan struktur sosial dan ekonomi sedikit saja pengaruhnya kepada perkembangan bahasa.

(Groups of words and the rules governing those words to form sentences. It is a system of sounds that signifies certain meanings ... In general, language does not depend on social structures. Changes in social and economic structures do not greatly influence the development of language.) (Shadily, 1980: 358)

There is no suggestion that *bahasa* has any direct or essential relationship with human beings. In fact, the relationship between language and social structures is explicitly denied. A reference to human beings is made in another Indonesian encyclopedia, *Ensiklopedi Umum*, but the separability between human thought/feelings and human language remains. Here, *bahasa* is defined as:

ungkapan pikiran dan perasaan manusia yang secara teratur dinyatakan dengan memakai alat bunyi. Perasaan dan pikiran merupakan isi-bahasa, sedangkan bunyi yang teratur merupakan bentuk-bahasa.

(the orderly expression of human thought and feeling as manifested in speech. Feelings and thoughts are the content of language, the orderly sounds are the form of language.) (Pringgodigdo and Shadily, 1973: 139)

In this view, thought/feelings can presumably exist outside language, and vice-versa. Significantly, no example of language-free thought or feelings (or thought-and-feelings-free language) is presented by proponents of this commonly held view. Although Hassan Shadily was responsible for preparing both encyclopedias, there is a striking difference between the two in their views on the relation between language and social structure. The second work notes that social factors are inherent in the structure of language. 'Linguistic expressions depend on the social milieu of their speakers' (Pringgodigdo & Shadily, 1973: 139).

To be fair, there are various views of language among Indonesian intellectuals. I have discussed this briefly elsewhere (Heryanto, 1987: 43). Nonetheless, it is fair to say that for many, language is merely a reflection of social structures (see e.g. Simatupang, 1983; Moedjanto, 1985: 299). More seriously problematic is the notion of language as primarily an objective instrument, detachable from human thought, social structures and worldly interests. This view informed the initial writings of one of the forefathers of Indonesian grammar, Sutan Takdir Alisjahbana (1959). It is also shared by Anton M. Moeliono (1982: 8), one of Indonesia's most eminent figures in the promotion of language planning at the height of the nation's Developmentalism. Other figures of importance who subscribe to the same view include Daoed Joesoef (1983), then a Minister of Education and Culture, and a number of other Indonesian thinkers, Gunawan Wibisono Adidarmodjo (1983), Harsja W. Bachtiar (*Kompas*, 1985) and Jujun S. Suriasumantri (1985). The same notion was presented by President-to-be General Soeharto in the embryonic year of the New Order (Soeharto, 1967: 37). Pushing further the orthodoxy of the day, Khaidir Anwar writes:

> as far as cognitive thought and knowledge is concerned, one's language acts mostly as an instrument rather than a shaper. Our *Weltanschauung* has not much to do with our native language, and our considered opinion of an issue having socio-political significance is not shaped by our mother tongue. (Anwar, 1980: 12)

Alternative views that acknowledge the inseparable links between language and social life exist among Indonesians. Unfortunately, such views are extremely rare, too much on the periphery of the discourse to draw the public attention they deserve, and are mostly presented in passing comments. Early examples worthy of mention include Slamet Iman Santoso (1983) and Sartono Kartodirdjo (1987). Contrasting views of language can also be examined by the way old communities and their descendants deal with words and names. Modern Indonesians are familiar with the English aphorism 'what's in a name?' (in translation *apalah artinya sebuah nama?*), emphasising the arbitrary relationship between a name and the person or thing being named. By contrast, more traditionally-inclined Malays and Javanese acknowledge certain divine links between at least selected words and events. Theirs is a world where proper names and formulaic words have real or potential supernatural power. Their *mantera*, 'magic formulas,' charms and spells are deployed to create, prevent, negotiate or control events of major importance. There are taboos on uttering certain names (e.g. of deities, royal families, spirits, heirlooms and certain animals).

Within such communities that can still be found in many parts of Indonesia, people are very careful about naming children so as to avoid misfortune. Thus, the relationship between a name and the named is not considered arbitrary. To many Javanese, each name has what is called *bobot* (weight). *Bobot* in relation to naming a person refers to the quantity and quality of supernatural power it carries. Parents want to make sure that each of their children has a benevolent and auspicious name. However, each person in this community is entitled to only a particular range of possible names in accordance with his or her status. When a child often gets sick or goes through other major difficulties, the common practice is to change the child's name to lighten its spiritual burden. The child is thought to suffer from bearing a name with too much *bobot*.

It is tempting to account for such contrast by adopting the familiar categories such as 'traditional' communities versus 'modern' societies. While there is admittedly some value in using these categories, it is important not to assume that they are mutually exclusive, distinguished objectively by levels of achievement and superiority, and that one category will inevitably replace the other in consistent and predictable ways (the variations across the world being only in pace and styles). The process is obviously much more complex and messier than that. Despite this, by and large the global process invariably undermined indigenous definitions and imposed a new set of definitions, a new ordering of meanings. It is also observable that the major source of energy in these social changes came predominantly from the modern West. The experience of Malay or Javanese communities is not unique. The vast and interrelated corpus of writings on colonialism, imperialism, under-development, dependency, post-colonialism, subalternism and globalism seeks to explain the Western cultural domination of various communities in the world, its varied local manifestations, and also the responses it provokes. Unfortunately, a common feature of these writings is their tendency to make sweeping generalisations about the histories of different non-Western communities. More seriously from the point of view of our concern here, the questions of language are inadequately or poorly treated, if at all. One recent attempt to rectify this has come from the collaborative work of Rigg *et al.* (1999). These authors seek to offer a better understanding of local perceptions and languages of Development in South-East Asia in the 'post-developmentalist' era. They shed new light on local variations of certain Developmentalist keywords in Thailand, Burma and Indonesia. But they stop short of asking the more fundamental issues of the mode of communication ('languages') that gave birth to selected keywords they analyse.[5]

Discussing the early rise of nationalist consciousness in Indonesia, Benedict Anderson (1996) notes the impact of Western contact with Java. He describes the shattering of the old Javanese cosmology after the introduction and rapid expansion of trains, clocks and the newspaper industry in late 19th century Java. The traditional perspective of time, space, human beings and all other realities was radically and fatally challenged by a new 're-presentation' of reality: maps, calendar, statistical figures and the print alphabet. Anderson shows how confident the Javanese had been in their relatively autonomous and closed cosmology.

> In the 18th and 19th centuries, Javanese rulers had called themselves *Pakubuwono* (Nail of the Cosmos) and *Hamengkubuwono* (Holder of the Cosmos) without much self-consciousness, though from today's perspective there is something irremediably laughable about rival rulers with capitals (Surakarta and Jogjakarta) less than 50 miles apart calling themselves by such world-conquering appellations. (Anderson, 1996: 27)

The extent to which the changes in the 19th century affected confidence in the old cosmology can be imagined from Anderson's next few lines:

> By 1990, however, Jogjakarta and Surakarta were, above all, railway junctions along the trunk-line between the great port cities of Batavia and Surabaya. These cities in turn were subordinates to The Hague; and The Hague was the capital of a speck on the northwest periphery of Europe ... there was no longer any place or person whereby the Cosmos could be nailed. In colonial classrooms cheap metal globes were being happily *spun* by 'native' children. (Anderson, 1996: 27–8)

Ba(ha)sa was under a great and growing threat. 'In the 1890s the colonial regime for the first time began a sustained effort to turn local elites bi- or trilingual through the institution of government primary and (later) secondary schools' (Anderson, 1996: 29). It was no longer possible for the Javanese to ignore the newly perceived fact that Javanese was no other than one of many existing languages. In lieu of the monopoly of *basa* in the Javanese cosmos, people began to speak more and more of *Ba(ha)sa Melayu*

('Malay'), *ba(ha)sa Belanda* ('Dutch') and later *Bahasa Indonesia* ('Indonesian'). It is now common for Javanese to speak of *Bahasa Jawa* ('Javanese'). The use of dictionaries among the schooled elites from near the end of the 19th century led to a further conviction that 'languages are translatable' (Anderson, 1996: 29). Still more fundamental to our concern than these all-encompassing changes, something that lies beyond Anderson's immediate interest, was the idea and practice of learning a powerful language in state-sponsored formal schooling.

The demise of the old *ba(ha)sa* and the rise of *bahasa* as 'language' can be seen as part of the process of both globalisation and Westernisation. In this we see not only the application of industrialised definitions of language and human beings globally, but we also see a particularly Western mode of language practice occupying the dominant positions in the global social hierarchy. Western languages – Western *standardized* languages, to be more precise – become the model for language studies. A high correlation between student's achievement of mastering Indonesian and English was evident by the early 1980s (see *Kompas*, 1984), well before MTV 'Americanised' the language of urban youths, advertisements and entertainment industry more broadly. While painfully, though not always coercively, unlearning their own traditions, indigenous communities began to learn what appears to be the more powerful and more materially rewarding 'knowledge' and 'truth' available in Western languages and world-views.[6]

The shift of fundamental meanings of *bahasa* from being specifically Javanese or Malay into that of being a generic, abstract and universal category strips off people's vernacular world-views without the service of a new vocabulary. It is not a quantitative change (in addition to the familiar Javanese *basa* they now discover a number of other kinds of *bahasa*), but a qualitative one. Speaking of both ancient and modern colonialism, Becker (1984: 145) notes that one of its most subtle forces 'is the undermining of not just the substance but the framework of someone's learning'. The industrial Western domination in bahasa is subtle, for it expresses itself in what appears to be an 'indigenous' word.

As we shall see, this Westernisation is not totally covert or subtle. Neither is its conquest taking place without resistance.[7] For the moment, we need only to note how this redefinition of *bahasa* implies a redefinition of human beings in the world (Williams, 1977: 21) and how the new redefinition relates to Development.[8] The breakdown of the old meanings of *bahasa* implies a serious challenge to the former concept of esteemed human beings. Nowadays, one's failure in performing the proper *bahasa*, as indicating that one has not yet achieved the status of becoming Javanese or Malay, hardly has any validity. Every Javanese and Malay is now taught to view and define his/her essential being and that of others anew: all are indiscriminately and universally 'human beings', regardless of abundantly re-newed inequalities. In the 1940s Javanese nationalists joined the confident advocacy of their fellow countrymen in propagating the idea of 'humanism' in the Constitution and the official state ideology, *Pancasila*. Today, *Kemanusiaan*, 'humanitarianism' has become one of the most respected and glorified notions, at least in formal speeches; its value has certainly outweighed the importance of being *nJawani* or keeping one's *budi bahasa*.

A case in point that best illustrates the experience of contemporary Bahasa Indonesia is the impressive widespread use of the pronoun *Anda*, after the English pronoun 'you'.[9] The word was introduced with the specific aim to stamp out and replace the many existing options for the second-person pronouns, which modernists often have perceived as confusing and 'non-democratic' in character. In the 1970s a colleague of mine collected over 50 different second-person pronouns in use in the small town of Salatiga, each designating a different interpersonal relationship. The successful promotion of *Anda* cannot be fully explained merely in terms of cultural assertion by one section of the nation's elite or the aggressive invasion of English. Rather, it must also be attributed to technological development in the expanding mass media in New Order Indonesia: messages must be communicated to a mass and abstract audience. How else should a presenter address this newly constituted and widely varied audience but by the neutral term *Anda*?

As *bahasa* was perceived to be a generic category and global phenomenon, persons became individual human beings, and vernacular communities were transformed into a nation. In sum, in contrast to the major features of vernacular worlds discussed above, standardisation, abstraction and globalisation have now prevailed. Although some 'localisation' has lately become a necessary element in the gambit of global capitalism, and 'multi-culturalism' was for a while politically correct, these have come and gone as dictated at a higher level by the logic of centralised efficiency, accumulated profit and global domination.

Developmentalism Revisited

The global standardisation of what were formerly exclusive, autonomous and heterogeneous beings laid the foundations for what in subsequent years became Development programmes. Advancing the idea of modernisation and standardisation of Bahasa Indonesia, Alisjahbana (1976: 59) 'consider[s] the plurality of languages in the modern world ... a great handicap.

It hampers ... understanding between individuals as well as nations'. He asserts this with full awareness that standardised language entails standardised general behaviour, which he values highly (Alisjahbana, 1976: 101). The 1980s saw the imposed standardisation of traditional arts and ritual practices, which had long been independent of elite engineering (see *Surabaya Post*, 1986; *Kompas*, 1986; Zurbuchen, 1990). Following the idea of normatively homogenous beings is the idea of standardised 'basic human needs.' As Illich (1979, 1982) argues, we have now come to a point where presupposed basic human needs translate materially into a set of consumption patterns. Fulfilment of these basic needs is defined as consuming an increasing amount of mass-produced industrial commodities.

The use of the term 'Western' to designate the current world hegemony has become increasingly unsatisfactory. Words like 'industrialisation', 'Development' and 'globalisation' have all had their currency for a while. They indicate that the Western world still dominates but not exclusively so. In global capitalism, industrialisation requires a significant degree of standardisation to make mass production and market exchange faster, easier and more economical. Variations of 'localisation' are tolerated and at times necessary, but they are tolerated as long as they operate under control and pose no threats to the overall system. Progress demands the demise of autonomous diversity, including vernacular activities, social institutions and worldviews.

This is not to romanticise what – at a distance – appears exotic, especially after Asian dictators misappropriated history to launch the propaganda of nativist identity (e.g. Asian values). Many modern schooled Javanese accept the popular condemnation of (real or imaginary) 'Javanese traditional culture', where inequity was justified and popular participation denied. Some of the Developmentalists' critiques of traditional culture have been refreshing and empowering to them. The point is that having claimed to liberate millions of people from 'backwardness' and to bring equity, democracy and enlightenment, Development and more recently neo-liberalism have evidently led them to another series of alienation, disempowerment and dependence, this time of an even greater scale. Once 'liberated' from their vernacularity, Javanese or Malay words can now be translated into any industrial languages across the globe; the speakers become ostensibly 'free' individual wanderers whose labour is theoretically but never wholly freely exchangeable in the ruthless market.

The constitution and reproduction of this hegemony relies heavily on the mass standardised consumption of its products. That mass consumption in turn rests on the assumption of scarcity of basic needs and on modern economics, which is based on that same assumption. Thus, no longer do members of the Javanese or Malay communities – at least their elite – attempt to achieve 'self-defined' states of being (for example, to be *nJawani*, or to acquire *budi bahasa*). They must now compete with other 'human beings' for the same universally standardised and scarce attainments. As industrialisation has developed hand-in-hand with capitalism, communities across the globe have been made to consider greed as respectable (Benjamin, 1988: 13). Equity is now seen to mean (re-)distribution of the new privilege to consume what is scarce. Even words and meanings have become 'scarce' industrial commodities in a way that would have been unthinkable in the communities of the East Indies archipelago during the 19th century. Prerequisites that were formerly sensible only in limited activities, such as construction and industry, are now regarded by a former head of the nation's Language Centre as indispensable requirements for sustaining Bahasa Indonesia: 'man-power, material, management and money' (Halim, 1981: 335).

The distinguishable communities in what is now Indonesia are losing not only their own definitions of what constitutes their basic needs, but also the productive competence to satisfy such needs. They are now dependent on the products of industries. They can only hope to consume what they cannot produce. Significantly, Javanese has one verb, *(ng)gawe*, to refer to what would be two opposite notions in English or Bahasa Indonesia: 'to produce', *membuat*, and 'to consume', *memakai*. But even to say that *(ng)gawe* is both 'to produce' and 'to consume' is inappropriate. The expression *nduwe gawe* ('to have a *gawe*') does not simply refer to some physical behaviour, but to a religious ritual and festivity. When the Javanese strove to be fully *nJawani* or the Malay endeavoured to acquire sufficient *budi bahasa*, they depended on no one, let alone outsiders (the Gods and spirits of ancestors being the exception). Neither *budi bahasa* nor being *nJawani* was economically scarce. In the contemporary language of Development, exclusive and distinct vernacular values are disappearing.

The early years of Indonesian nation-building witnessed the beginning of a phenomenal proliferation of new words circumfixed by *ke- -an* and *pe(r)- -an* (Poedjosoedarmo, 1981: 155), a tendency which Alisjahbana (1976: 58) considers a desirable indication of the modernisation of Bahasa Indonesia. These circumfixes are nominalisers, significantly referring to abstraction and generalisation. The construction of *Pembangunan* in early decades of the 20th century was only a case in point.[10] That word re-presents the old communities anew, as one of many 'developing' nations on the globe.

Communities of human beings across the globe are put in a hierarchy by their degree of industrial Development. Some are commonly termed 'underdeveloped', others are 'developing' and still others are already 'developed'. In the contemporary language of Development, there is only a single phrase to designate the best projected possible future of these 'developing nations': being 'developed', an appellation traditionally identified with the modern West and only recently extended to accommodate newly-industrialised countries. Seen in this light, the so-called 'New Industrialising Countries' are posing a challenge to their Western rivals only in terms of a game the West initiated, not a radically alternative redefinition of living. A bird's-eye view of Development Studies literature (Goldsworthy, 1977) suggests that critiques of conventional-modernist Development are often followed by attempts to reform, redefine and modify Development (see Rigg *et al.*, 1999). De-Development and anti-Development are hardly considered.

Other forms of resistance and defence on the part of the Indonesian communities are worth considering.[11] Much of James Siegel's (1986) observation of the Javanese in Surakarta during the New Order period attests to the residual vitality of the old idea and practice of *basa* that he disapproves. As Siegel (1986: 18) says, when the Javanese speak *basa*, the appropriate tone chosen is 'not to match one's feeling to one's words, but to one's listener's sensibility'. The words are chosen 'not according to [one's] listener's capability to understand, but as though languages are not arbitrary matters' (Siegel, 1986: 19). In speaking *basa*, the Javanese 'has to find out where the hearer fits in society, and then speak as though the words were attached to the status, part of the nature of the world' (Siegel, 1986: 19). Preserving their own definitions of *basa* as separate from 'language,' according to Siegel (1986: 298–9), the Javanese would acknowledge only those translatable into Javanese as 'language.' And when they are seen as languages, they are treated 'as though they were Low Javanese' that must be suppressed by way of translation into High Javanese (Siegel, 1986: 301).

Despite the strong position of the Javanese in Indonesia, Javanese and 'Javanism' are not what Indonesia is all about.[12] Unlike the Javanese that Siegel observed in Surakarta, the nationalist elite is more self-conscious in confronting what they see as undesirably Westernised standard grammars and studies of Bahasa Indonesia. Throughout the history of the nation, the idea of indigenising the national language has been expressed repeatedly, but, as is evident, to little avail.[13] Some of the most important and common concerns among these critical intellectuals, themselves products of Western-style education, are the applicability of Western linguistic categories such as subject/predicate/object, nouns/verbs/adjectives, or passive/active voice. Reflecting on this issue, Alton L. Becker (1983: 11) asks why South-East Asians did not evolve their own 'meta-language' in the sense of 'the language of the grammar'. He suggests that there are at least two answers.

First, 'grammar comes with writing' and basic writing systems in Indonesia (Indic, Arabic, Roman) came from elsewhere. The second answer, one less obvious, is closer to the main argument of this chapter. 'Southeast Asians have traditionally taken a different approach to the description of language, one more appropriate to an oral poetic economy' (Becker, 1983: 11). Attempts at the indigenisation of Indonesian grammar are doomed to failure as long as the historical construction of what constitutes 'language' remains unquestioned.

Conclusion

Westernisation of the Indonesian language has long been a point of concern among some circles of the nation's emergent *literati*. However, as mentioned several times earlier, the process of Westernisation was and is not wholly one of coercion. For other and more influential intellectuals, of whom Sutan Takdir Alisjahbana became a key spokesman, Westernisation was/is not only legitimate but also necessary and desirable. In one of its early issues, the journal *Pembangoenan*, directed by Sutan Takdir Alisjahbana, stated that,

> *Seperti bangsa Timur yang lain, bangsa Indonesia dengan sengaja pula menyongsong kebudayaan Eropah, dengan jalan memasuki sekolah yang didirikannya, membaca bukunya, menjadi pegawai dalam perusahaannya, turut menyertai perdagangan internasional dan lain-lain.*
> (Just like other nations of the East, the Indonesian nation consciously welcomes European culture by attending the schools it founded, reading its books, becoming employees at its firms, taking part in international trade, and so forth.) (*Pembangoenan*, 1946),

Denouncing some strong tendencies in the Indonesian language of his time, Nur Sutan Iskandar, a prominent author in the first quarter of the 20th century, lamented in a 1956 article, 'there are many more peculiarities in the use of words and sentence constructions which only Western-educated intellectuals can grasp the meaning of' (cited in Anwar, 1980: 117–8). This kind of stance was seen as ignorantly conservative by many leading intellectuals of the time. A quarter of century later we find Khaidir Anwar expressing the elitist view, that 'ordinary readers tended to have much simpler ideas than the sophisticated writers' (Anwar, 1980: 118). Furthermore, he explains that those Indonesian writers,

> Regarded themselves as intellectuals in the true sense of the word ... they did not want to give the impression that they were not acquainted with the sophistication of the Western ideas. They even regarded themselves as legitimate heirs of world culture ... [and they] by and large wrote care-

fully-thought out Indonesian prose because they took pains to do so relying mainly on a Western language as a mode. (Anwar, 1980: 118)

As all communities across the globe are seen to possess their own languages, we have seen a diagram, 'a family tree' of languages, and a map of nations of the world. A century ago Javanese and Malay elites acquired a new literacy that enabled them to read and locate their newly redefined *ba(ha)sa* within the global map of languages. Since the beginning of the 20th century, they have accepted the self-fulfilling conviction that languages are more and more translatable. Once their *bahasa* was redefined in Western terms, they made vigorous efforts to find the 'knowledge' and 'truth' discoverable only in Western languages, by way of translation and adoption. In 1945 Indonesian modernists proudly published a new 'World-List' in which 8000 new words (mostly for scientific discourse) were introduced after being 'legalised by the Indonesian Language Committee' (see *Pembangoenan*, 1945).

Commenting on what he calls 'industrialised' languages, Ivan Illich (1982: 6, 8) notes that they 'translate easily from English into Japanese or Malay'. What must be added is the fact that 'industrialised' languages, like nations, have been sharply stratified into a new and ugly hierarchy. Contemporary Indonesian elites are quite convinced that some languages, like their own, are less 'developed' than others. To quote the title of Kuntoro's (1984) essay, *'Bahasa Indonesia Belum Berkembang'* ('Indonesian language is still underdeveloped'). To redress the 'shortcomings' of their own language, they have launched nationwide programmes for Developing the language and have chosen Western standardised languages as models of what a 'developed' language should be like (see Alisjahbana, 1976: 55; Moeliono, 1977; Badudu, 1985).[14] Ironically, it is the very notion and success of language Development that has engendered the conviction among contemporary Indonesians that their language is 'bad and incorrect.' Thus, with the growing investment in state-sponsored programmes for language Development, Bahasa Indonesia has become a national language that the nation does not – according to the official assessment – speak and write properly.

Acknowledgements

The author gratefully acknowledges the benefits of having the comments on an earlier version of this chapter from those who do not necessarily agree with the arguments presented here: Alton L. Becker, Joel S. Kahn, Francis Loh, James Scott, Benedict Anderson and the two co-editors of this book, Alastair Pennycook and Sinfree Makoni. Thanks are also due to Nina

Heryanto for her typing assistance when an earlier version of this chapter was prepared. Unless indicated otherwise, all translations of phrases and citations are the author's. The author alone is responsible for shortcomings in this chapter.

Notes

1. I purposefully spell 'Development' with a capital 'D'. This is to underscore its newly-acquired status as an independent noun (e.g. '... of Development'), in contrast to its older sibling 'development,' a noun of process (e.g. 'development of ...'). An earlier version of the arguments (significantly altered and updated here) can be found in Heryanto (1990). For a more elaborated account see Heryanto (1995).
2. Interestingly Wilkinson's (1901: 136) old dictionary translates the expression as those who have 'no breeding'. It is possible that has been more than one salient rendering in the past, or a major semantic shift has taken place since then.
3. Reportedly there have been attempts to standardise the gamelan in Bali, but their scale and appeal have been limited. Such attempts have not necessarily been motivated by the logic of industrialisation as elaborated in a moment or commercial pursuit. One reason has to do with the increased desire to experimentally create new fusion music, where Western musical instruments dominate, and ethnic flavours such as the gamelan occupy some decorative space.
4. For more examples of conceivably 'language-free' or 'unstandardised universe', see Milroy, 2001: 539–43).
5. Curiously, these authors rely mainly on non-Southeast Asian writings when they claim to study locals' views and languages. Unlike their analysis of the Thai case, the analysis of language of Development in Indonesia is presented without a single reference to text in Indonesian or by Indonesians. For a critique of orientalist tendencies in South-East Asian studies see Heryanto (2002).
6. See Milroy (2001) for an excellent account of the ideology of the standard language and how linguists have been affected by and contributed to such ideology.
7. Though not immediately relevant to the discussion at hand, see Blommaert (1999) for cases of the ideological battle in language practice across the globe.
8. For the next few paragraphs I am indebted to the insight of Ivan Illich (1982).
9. Elsewhere I made a modest attempt at examining the significance of the use of *Anda* (Heryanto, 1978).
10. For a further account of the historical construction of the New Order keyword, *Pembangunan*, see Heryanto (1988).
11. Owing to the unavailability of sufficient data, in the following I consider only examples of resistance from Javanese and Westernised cosmopolitan Indonesians. For some brief comments on the case of Malay communities, see Benjamin (1984/5).
12. For more on the recent engineering of Javanese in Java see Errington (1998: 278–81).
13. A collection of works by Armijn Pane (1953) presents an early and serious questioning of this issue, but suggests no substantial and comprehensive alternative. Most other writers make only passing comments on the matter. A

more recent published study on this issue is that of Bambang Kaswanti Purwo (1988). Although no sweeping generalisation can be made, many of the indigenisation projects and desires are paradoxically indebted to, and derived from, Western colonial thoughts. The Asian values rhetoric is a case in point. Advocates of the Asian values argue for both the existence and desirability of some imagined native or authentic moral heritage, which may in fact be no more than an invention of Western colonial knowledge, reinvented in the post-colonies by a strongly Westernised, but anti-West, Asian political elite.

14. Soon after East Timor gained independence from Indonesia, the new nation's Prime Minister visited Jakarta and during his visit proposed that Indonesia help set up a language centre in Dili (*The Jakarta Post*, 2003).

References

Adidarmodjo, G.W. (1983) Bahasa Indonesia sebagai pembentuk jalan pikiran. *Suara Karya*, 18 November.
Alisjahbana, S.T. (1959) *Tatabahasa baru Bahasa Indonesia* (Vol. II, 19th edn). Jakarta: Pustaka Rakyat.
Alisjahbana, S.T. (1976) *Language Planning for Modernization*. The Hague: Mouton & Co.
Anderson, B. (1996) Language, fantasy, revolution: Java 1900–1950. In D. Lev and R. McVey (eds) *Making Indonesia: Essays on Modern Indonesia in Honor of George McT. Kahin* (pp. 26–40). Ithaca: Southeast Asia Program, Cornell University.
Anwar, K. (1980) *Indonesian: The Development and Use of a National Language*. Yogyakarta: Gadjah Mada University Press.
Badudu, Y.S. (1985) Bahasa Indonesia, bahasa kita. *Kompas* 15 May, p. 4.
Becker, A.L. (1983) Language construction and poetic change: Observations on the Indonesian National Center for Language Development. Unpublished paper for a seminar held by Pusat Pembinaan and Pengembangan Bahasa, Jakarta.
Becker, A.L. (1984) Biography of a sentence: A Burmese proverb. In E. Bruna (ed.) *Text, Play and Story* (pp. 135–155). Washington: American Ethnological Society.
Benjamin, G. (1984/5) Meaning, morphology and history in the Malay dialect: Continuum. A paper for the Fourth Eastern Conference on Austronesian Linguistic, Ann Arbor, August 1985.
Benjamin, G. (1988) The unseen presence: A theory of the nation-state and its mystification. *Working Paper No. 91.* Singapore: Department of Sociology, National University of Singapore.
Blommaert, J (1999) (ed.) *Language Ideological Debates*. Berlin: Mouton de Gruyter.
Errington, J. (1998) Indonesian('s) development; On the state of a language of state. In B. Schieffelin, A. Woodland and P. Kroskrity *Language Ideologies: Practice and Theory* (pp. 271–284). Oxford: Oxford University Press.
Errington, S. (1974) A disengagement: Notes on the structure of narrative in a classical Malay text. A paper for conference on Modern Indonesian Literature, Madison, 28–29 June.
Goldsworthy, D. (1977) *Analysing Theories of Development*. Clayton: Centre of Southeast Asian Studies, Monash University.
Halim, A. (ed.) (1981) *Bahasa dan pembangunan bangsa*. Jakarta: Pusat Peembinaan dan Pengembangan Bahasa.

Heryanto, A. (1978) Benarkah Bahasa Indonesia memerlukan 'Anda'? *Surabaya Post* 7 October.
Heryanto, A. (1987) Kekuasaan, kebahasaan, dan perubahan sosial. *Kritis* 1 (3), 1–53.
Heryanto, A. (1988) The development of 'development' (N. Lutz, trans.). *Indonesia*, 46 (October), 1–24.
Heryanto, A. (1990) The making of language: Developmentalism in Indonesia. *Prisma* 50, 40–53.
Heryanto, A. (1995) *Language of Development and Development of Language*. Canberra: Pacific Linguistics.
Heryanto, A. (2002) Can there be Southeast Asians in Southeast Asian Studies? *Moussons* 5, 3–30.
Illich, I. (1979) The new frontier for arrogance: Colonization of the informal sector. Paper for the General Assembly of the Society for International Development, Colombo, Sri Langka, August 15.
Illich, I. (1982) *Gender*. New York: Pantheon Books.
Jakarta Post, The (2003) RI asked to set up language center in East Timor. 13 June.
Joesoef, D. (1983) Bahasa akademik, bahasa asing, Bahasa Indonesia. *Sinar Harapan* 28 October, p. 6.
Kahn, J. (1989) Culture: Demise or resurrection? *Critique of Anthropology* 9 (2), 5–26.
Kahn, J. (2001) *Modernity and Exclusion*. London: Sage.
Kartidirdjo, S. (1987) Fungsi humaniora dalam pembangunan nasional, in three parts. *Kompas*, 26–28 February.
Kompas (1984) Dr Jawasi Naibahoi korelasi Bahasa Indonesia dengan Bahasa Inggris positif. 15 October, p. 9.
Kompas (1985) Kemampuan berbahasa rata-rata siswa memprihatinkan. 10 May, p. 1.
Kompas (1986) Festival reog Ponorogo mencari pembakuan. 21 September, p. 6.
Kuntoro, S. (1984) Bahasa Indonesia belum berkembang. *Pikiran Rakyat* 29 October, p. 7.
Moedjanto, G. (1985) Konsolidasi kedudukan dinasti mataram lewat pengem bangan bahasa Jawa. *Basis* 24, 24–8.
Milroy, J. (2001) Language ideologies and the consequences of standardization. *Journal of Sociolinguistics* 5 (4), 530–55.
Moeliono, A.M. (1977) Bahasa Indonesia dan ragam-ragamnya (Part II). *Kompas*, 26 October.
Moeliono, A.M. (1982) Bahasa dan struktur sosial. *Analisis Kebudayaan* 1 (3), 8–15.
Pane, A. (1953) *Perkembangan Bahasa Indonesia: Beberapa tjatatan*. Djakarta: Pustaka Kita.
Pembangoenan (1945) Kamoes-Istilah. An advertisement 1 (1), 10 December.
Pembangoenan (1946) Kesoesasteraan: Poeisi baroe sebagai pantjaran masjarakat baroe. 1 (4), 68–70.
Poedjosoedarmo, S. (1981) Problems of Indonesian. In A. Halim (ed.) *Bahasa Dan Pembangunan Bahasa*. Jakarta: Pusat Pembinaaan dan Pengembangan Bahasa.
Pringgodigdo, A.G. and Shadily, H. (eds) (1973) 'Bahasa'. In *Ensiklopedi Umum* (pp. 139–142). Jogjakarta: Jajasan Kanisius.
Purwo, B.K. (1988) Menyibak Alisjahbana dan Keraf: Ke arah jalan keluar. *Kritis* 2 (4), 7–22.
Rigg, J., Allot, A., Harrison, R. and Kratz, U. (1999) Understanding languages of modernization: A Southeast Asian view. *Modern Asian Studies* 3 (3), 581–602.

Santoso, S.I. (1983) Bahasa Indonesia dalam proses pengebirian. *Sinar Harapan* 6 (December), 4.
Shadily, H. (chief ed.) (1980) *Enslikopedi Indonesia* (Vol. 1). Jakarta: Ichtar Baru and Van Hoeve.
Siegel, J. (1986) *Solo in the New Order: Language and Hierarchy in an Indonesian City.* Princeton: Princeton University Press.
Simatupang, M.D.S. (1983) Aspek sosial budaya dalam berbahasa. *Suara Karya*, 28 October.
Soeharto (1967) Bahasa dan sastra Indonesia amat penting dalam pembinaan Orde Baru. In L. Ali (ed.) *Bahasa dan Kesusastraan Indonesia sebagai Tjermin Manusia Indonesia Baru* (pp. 37–39). Djakarta: PT. Gunung Agung.
Surabaya Post (1986) Topeng Malangan sedang dibakukan dua sanggar. 27 November, p. 11.
Suriasumantri, J.S. (1985) Peningkatan Sarana Berpikir Ilmiah. *Sinar Harapan*, 13 August, p. 6.
Teeuw, A. (1979) *Modern Indonesian Literature* (Vol. 1; 2nd edn). The Hague: Martinus Nijhoff.
Toer, P.A. (1980) *Anak Semua Bangsa*. Jakarta: Hasta Mitra.
Wilkinson, R.J. (ed.) (1901) *A Malay–English Dictionary*. Singapore: Kelly & Walsh Ltd.
Wallerstein, I. (1988) The bourgeois(ie) as concept and reality. *New Left Review* 167 (Jan–Feb), 91–106.
Williams, R. (1977) *Marxism and Literature*. Oxford: Oxford University Press.
Williams, R. (1983) *Keywords* (2nd edn, revd). New York: Oxford University Press.
Windstedt, R.O. (ed.) (1939) *An English–Malay Dictionary* (3rd edn). Singapore: Kelly Walsh Ltd.
Wolff, J. and Poedjosoedarmo, S. (1982) *Communicative Codes in Central Jawa.* Linguistic series VII. Ithaca: Southeast Asia Program, Cornell University.
Zoetmulder, P.J. (1974) *Kalangan*. The Hague: Martinus Nijhoff.
Zoetmulder, P.J. (ed.) (1982) *Old Javanese–English Dictionary* (Part I). 'S-Gravenhage: Martinus Nijhoff.
Zurbuchen, M.S. (1990) Images of culture and national development in Indonesia: The Cockroach Opera. *Asian Theatre Journal* 7 (2), 127–49.

Chapter 3
Critical Historiography: Does Language Planning in Africa Need a Construct of Language as Part of its Theoretical Apparatus?

SINFREE MAKONI and PEDZISAI MASHIRI

Introduction

Our main objective in this chapter is to explore the implications of adopting a 'human linguistics' (Yngve, 1996: 80) on language planning in Africa. From such a perspective 'language is not a thing that leads a life of its own outside and above human beings, but it has true existence only in the individual, and all changes in the life of a language can only proceed from the individual speaker.' (Yngve. 1996: 28). In a 'human linguistics' perspective it is people and the activities that they are engaged in which should be central to a study of language so from such a perspective the primary goal of language planning in Africa would be to promote and change the political and economic status of people by enhancing the nature of communication between them. Enhancing communication between people is valuable because 'communicative tasks are often subtasks of nonlinguistic tasks ... and interface naturally with practical affairs' (Yngve & Wasik, 2004: 23), so the ultimate objective of language planning would be to create communicative contexts that would enhance people's abilities to carry out their activities to improve their social welfare. If the ordinary objective of human linguistics is to enable people to carry out their activities, and language is a sub-task within that process, language cannot exist in 'splendid isolation' (Yngve & Wasik, 2004: 23). In a 'human linguistics' perspective in which people are of primary importance, people are seen as using language and not as language users. To call people language users is therefore 'perverse' because we are defining people in terms of language (Yngve, 1996: 77).

Many scholars working on Africa have observed frequently that African governments are either reluctant or unwilling to comprehensively implement language policies that seek to promote what are regarded as indigenous languages (Stroud, 2001). The alleged failure by African governments to implement such language policies is attributed to their preference for English or French, which in turn is construed to be a result of neo-colonialism. Unfortunately, that argument is historically wrong. The argument is based on the assumption that one of the primary objectives of colonial governments was to promote either English or French. The argument is not historically valid because colonial governments were much more inclined to promote African languages than either English or French. Contrary to the neo-colonial argument it was African parents themselves who strongly argued for the use of English in education (Summers, 2000; Makoni & Truddell, 2006). The main thrust of our argument in this chapter, however, is not on the historical aspect of language planning, illuminating though such an analysis might be, but on the theoretical notion of language in African language planning and the implications of reframing language from a 'human linguistics perspective' in language planning in Africa.

The oft-reported failure of African language planning policies in Africa has paradoxically created unique opportunities for us to critically examine some of the assumptions made about African languages. The lack of success of language planning policies in Africa is not due to an unwillingness or inability on the part of African governments to implement language policies but is due to a theoretical tendency to treat African languages as if they were real objects. We are neither the first nor the only scholars to be skeptical about the belief that languages are entities in the real world, arising from a conflation of natural and artificial objects (see Yngve, 1986, 1996; Yngve & Wasik, 2004; Danzinger, 1997). While a number of scholars have questioned the existence of languages in the real world, such skepticism has rarely been articulated in the African context in research in language planning. If African languages are not entities in the real world, for language planning to succeed it has to reorient itself away from assuming that it is dealing with real entities, and to seek to enhance communication between people. Our position is not that we should dispense with language planning as an enterprise in Africa, but that we should reorient ourselves away from a reification of languages as if they existed in the real world, towards frameworks whose primary objectives would be, first, to promote people, and second, to enhance communication between them. An African Linguistics carried out from a 'human linguistics' perspective leads us to reformulate our questions even in other areas of African languages: 'We could say that we are interested in how children learn to talk and that we are curious about how the way we view the world (and we could add people) depends on the way we have to talk about it' (Yngve, 1996: 73).

The position we are adopting is the converse to conventional models of language planning, whose main goals are to promote the status of languages. Such models do not pay much, if any, attention to how people talk about the world and each other. The models assume that, by changing the status of a language we will be able to alter their social and economic status. We are arguing that changes in the status of language can occur as a result of changes in the social, political and economic status of its speakers. The converse does not necessarily occur. People's social-economic status will not necessarily improve because the status of their languages has been changed.

If our conceptualizations of African languages are to change, we have to *disinvent* the discourses of African languages. For *disinvention* to take place, it is necessary to intervene at a level of discourse, at the level of representations, and by implication at a level of conceptualization. The ultimate objective of *disinvention* is to facilitate alternative ways of framing and conceptualizing African languages. In this chapter we therefore *disinvent* five dominant ways of conceptualizing African languages:

(1) linguistic diversity as enumerability;
(2) the naming game;
(3) conceptualizing African languages;
(4) constructing indigeneity; and
(5) dictionaries as discourse and as a theory of African Languages.

The arguments we are putting across are not necessarily unique to Africa, although they may assume heightened significance in Africa. Not only may they resonate with minority language experiences in Europe and other ex-colonial situations such as India, but our arguments here have significance for how all languages are understood.

Linguistic Diversity as Enumerability

In this section we analyse the role of enumeration in the conceptualization of African diversity. Greenberg (1966) in *Languages in Africa* estimates that there are about 800 different African languages. Crystal (1997: 316) places the number of languages in Africa at about 2000. Mann and Dalby's (1987) estimate is relatively higher than that of Crystal: They suggest that Africa has approximately 2550 languages. There is an on-going debate among those in the linguistic community, anthropologists, aid groups, educational planners and African governments on the exact number of

African languages. Even well established linguists, with extensive experience in Africa working in a single polity, seem to be undecided about the exact number of languages. For example, Whiteley (1974) assigns 47 languages to Kenya on page 21, and then he mysteriously reduces the number to 34 on page 27 (Njoroge, 1986: 330). According to the Kenyan government, Kenya has a total of 39 languages. The estimates for languages in Malawi are said to vary between 12 and 35; such a wide variation is not peculiar to Malawi. Estimates of the number of languages in Zambia vary even more widely. Sometimes it is suggested that there are 20 languages in Zambia, at other times as many as 73 (!) (Williams, 1992).

The variability in the number of African languages is not peculiar to either southern Africa or East Africa. Grimes (1974) estimates the number of languages in Cote D'Ivoire to be 58. A year later, the 1975 official census reports that Cote D'Ivoire has a total of 69 languages. The Summer Institute of Linguistics International (SILI) (an organization that has extensive experience in the codification of African languages) in 1995 listed a total of 74 languages for Cote D'Ivoire, 73 living and one extinct (Djite, 1993: 16). The controversy about the number of African languages foregrounds important theoretical issues that have a direct bearing on applied areas such as language planning and language in education. It is highly unlikely that we will ever come to a general agreement on the exact number of African languages.

Mühlhäusler (1996: 36), with his mind focused on the Pacific region, suggests that the lack of agreement on the numbers of languages does not so much reflect the inability of linguists to distinguish between communalects, languages and dialects but the non-existence of languages as constructed in a formal Western sense. Although Mühlhäusler did not have Africa in mind, his argument is equally relevant there. Paradoxically, the discrepancy and controversy in the number of African languages is not an unfortunate situation. It is, indeed, a situation that should be encouraged. It compels us to rethink some of the foundational concepts in African linguistics such as whether we need notions about language as a way to frame and describe African sociolinguistic contexts. If the appropriateness of the notion of language is open to question in African contexts, we perhaps need to examine not only the notion about language, but to go even further and question the appropriateness of concepts such as sentence, phrase, form and content widely used as a basis for analysing African languages.

The numbers game in African languages is symptomatic of the powerful influence of *census ideology* in African linguistics. *Census ideology* is the backbone of the enumerative modality, one of the five modalities used to frame colonial and post-colonial narratives about Africa. The other four modalities are: (1) *historiographic*, (2) *observational/travel modality*, (3) *survey modality* and (4) *museological* (Cohn, 1996: 8). The enumerative modality, unlike other modalities, is based on the idea that African languages can be converted into countable forms, are describable, and can thus be prescribed. In short, the enumerative modality is predicated on the belief that languages in general, but African speech forms in particular, can be contained and controlled. In order for the counting to take place, the languages are labeled, even though 'naming languages is a type of consciousness, an artifact embedded in the consciousness of Western formal education' in a continent in which a majority are not formally literate in a Western sense of the term (Makoni *et al.*, 2003: 3). Ideologically, the numbers play a dual role. In some cases the numbers are used to oppress the speakers of those languages, while on the other hand, Phillipson (2003) and Skutnab-Kangas (2000) and other like-minded scholars evoke the same numbers to demand redress and compensation.

The Naming Game

In this section we illustrate how the notion that languages have names emerged, and the impact naming has on ways in which the African linguistic map is understood. Because the linguanyms often coincided with ethnonyms (the Shona spoke Shona, the Zulu spoke Zulu, the Bambara spoke Bambara) the production of linguistic maps also produces ethnic maps simultaneously. We illustrate how the naming, cataloguing and classifying was part of a project of developing encyclopaedic colonial inventories (Fabian, 1986). Linguistically, the variability in the number of languages (Table 3.1) is in part a consequence of the different names assigned to the 'same' speech variety (at times even within the same polity) resulting in counting the same speech variety more than once, thus inflating the number of African languages (Djite, 1993).

Because some of the African languages are spoken and used in a number of different polities, they have (not surprisingly) multiple names. For example, a Zulu-based pidgin spoken in mining towns in southern and central Africa, derogatively referred to by European colonialists as either

Table 3.1 Multiple names for certain varieties

Country	Names of languages
South Africa	Fanagolo, Isikula, Silngubi, Cilolo
Congo	Kituba, Ikeleve, Fiote, Monokituba
Cameroon	Nso, Lmaso, Bansaw

'kitchen kaffir' or 'mine kaffir' is referred to as *Fanagolo,* in South Africa, *Chilapalapa* in Zimbabwe, *Cikabanga* in Zambia, and *Kitanga* in the Democratic Republic of the Congo (DRC). There is also a tendency to regard mutually-intelligible languages as distinct because they are historically associated with different political dispensations (some of which predate colonialism). For example, *Kirundi* and *Kinyarwanda* owe their identities to different kingdoms that have evolved into modern day Burundi and Rwanda (Masagara, 1997: 385).

There is also a discrepancy between the names used by linguists and those by speakers themselves. The names used by applied linguists have generally been the versions created by colonialists; this is not surprising since, in Africa, applied linguistics is heir to colonialism. In ethnomethodological terms, the names of the languages used by colonialists and applied linguists do not necessarily correspond with those used by the speakers themselves. For example, Djite cites two languages spoken in west Africa, *Guere* and *Wobe*, which, on the basis of ostensibly objective linguistic criteria, can be treated as different languages, but are regarded as the 'same' language by *Guere* and *Wobe* speakers themselves. According to the speakers, the distinction between *Guere* and *Wobe* 'exist in the language of the white man' and the speakers identify themselves with the bigger Akan community (Djite, 1989: 6).

Evidence of the impact of European colonialism in shaping Africa's linguistic map is widespread across Africa and is not confined to west Africa only. In some cases the names were not only imposed, but they were pejorative as well. The pejorative nature of the labels has not escaped the colonialists themselves. For example, Springer, writing in 1909 about *ChiShona* in southern Africa, comments, 'Various terms have been invented by the white man, the most common being *Chiswina,* meaning, *the language of the filthy people'* (Springer, 1909: 4). In Malawi, 'the missionaries and early explorers were responsible for giving the language (*ChiChewa*) the name *ChiNyanja* during the pre-colonial era' (Mvula, 1992: 45). Mvula recounts how early Portuguese explorers entered south eastern Africa in the Quelimane region where they came across the Maravi or Chewa people. The Maravi people were nicknamed Amanyanja since they lived in the area near the lake or Shire River, commonly referred to as Nyanja. Hence, Anyanja meant *people of the lake* and ChiNyanja, *'the language of the lake people'* (Mvula, 1992: 45). In 1968, four years after independence, Malawi replaced the name ChiNyanja with ChiChewa.

The arguments by Djite (1989), Springer (1905) and Mvula (1992), among others underscore the need to pay close attention to how speakers construct their languages, and the need to build descriptions and classifications that

Table 3.2 Reconstructing the ancestor language

Language	Word for 'three'
Proto-Bantu	tatu
Modern Bantu: Sepedi	raro
kiSwahili	tatu
Konde	thathu
Zulu	thathu

take into account the perspectives of the users, as part of a project of decolonizing the thinking that shaped the so-called indigenous languages. The perspectives of the users normally reflect the nature of the social relationships among the speakers from the 'allegedly' different groups (Hymes, 1983), unlike those used by linguists which are ostensibly built on 'objective' linguistic criteria whose accuracy in some cases is open to question. The legacy of objectivism is apparent in how African speech forms are divided into distinct 'languages' and the languages further subdivided into 'families'. At times the 'languages' are traced to a common ancestor, a proto-Bantu (Guthrie, 1972) or ur-Bantu (Carl Meinhof, 1932). Proto-Bantu and ur-Bantu are historical reconstructions, linguistic fictions, and not real languages. They are reconstructions based on the assumption that all Bantu languages developed from a common ancestor. The examples in Table 3.2 demonstrate how the reconstruction of the ancestor language is carried out.

The analysis of the neogrammarian, Carl Meinhof, demonstrates that Bantu languages are 'related' and belong to the same *family* and that there was historical continuity with proto-Bantu. The comparative method, which was applied to African languages, has been used in other regions of the world – for example, in the Pacific region (Crowley, 1989). The classification, however, excluded 'mixed language' contact, vehicular languages and creoles, which went undescribed because they were treated as ideologically marginal. They were marginal ideologically because they were used mainly between Africans and not between Africans and Europeans (Errington, 2001: 29). The reconstruction of proto-Bantu languages also created a linguistic interpretation of history, based on an idealization of historical processes, a simple juxtaposition of present states and hypothetical states without any reference to intermediate states. Thus, a whole range of data endowed with variation has been excluded from historical analysis. Cohn levels a much more powerful critique of the comparative method when he writes:

The power of comparative method was that it enabled the practitioner to classify and control variety and difference. At a phenomenological level the British discovered hundreds of languages. As with genealogies, which could represent all the members of a family or descent group visually as a tree with a root, trunk, branches, and even twigs, so could dialects and languages be similarly represented and grouped. Significantly, the trees always seemed to be *northern European ones, like oaks and maples*, and the British never seemed to think of using the most typical south Asian tree, the banyan, which grows up, out, and down at the same time. (Cohn, 1996: 55; our emphasis).

Bantu languages are the biggest language group within the Niger-Congo languages. The Niger-Congo is the biggest 'language family' in Africa south of the Sahara, and (so it is claimed) is spoken by about 260 million people in western, central, eastern and southern Africa (Webb & Kembo-Sure, 1999: 33). The linguistic relationship between the languages is apparent if the words used for the same concept are analysed as illustrated in Table 3.2 above.

The discourse of language classification of African languages is an object of analysis because, as a type of discourse, it shapes our images of and conceptualizations of African languages. From a feminist perspective, the discourses on the classification of African languages are striking. 'Family' imagery is used to enframe relationships between African languages. The metaphor of a 'family' is an extremely powerful and emotive one even when used analytically (Irvine & Gal, 2000). Unfortunately, as an idiom it might be ill suited to describe relationships between 'languages' because like any metaphor it carries baggage, extra implications about languages and their speakers – such as whether those speakers share a common interest, whether they are co-participants in some global community, and whether their participation is inevitably differentiated according to a social hierarchy. In some cases, related languages are described as 'sister' languages. The feminization of African languages is obvious when 'languages' such as Hausa, are said to be 'impregnated with semiticism.'

Methodologically, the classification of African languages into distinct, hermetically sealed units (Makoni, 1998), although ostensibly based on objective linguistic data, unfortunately excludes the perspectives of the speakers. It furthermore conceals the role of the analyst. Linguistic objectivism arises from a double demand. On the one hand, the analyst is expected to be objective, while at the same time s/he is expected to be immersed in local life. The labels/names assigned to the languages subsequently shape the sociocultural identities of speakers of African languages.

The issue, therefore, is not one of simply getting the right name for what one speaks, but an awareness of the constitutive nature of naming. The labels are not merely *descriptive*, they are *constitutive* (Danzinger, 1997), resulting in Africans seeing themselves through the lenses assigned to them. Historically, such invented labels are frequently mobilized in nationalistic and ethnic politics. For example, Webb (2003: 289) remarks on a growing consciousness of linguistic identity in South Africans producing self-identifying statements such as 'I speak Tswana, not Northern Sotho' using exactly the same categories invented by colonial administrators. Yet, as van Warmelo (1974: 74, cited in Herbert, 1992: 2) rightly observes, 'It is difficult to draw any real boundary between Tswana and Northern Sotho, and further, the Northern Sotho "cluster" contains sufficient diversity to raise some doubts about its essential unity'. The linguistic consciousness arises as a result of speakers' experiences of their languages in written form. The impact of print on the formation of ethnic identities is neither a recent phenomenon nor is it peculiar to South Africa as Webb implies. Ranger (1989), a well-known historiographer of colonial Rhodesia (now Zimbabwe), reports on the emergence of a similar consciousness in the early 20th century among missionary and European-educated Africans in Zimbabwe.

Conceptualizing African Languages

Conceptually, African linguistic diversity is an artifact of constructing separate languages whose boundaries may not necessarily have any social or functional reality. A demarcation based on purely linguistic criteria does not necessarily translate into boundaries of communication (Djite, 1993). If the African map was designed on the basis of communication rather than imagined language differences it would be relatively easier to produce workable language planning solutions (Djite, 1993). In the African continent, the issue of redrawing African linguistic boundaries has ramifications that go beyond language. Chimhundu argues:

> What the Europeans actually did when they partitioned Africa was effectively to stop the perpetual movements of groups of people. The result was to freeze the geopolitical and ethno linguistic maps which the Europeans themselves created by their own rules during the early stages of colonial rules. African linguists and historians need to look at these maps again. (Chimhundu, 1985: 89)

Stroud (2001) elaborates on the lack of 'fit' between the construct of 'language' and multilingual environments. He argues that the construct of 'language' may be poorly attuned to multilingual developing nations. The construct of multilingual networks may be better suited to describe the nature of the language practices that one encounters within an African context. African speakers 'move into, between, and across many different semiotic practices, exhibiting multiple and varied practices of language use, such as language crossing and mixed registers' (Stroud, 2001: 350). Interest in the problematic nature of 'language' has implications for other important areas such as Linguistic Human Rights. The rights discourse seems to treat notions about 'language' as having an ontological validity independent of the discourse in which they are articulated. The meaning of 'language' (its significance) is very much a strongly contested area of inquiry, the outcome of divergent and conflicting ideological positions. The word language is used in several senses and it is not obvious that the senses are compatible with each other. Language is construed as a:

> natural phenomenon, the object of science, a type of faculty, a type of system, as voluntary behavior, as something used, as something taught and learned, as having learned elements, as having patterns, as something spoken, heard, and learned as something processed, as something organized and structured, as something produced and comprehended as data. (Yngve, 1996: 10)

It is not clear that each of the aforementioned notions of language is necessarily compatible with the notion of linguistic 'rights'. Stroud (2000) tries to address the problematic nature of the notion of language by proposing the notion of 'linguistic citizenship'. This is a potentially useful framework since it enables Stroud to reframe language in a way that emphasizes how 'language, its meanings and significance, is very much a constrained and contested object and the sociohistorical outcome of debate, legislation, divergent ideologies and social conflict' (Stroud, 2000:348). The notion of linguistic citizenship is a powerful corrective that challenges the overwhelming hold of a structuralist view of language, a view which has a powerful impact on how African languages are imagined. If our imagination of African sociolinguistics is organized around discrete, countable, unitary languages, we end up conjuring an image of 'exceptional linguistic African diversity' (Breton, 2003: 204) which may lead us to formulate inappropriate language policies.

Constructing Indigeneity

Mudimbe in *The Invention of Africa* and subsequently in *The Idea of Africa*, argues compellingly that the idea of Africa was an invention (Mudimbe, 1988, 1994). He argues that the invention was carried out through a deployment of a series of Eurocentric and conceptual tropes and discourses commencing with Greek narratives about Africa, through to anthropological and missionary discourses and philosophy. Africa was therefore being imagined and embedded in foreign discourses. Even though the idea of Africa as an invention is widespread in African studies, indigenous languages in African linguistics have been treated as if they were primordial. This has had major policy implications in which the goal of the projects was the promotion of the so-called indigenous languages. In the following section we argue that the ways in which indigenous languages are constructed is an invention. The process of invention is not restricted to the colonial era, as the construction of chiChewa in Malawi and Runyakitara in Uganda demonstrates. Bernstein illustrates how during the heydays of the Buganda kingdom, Runyakitara was regarded as a single language, but after the advent of missionaries, it was divided into two. In the early period after the attainment of Ugandan independence in the 1970s it was further divided into four separate languages. Currently, there are attempts to reduce it into a single language. The history of Runyakitara therefore illustrates how a single language moved from one to two, to four and then back again to one (Bernstein, 1998).

The concept of *indigenous languages* is one of the key concepts through which African sociolinguistics is narrated and imagined. Its significance is apparent in how it is frequently evoked to frame decisions on language planning and policy within African polities. In terms of language planning, when African countries are selecting language policies they typically choose among three options: (1) to opt for a colonial language, (2) to opt for an ex-colonial language or (3) to choose a combination of indigenous and ex-colonial languages. The main objective of this chapter is not to debate whether or not English can still be defined as a colonial language (although that is an interesting issue in its own right), but to argue that the opposition between English and African languages, frequently constructed as one between colonial and indigenous languages, is conceptually flawed and is historically unsustainable because the so-called *indigenous* languages are a colonial creation themselves. The concept of indigenous languages is a post-colonial response to the consequences of colonialism. Indigenous languages are therefore a post-colonial prism through which pre-colonial Africa is imagined.

Paradoxically, the languages that are defined as *indigenous* in post-colonial Africa were construed as inauthentic during the colonial era by missionaries, their African assistants, colonial administrators and local Africans themselves. For example, Africans referred to the version of ChiShona used in the educational system (chiShona is spoken mainly in

Zimbabwe, Mozambique and South Africa) as *Chibaba* – the language of the priests. The priests were even more candid, defining one of the ChiShona dialects as *Jesuit language* (Ranger, 1995). It is these indigenous languages that were framed as colonial languages and not English by educated Africans (Ranger, 1985). The process of invention was not restricted to colonial Africa; it was part of a general process in British colonialism. Breckenbridge and van der Veer, writing about India, comment in ways that resonate with the African experience: 'The very languages that are called "native" are products of an intricate dialectic between colonial projects of knowledge and the formation of distinctive group identities' (Breckenbridge & van der Veer, 1993: 6). In southern Africa, sociohistorical investigations of languages like Tswana, Zulu, Xhosa, Tsonga and Ndau were recently reconstructed, hence in need of *disinvention* and *reconstitution* (Makoni, 1998, 2003; Cook, 2001; MacGonagle, 2001)

The process of invention, unlike most other language standardization situations, was NOT one of converting a linguistic continuum into discrete languages, but that of actively creating 'ideal languages' (Eco, 1995) which reflected more European epistemology than prevailing local social realities (Harries, 1995: 40). The creation resulted in a production of African languages that were not anybody else's mother tongue. Invented African languages have their socio-genesis as second languages. In Zimbabwe the creation of complex orthographical rules (word division) and spellings was part of the harmonization of chiShona by Clement Doke (1931). The ChiShona language committee and Fortune (1972) produced a type of ChiShona that no one used successfully outside the context of an examination (those who use it are likely to view it more as a second language than as their first language).

The process was not one of simply reducing African speech forms, but in Harries' (1989: 87) felicitous terms, that of 'compiling' an inventory of linguistic forms and regulating meaning through the production of dictionaries. For example, Swiss missionaries created a language called Tsonga 'as a lingua franca for a dauntingly confusing pot-pourri of refugees, drawn from the length and breadth of coastal south-east Africa, who shared no common language and lived in scattered villages that were independent of one another' (Harries, 1995: 29). Tsonga is currently spoken in northern and eastern Transvaal in South Africa and the southern part of Mozambique. The people who occupied this region were not a coherent social and linguistic entity. They were made up of refugees from a series of political and ecological upheavals prompted by Gaza civil wars in the 1860s and the Shakan refugees (hence Harries' assertion that they were a pot-pourri of refugees).

After the compilation of a linguistic inventory, and now referred to as Tsonga, it was subsequently reintroduced into the area to give what was originally a heterogeneous area the appearance of linguistic coherence. The term Tsonga is pejorative, Zulu in origin, and literally means *'conquered peoples'*. The inhabitants of this geographical region were then for practical purposes to be appropriated by an indigenous language assigned to them. The important issue to emphasize here is that the missionaries, through their positivistic orientation, failed to see that the linguistic inventories (which were to be subsequently defined as languages) were human constructs that were not scientifically objective. 'Unlike microbes or river moths, the Ronga and Thonga/Shangaan languages were not awaiting discovery; they were very much the invention of European scholars and, perhaps even more so, of their African assistants' (Dwyer, 1999). The compiled inventories, which were to subsequently pass for languages, were to also subsequently shape the oral language, particularly for those who were to be educated through the medium of indigenous languages. Historically, the compiled inventory called Tsonga was to develop three discrete dialects as part of its process of compilation and development.

The compilation of the inventory was part of an imperial hegemony, an attempt to control and bend African realities to suit European epistemology (Harries, 2001: 410) which created a context in which *descriptive appropriation could become an avenue for linguistic imposition* (Fabian, 1986). Did the missionaries, colonial administrators, and their African collaborators succeed in shaping African realities to suit European epistemology? The answer has to be a qualified, no. Even hegemony has its limits, as Said, with his mind on a different context, said:

> ... reality is neither at the individual's command (no matter how powerful) nor does it necessarily adhere more closely to some peoples' mentalities than to others. The human condition is made up of experience and interpretation, and these can never be completely dominated by power: they are also the common domain of human beings in history. (Said, 2003)

The process of creating 'new' versions of African languages entailed not only developing an orthography but constructing grammatical rules and regulating words through lexicography. 'Once established, the grammatical rules were subsequently portrayed as operating autonomously of their creators. Their person-made origins were forgotten and they were conceived as givens operating according to the laws of science' (Harries, 1995: 43). According to Irvine, because of academic pressures for 'objectivity' in linguistic science, the

... personal, or socially situated character of authors and speakers disappeared – or was made to disappear – from African linguistic analysis at both the speaker end and at the linguist end, in pursuit of a science of language, pursued within the conditions of an imperial system. (Irvine, 2001b: 87)

From a constructionistic perspective, the danger of effacing the social situated nature of knowledge construction is that a constructed linguistic phenomenon assumes an ontological status independent of the analysts and producers. The constructed knowledge is presented as natural knowledge. Colonial knowledge is therefore made to pass for official knowledge (Prah, 1999).

From the perspective of the missionaries and colonial administrators, they 'owned' Tsonga and used their control and influences over the colonial state to 'promote' their versions of African languages in collaboration with missionary-educated Africans. The monopoly held by the mission, and later by the government, over the publication of Tsonga books and African books crucially shaped and determined what Africans read. In colonial applied linguistics, as in anthropology and folklore, Africans were readers, consumers of texts (Yankah, 1999). They generally were not expected to be authors (Irvine, 2000). They were, in Said's terms, expected to be at best 'compliant natives' (Said, 1997: 172). Print literacy was taught so that Africans could read the Bible, not so that they would write books of their own. Africans might be translators, interpreters or copyists; they might offer (oral) sermons to fellow Africans (if supervised), but they were not to sermonize to Europeans, or hold authority over them (Ranger, 1995; Irvine, 2001: 80). When Africans were subsequently to be writers they did so initially based on colonial epistemological assumptions. For example, using 'invented languages' and 'dialects', Africans produced 'tribal pasts' and 'tribal histories' (Ranger, 1985: 15). Europeans tried to shape how Africans conceptualized themselves by articulating European world views through African linguistic forms, a process analogous to what Franz Fanon (1967) called *Black Skin White Masks*.

Dictionaries as Discourse and as a Theory of African Languages

The notion of 'dictionaries as discourse' is unusual because it runs counter to assumptions about dictionaries and language. Dictionaries are widely regarded as a type of list or listing whose organizational principles differ substantially from discourse in the everyday sense (de Beaugrande, 1997). The discrepancy recedes, however, if we define discourse not as an artifact of language based on the model of everyday conversation, but as any communicative event among participants. We shift our focus from dictionaries as tangible artifacts of paper and ink, over to the compilation and use of dictionaries as communicative occasions occurring under characteristic circumstances (de Beaugrande, 1997; Benson, 2001). In an African context, dictionary production has to be understood within a broader context of colonialism, neo-colonialism and Black Elite Supremacy.

The development of lexicography in African applied linguistics has been driven by Christianity, colonial expansion, and anthropology – rendering any avoidance of issues about political imperialism in African applied linguistics an historical and intellectual impossibility. Recently lexicography has been driven by developments in descriptive linguistics, specifically corpus linguistics (Prinsloo & de Schruyver, 2001, 2002). Corpus linguistics has led to the launching of ambitious lexicographical projects. To date, corpora have been developed for at least 15 different 'languages' including Ciluba, Swahili, ChiShona, isiZulu and isiXhosa (Prinsloo & de Schruyver, 2000).

Most of the early dictionaries in African languages were bilingual. For example, one of the earliest dictionaries (published before Johnson's famous English dictionary) was a quadrilingual dictionary comprising Italian, Latin, Spanish and kiKongo (1650). Other significant bilingual dictionaries include Biehler's *English/Chiswina* dictionary (1927), his *Shona Dictionary* (Biehler, 1950) and a *Zulu/Kaffir* dictionary (1953). Lexicographical research is becoming increasingly monolingual. For example, in Zimbabwe, the agenda set in 2000 for the African Languages Research Institute (ALRI) was, amongst other things, to produce monolingual dictionaries in ChiShona and SiNdebele as apparent in Chimhundu *et al.*'s *Dictionary Duramzwi reChishona* (1996), and Hadebe *et al.*'s *Isichazanazwi SesiNdebele4* (2001). ALRI's' agenda dovetails with, and is inspired by, those of the national terminology services and the lexicographical unit for siNdebele in South Africa, and the National kiSwahili Council in Tanzania and the Center for Language Studies in Malawi.

The shift from bilingual dictionaries to monolingual dictionaries warrants an explanation. Most of the bilingual dictionaries were modeled around European languages; bilingual lexicography created a space that enabled Europeans to exercise authority over African languages. If bilingualism enabled Europeans to exercise authority over African languages, monolingualism created opportunities for African scholars to exercise counter authority over African languages. Monolingualism literally provided opportunities to 'write back'. In an intellectual context in which bilingualism is celebrated, it is important to resist the tendency to villainize 'monolingualism'. It is necessary to take cognizance of the intellectual strategies that the researchers are pursuing and to avoid an uncritical celebration of bilingualism. A shift from bilingual to monolingual dictionaries is taking place against a background in which the relationships between African expertise and western scholarship are radically being reconfigured. Ranger makes an astute observation when he writes, ' ... in contemporary Africa and Asia expatriate scholars have to accept partnership or apprenticeship as a condition of doing research at all as part of an effort to replace old colonial relations of dominance' (Ranger, 1995: 272). The bold effort to insist that Western scholars serve as apprentices to African scholars as a prerequisite for carrying out research is taking place in a context in which, paradoxically, powerful donor agencies exercise an influence over African intellectual agenda in ways more powerful than in earlier decades.

African applied linguists, as with other African intellectuals, are concerned that their agenda is in danger of 'being domesticated' (Hyden, 1993. 252) by outsiders, a majority of whom do not empathize with their predicament. Because they cannot always represent themselves, they continue seeing themselves through other people's lenses, images and an external intellectual idiom. The apprehension which African scholars feel has to be understood within a context in which most of what the West knew about the non-Western world, it knew in a framework of colonialism and approached the African 'subjects' in a position of dominance. It is this position of dominance that African scholars are seeking to challenge as they insist on making research apprenticeship a precondition for research involvement by Europeans in Africa.

Dictionaries during the colonial era were part of a process that encouraged Africans to internalize European epistemology about themselves, creating a new view about their current affairs and superimposing new values on their past (Makoni, 2003; 142). These dictionaries invented fresh and ideologically laden relationships between words and meanings, giving European meanings to African words. The internalization of European epistemology by African-educated speakers resulted in rural and educated Africans not being able to readily relate to each other's worldviews, although ostensibly speaking the 'same' languages. Dictionaries in the colonial era can be construed as a perfect example of Bentham's *Panopticon* (Foucault, 1977). An analysis of dictionaries written between 1890 and 1931 in Southern Rhodesia (now Zimbabwe) demonstrates the role of dictionaries in providing an important epistemological and Foucauldian lens through which African societies were observed, surveyed and controlled. Hartman in his 1893 dictionary translates *'gentle-*

man' as *murungu* which in Shona vernacular refers to whites, thus implying that the only people who could be 'gentlemen' were Europeans. Incidentally, a century after Hartman's dictionary, Mawadza (2000: 95; Mashiri, 2003: 123) demonstrates that urban ChiShona has now the same meanings as the ones invented by Europeans in formations of European meanings of African words.

The colonialists were preoccupied with raising revenue through wage labor and at times imposing hut taxes on Africans. People who refused to be engaged in wage labor were defined as 'lazy' or 'dishonest'. Holy Spirit was translated as *mudzimu unoyera*; *mudzimu* in African cosmology refers to the spirit of the deceased. Other dictionaries went so far as to define God as *mudzimu*, an interpretation that is inaccurate even from an Africanist perspective because *mudzimu* is an intermediary and not an ultimate being.

Jeater aptly describes the process that took place in the embedding of European epistemology within African languages when she comments:

> To find a word for '*god*' or '*sin*' or '*spirit*' in a local vernacular that did not do damage to the concept as understood by Christians was a powerful method of forcing missionaries to think deeply about the spiritual ideas of those they hoped to convert, and so to identify points of connection, entry points between the two cosmologies. The missionaries were not just recreating the languages in textual form, making decisions about phonetics, orthography and word division based on European languages, they were bending the vernaculars to their will and making them do new things. The language projects were important, not because they helped missionaries to converse with Africans, but because they enabled them to appropriate African languages, and to reinvent them within the Christian tradition. (Jeater, 2000: 457)

An analysis of colonial dictionaries demonstrates that there was a systematic effort to 'bend' African words to express European epistemological views. Unlike other African scholars (Mazrui & Mazrui, 1998), we are arguing that colonial images are covertly inscribed in the so-called indigenous languages. The argument that indigenous languages have been bent to embody European meanings clearly has implications on how relationships between 'signifier' and 'signified' within those languages can be conceptualized. From the perspectives of the compilers of the colonial dictionaries, the relationships between 'signifiers' and 'signified' were clearly NOT arbitrary, but were socially motivated.

A different set of claims is being made for dictionaries designed on electronic corpora; 'Compiling and querying electronic corpora has become a sine qua non as an empirical basis for contemporary linguistic research' (de

Schryver & Prinsloo, 2000: 89). Taking the suggestions of some of the key protagonists of corpus linguistics and lexicography seriously, we 'query' some of the claims of corpus linguistics as a type of dictionary discourse. Electronic corpora aspire to build corpora that are both 'representative' and 'balanced', and are based on 'authentic' as opposed to 'invented'/'concocted'. The categories of analysis, ('authentic', 'representative', 'balanced') are terms of reference used in relation to English corpus linguistics and have been a source of much controversy (Sinclair, 1991; McCarthy & Carter, 1995; de Beaugrande, 2001; Widdowson, 2000). The terms are potentially 'ethnocentric' because more research has been carried out on corpora in English. Conceptualizations about English corpora are unintentionally foisted on corpora of other languages (Makoni & Meinhof, 2003). Hegemony is being defined here as the imposition on African languages of the staple discourses associated with English (Fardon & Furniss, 1994: 16). The danger of the hegemonic relationship is not only the unwitting imposition of English discourses on African languages, but that the nuances within 'English discourses' are stripped of that complexity when they are transferred to other languages. .

The discourse of dictionaries creates the idea that the texts that make up the corpora on which the dictionaries are based are 'representative' of the language in use. The corpus is therefore presented as representative of language in use, when it is, in reality, a collection of texts, a magna vocabulary. The magna vocabulary of the corpora that form the basis of the dictionaries cannot be said to be representative because they do not constitute the vocabulary of any native speaker. If the dictionaries are based on 'texts' as contained and assembled in a corpus, then the meanings are derived from texts and not directly from language in use because, in a written ecology, languages are 'measured by authoritative collections' and not by how they are used. Because the 'magna vocabulary' as contained in dictionaries has an authoritative status, it entrenches a prescriptive tendency within language.

The blurring of the distinction between *language as actually used*, and *language as assembled* in a collection of texts is an artifact of language as an 'Autonomous Text' (AT) in which the meaning is encoded in a text, and no other information is necessary for its interpretation, such as who the speaker is, whom she is addressing, (who else may be listening, the mood of the speaker, etc.) (Grace). ATs are typically used to encode and decode propositions, and to communicate factual information. 'The nearest approximations to AT language can be – and are sometimes – spoken, its prototypical medium is writing. The spoken forms are derivative. AT languages are not natural languages' (Grace). If AT languages are not natural languages, then the language in corpora cannot be read as exemplars of 'authentic language'. They are an artifact of an AT language.

The development of metalinguistics is necessary because it is difficult to separate our knowledge of African languages from the categories that are used to describe them. In other words, it is difficult to maintain a clear distinction between the *language under description* from the *language of description* or to maintain a distinction between *language* and metalinguistics (Harris, 1981). If a language cannot be successfully separated from its metalinguistics, and the metalinguistics we are using in African languages has come to us from English via Latin, it means we are viewing African languages through the prism of English. African languages even at a linguistic level cannot be said to be equal to English. If the objective of language planning is to promote African languages so that they are equal to English, then the intervention has to take place at an analytical level in terms of how we construe and frame African languages. (see Makoni & Pennycook, this volume).

Toward Disinvention and Reconstituting African Languages: An Argument for Critical Historiography

In the following section we argue against a pluralistic view of multilingualism as providing building blocks of disinvention. One of the most articulate proponents of African multilingualism is Alexander (1998, 2000), who treats African multilingualism as a 'resource', a view best encapsulated in his astute rhetorical move that turns the Tower of Babel inside out when he talks NOT about the Tower, but the Power of Babel. The metaphor of indigenous languages as a resource has not gained much traction from the people on whose behalf it is articulated. To argue, for instance, that even the language one neither speaks nor understands is a resource might make sense if one subscribes to a notion of universal ownership of resources. From the perspective of those that speak the language, however, it sounds strange to insist that one has a claim to a language that one does not even speak, and might not even have any intention of learning. Universal ownership may be construed as a strategy to conceal the control of the world's resources including language by a small but powerful group of people in a globalizing world.

Even though we are critical of the pluralistic view of multilingualism articulated in the 'language as a resource' metaphor, we concede that multilingualism in Africa as an intellectual project has to some extent succeeded in so far as it has forcefully drawn our attention to the potentially beneficial impact of African languages in education, health, and the economy. The multilingual argument has also forcefully drawn our attention to the fact that the acquisition and use of English is not necessarily a panacea to Africa's social and educational problems. Unfortunately, the multilingual argument has severe limitations apparent in its failure to gain much traction amongst the urban poor Africans who, in spite of the rhetoric of indigenous languages as a resource, are shifting away from the so-called resources towards urban vernaculars in southern, east and west Africa (Cook, 2001; Ngom, 2005; Mufwene, 2002).

In spite of the way multilingualism has enhanced our understanding of the language situation in Africa, the epistemological construction of language in African multilingual contexts is questionable. The issue is not only epistemological: it has real effects in so far as the way languages are constructed has an impact on the material life circumstances of Africans. Firstly, in what sense is Africa a Power of Babel? In a massive Pan African Project Prah (1999) directly challenges the idea of Africa as a Tower of Babel that forms the basis of Alexander's argument. He argues that over 80% of Africans speak no more than twelve key languages or clusters that are 85% mutually intelligible. It is not clear, however, what criteria he uses to determine what constitutes a language. Furthermore, it is not obvious what criteria he has used to determine what constitutes a 'key' language, and how acceptable such a criteria will be to other scholars working on language in Africa. The criteria of what makes one language a key language and another a non-key language is not self-evident. Sociolinguistically, Prah's project is also open to question. For instance, sociolinguistically it is not obvious how he could determine with such confidence that African languages are 85% mutually intelligible. Prah is also making a questionable assumption that it is languages that are mutually intelligible, as if languages were things that had a life of their own 'outside and above human beings' (Yngve, 1996: 29).

Prah is inadvertently defining Africans in terms of Western framings of language. He has succumbed to the belief in the existence of African languages as entities in the real world. Starting from the assumption that African languages exist, the main objective of his research project is to improve the linguistic description of languages. To us, improving the description of African languages does not necessarily resolve the problem if the existence of African languages is an illusion, a fiction. Prah is therefore taking for granted the very building blocks that his theory should subject to serious critique. He has succumbed to 18th and 19th century Western philosophical assumptions about language and consequently fails to question the validity of a concept such as language and, by extension, other constructs frequently used in a description of African languages, such as phonemes, words, grammars etc. If African linguistics is to make progress, we therefore need not better descriptions but questions about the very basis of the concepts that we are using. The critique is necessary because 'while physicists study objects of the real world given in advance, language is not an object given in advance that can be studied scientifically' (Yngve, 1996: 69).

The starting point for a disinvention project should be the mixtures rather than the indigenous languages, and the ability of Africans to draw upon linguistic material from different social/linguistic systems to communicate. Comaroff and Comaroff (1991) demonstrate how the ability to mix and draw from different languages and semiotic systems, which is increasingly being reported upon in many studies in urban vernaculars, is not novel. It was characteristic of African social and linguistic behavior even in pre-Colonial Africa. Mixing is therefore socially embedded in African historical and contemporary social experiences and uses of language.

If Africans are shifting away from indigenous languages towards urban vernaculars, it is a contradiction to therefore argue that the promotion of indigenous languages facilitates the retention of African cultural practices. A disinvention project has to address the factors that are facilitating the shift away from indigenous languages towards urban vernaculars and the consequences of such shifts on language planning projects. This shift is not necessarily a bad thing if, on the one hand, indigenous languages are associated with specific ethnicities and conservative social and political ideology while, on the other hand, urban vernaculars are 'an embodiment of the hybrid identity of city dwellers ... where people from different ethnic and religious backgrounds in the country are unified (Ngom, 2005: 284). The urban vernaculars are also used in rural communities by rural people seeking to reflect urban identity (Cook, 2001). The fact that the urban vernaculars are also extensively used in rural areas shows the importance of combining both urban and rural social histories in Africa because many people live in both places simultaneously, suggesting that distinctions between rural/urban, indigenous and modern might not be a very useful way of proceeding with our analysis (Coquery-Vidrovitch, 2005).

Another major advantage of using urban vernaculars as a basis for a disinvention project is their extensive use by urban African youth. The African youth constitutes a majority in most African countries, so the languages that they use rapidly spread to the rest of the population (Salm & Falola, 2005). From a critical historiographical perspective it is important to stress two significant factors. Cities in Africa have always played a crucial role in the formation of new ethnicities and languages. Swahili is the best example of a city language. Lingala, a trading language, was most likely born before some of the invention of indigenous languages whose invention was a consequence of colonialism (Coquery-Vidrovitch, 2005). The process of the creation of urban vernaculars therefore requires a *longue-durée* view of language and social change.

Most language-planning projects in Africa are based on the notion of the state. We need to move beyond a state-centric perspective of language planning. By this we mean shifting away from the perspective of those who are representing the state or the language policy towards those who are subjects of the activation (Williams, 1992: 178). While the state and linguists might frame their discourse in terms of language, non-linguists might frame their activities in terms of communication. In a disinvention project we are arguing that most of the subjects of the language policy are likely to have social networks that might be situated in cities, which is not to deny that those networks might extend to rural areas well. Including cities as one of the key players in language planning is important because cities rather than states should form the basis on which language-planning projects are founded. This is because most African states are dysfunctional, while city dwellers constitute more than half of the African population, and the percentage of African city dwellers is likely to increase 'Citie(s) most of the time, exist as leading to or incorporated into a network of paths, roads, railways, rivers etc resulting in a network of other cities, what we call in French *tissue urbain*' (Coquery-Vidrovitch, 2005: xx). Cities have a long and extremely complicated history in Africa. Some African cities predate colonialism. The first urban revolution in Africa occurred when prehistoric hunting and gathering societies became sedentary, which allowed domesticated agriculture. 'Cities thus became multipurpose centers from the beginning. This was the case of Jenne-Jeno in the Niger River valley, at the dawn of the 1st century AD' (Coquery-Vidrocitch, 2005: 17).

A disinvention program has to take into account the historical and contemporary realities we have been describing above as a starting point, rather than accepting the assumptions about the promotion of indigenous languages based on the belief that they are promoting unitary and discrete phenomena with objective realities rather than fuzzy-edged constructs (Gardner-Chloros, 1995). A view of indigenous languages as unitary constructs is part of the legacy of the construction of African languages in the 19th century, which has the effect of reifying languages (Errington, 2001; Williams, 1992). The tendency to reify languages leads to a formulation of ineffective social strategies to redress inequalities because the social status of the speakers of the language or variety is construed as derived from the language itself rather than the social status of those who speak the language (Williams, 1992). If the status is attributed to the language rather than the speakers, the logical but wrong strategy to adopt would be to change the status of the languages as a strategy for shifting the status of the speakers of those languages. We are arguing that changes in the status of the speakers of the variety or language in question will most likely contribute towards a shift in the status of the language spoken by the group whose status has changed. The converse does not necessarily apply. A shift in the status of languages does not necessarily result in a shift in the status of the speakers. Theoretically, we are therefore arguing for an African linguistics that seeks explanations in terms of people, who they are, where they live, their migration and so on (Yngve, 1986).

We could say that we are interested in how it is that people differ in the way they talk in different parts of the world, and how it is that we differ in the way we talk from earlier generations. All this would be easily understandable to the general public and to our new students: it can be said without recourse to obscure references to language. (Yngve, 1996: 73)

If our argument is valid, then the failure of the multilingual movement in Africa frequently lamented by many African commentators (Stroud, 2000; Ngom, 2005) should be welcomed because advocates of African multilingualism inadvertently sought to continue a top-down tradition of language promotion that was a product of colonial thinking, which does not adequately take into account the perspectives of those who are the targets of the policy. Orthodox sociolinguistic research in Africa is likely to describe Africans as multidialectal, but we feel that a notion of verbal repertoire has the advantage over a notion of a multilingual/multidialectal because it is not founded upon a notion of competence in distinct languages. In a verbal repertoire a speaker may have control over some linguistic forms associated with different 'languages', but this does not necessarily mean that the speaker has anything approaching full competence in the languages from which the speech forms are drawn. The term 'verbal repertoire' captures a 'totality of linguistic forms regularly employed in the course of socially significant interaction' (Gumperz, 1972: 152). For example, Cook (2001) identifies Ezra, aged 65, who has lived most of his life in rural areas, but came to Thlhabane in the 1980s to find work as a plumber. He speaks SeTswana and Afrikaans fluently, as well as a little English. He also speaks Tsotsitaal, and some Xhosa and Zulu. If Mr Ezra says he speaks SeTswana or Afrikaans, we cannot make the claim that he is in control of all codes and norms contained in either SeTswana or Afrikaans. We can however say that he is able to manipulate and draw upon different linguistic fragments from his repertoire – depending upon what he is seeking to accomplish – which enable him to communicate, and to carry multiple linguistic allegiances and cultural belongings (Jacquemet, 2005).

It is these linguistic amalgams and transidiomatic expressions typical of the speech of people like Mr Ezra which should form the basis of a disinvention project. By placing these urban mixtures as the focal point of language planning we are able to address contemporary African realities: 'From the point of view of any individual born into that community, what others call a mixture is the given, the starting point; we should not lose sight of the fact that our so-called standard languages are all mixtures in origin' (Gardner-Chloros, 1995: 69). If the mixtures and urban varieties are to form a basis for language planning, they can be standardized in a way that makes it possible to capture their heteroglossic nature. In a disinvention project we are therefore arguing for a non-normative standardization of urban vernaculars (Williams, 1992: 147).

Concluding

In this chapter, we have analysed the various ways in which African languages are conceptualized, from discourses of enumerability, naming and conceptualizing, to constructions of indigeneity, and dictionaries as discourse theory of African Languages. We have argued that it is only by revising the different discourses about language that we can shift our conceptualizations of language and formulate a more coherent response to Western discourses about Africa.

... departing from the premise that contemporary African intellectual practice takes place within the format and formulas dictated by western epistemological categories and principles ... African intellectual practice has to break away from its Western conditionings to be able to make sense to Africans themselves. (Masolo, 1994: 147)

References

Alexander, N. (1992) South Africa: Harmonising Nguni and Sotho. In N. Crawhall (ed.) *Democratically Speaking: International Perspectives on Language Planning.* Cape Town: National Language Project.

Alexander, N. (2000) English unassailable but unattainable: The dilemma of language policy in education in South Africa. *Praesa Occasional Papers* 3. Cape Town: Praesa/University of Cape Town.

Benson, P. (2001)*Ethnocentrism and the English Dictionary.* London: Routledge.

Bernstein, B. (1971) *Class, Codes and Control* (Vol. 1). London: Routledge & Kegan Paul.

Bernstein, J. (1998) Runyakitara: Uganda's new language. *Journal of Multilingual and Multicultural Development* 19 (2), 93–108.

Biehler, E. (1927) *English-Chiswina Dictionary* (s.l): The Jesuit Fathers

Biehler, E. (1950) *A Shona Dictionary with an Outline Shona Grammar* (rev. edn). The Jesuit Fathers
Breton, R. (2003) Sub-Saharan Africa. In R. Breton (ed.) *Languages in a Globalising World* (pp. 203–217). Cambridge: Cambridge University Press.
Breckenbridge, C. and van der Veer, P. (eds) (1993) *Orientalism and the Postcolonial Predicament*. Philadelphia.University of Pennyslvania Press.
Chimhundu, H. (1985) Early Missionaries and the ethnolinguistic factor during the 'invention' of tribalism in Zimbabwe. *Journal of African History* 33, 87–109.
Chimhundu, H. *et al.* (2001) *Duramazwi guru rechiShona*. Harare: College Press.
Cohn, B. (1996) *Colonialism and Its Forms of Knowledge: The British in India*. Princeton, NJ: Princeton University Press.
Comaroff, J and Comaroff, J. (1991) *Of Revelation and Revolution: Christianity, Colonialism and Consciousness in South Africa*. Chicago: University of Chicago Press.
Cook, S. (2001) Urban language in a rural setting: The case of Phokeng South Africa. In G. Gmelch and W. Zenner (eds) *Urban Life Readings in the Anthropology of the City* (pp. 106–113). Prospect Heights, Il: Waverland Press.
Coquery-Vidrovitch, C. (2005) Introduction: African spaces: History and culture. In J. Salm and T. Falola (eds) *African Urban Spaces in Historical Perspective* (pp. xi–xv). Durham, NC: Carolina Academic Press.
Crowley, T. (1989) *The Politics of Discourse: The Standard Language Question in British Cultural Debates*: London: Macmillan.
Crystal, D. (1997) *English as a Global Language*. Cambridge: Cambridge University Press.
Danzinger, K. (1997) *Naming the Mind: How Psychology Found its Language*. London: Sage.
De Beaugrande, R. (1997) *New Foundations as a Science of Text and Discourse*. Stanford, CT: Ablex.
De Schryver, G. and Prinsloo, D.J. (2000) Electronic corpora as a basis for the compilation of African language dictionaries: The macrostructure. *South African Journal of African Languages* 20 (4), 291–309.
Djite, P. (1993) Correcting errors in language classification: Monolingual nuclei and multilingual satellites. *Language Problems & Language Planning* 12 (1), 14.
Doke, C. (1931) *Report on the Unification of Shona Dialects*. London: Stephen Austin and Sons.
Dwyer, D. (1999) The language/dialect problem. On WWW at http://www.msu.edu~dwyer/lgDialPr.htm.
Eco, U. (1995) *The Search for the Perfect Language*. Oxford: Basil Blackwell.
Errington, J. (2001) Colonial linguistics. *Annual Review of Anthropology* 30: 19–30.
Fabian, J. (1986) *Language and Colonial Power*. Cambridge: Cambridge University Press.
Fanon, F. (1967) *Black Skin, White Masks*. New York: Grove Publishing.
Fardon, R. and Furniss, G. (eds) (1994) Introduction: Frontiers and boundaries: African languages as political environment. In R. Fardon and G. Furniss (eds) *African Languages, Development and the State* (pp. 1–13). London: Routledge.
Foucault, M. (1977) *Discipline and Punish: The Birth of the Prison* (A. Sheridan, trans.). London: Penguin.
Fortune, G. (1972) *A Guide to Shona Spellings*. Harare: Longman.

Gardner-Chloros, P. (1995) Code-switching in community, regional and national repertoires: The myth of discreteness of linguistic varieties. In L. Milroy and P. Muysken (eds) *One Speaker, Two Languages: Cross-disciplinary Perspectives on Code-switching* (pp. 68–90). Cambridge: Cambridge University Press.

Grace, G. On WWW at http:www2.hawaii.edu/~grace. Accessed 01.06.06.

Greenberg, J. (1966) *Languages in Africa*. The Hague: Mouton.

Grimes, J. E. (1974). Word lists and languages. Technical report to the National Science Foundation, 2. Ithaca, NY: Cornell University

Gumperz, J. (1972) The communicative competence of bilinguals. *Language and Society* 1 (1), 143–154.

Guthrie, M. (1972) *Comparative Bantu: An Introduction to the Comparative Linguistics and Prehistory of the Bantu Languages* (4 vols). Farnborough: Gregg Press.

Hadebe, S., Mpofu, N., Maphosa, M. and Khumalo, L. (2001) *Ischazamazwi se siNdebele*. Harare: College Press.

Harries, P. (1987) The roots of ethnicity: Discourse and the politics of language construction in South Africa. *African Affairs* 86 (342), 25–52.

Harries, P. (1995) Discovering languages the historical origins of standard Tsonga in southern Africa. In R. Mesthrie (ed.) *Language and Social History* (pp. 154–176). Cape Town: David Phillip.

Harris, R. (1981) *The Language Myth*. London: Duckworth.

Hartman, A.M. (1893) *Outline of a Grammar of the Mashona Language*. Cape Town: St Leger Printer

Herbert, R.K. (1992) Introduction: Language in a divided society. In R.K. Herbert (ed.) *Language and Society in Africa: The Theory and Practice of Sociolinguistics* (pp. 1–19). Johannesburg: Witwatersrand University Press.

Hyden, G. (1993) The challenges of domesticating rights in Africa. In R. Cohen, G. Hyden and W.P. Nagan *Human Rights and Governance in Africa* (pp. 256–281). Gainsville: University of Florida Press.

Hymes, D. (1983) *Studies in the History of Linguistic Anthropology*. Amsterdam: John Benjamins.

Irvine, J. (2001) Style as distinctiveness: The culture and ideology of linguistic differentation. In P. Eckert and J. Rickford (eds) *Style and Sociolinguistic Variation*. Cambridge: Cambridge University Press.

Irvine, J. and Gal, S. (2000) Language ideology and linguistic differentiation. In P.V. Kroskrity (ed.) *Regimes of Language: Ideologies, Politics and Identities* (pp. 35–85). Santa Fe, NM: School of American Research Press.

Jacquemet, M. (2005) Transidiomatic practices: Language and power in the age of globalization. *Language and Communication* 25, 257–277

Jeater, D. (2000) Speaking like a native. *Journal of African History* 43, 449–468.

McCarthy, N. and Carter, R. (1995) Spoken grammar: What is it and how can we teach it? *ELT Journal* 49 (3), 207–218.

MacGonagle, E. (2001) Mightier than the sword: The Portuguese pen in Ndau History. *History in Africa* 28, 169–186.

Makoni, S. (1998) African languages as European scripts: The shaping of communal memory. In S. Nuttall and C. Coetzee (eds) *Negotiating the Past: The Making of Memory in South Africa* (pp. 242–248). Oxford: Oxford University Press.

Makoni, S. (2003) From misinvention to disinvention of language: Multilingualism and the South African Constitution. In S. Makoni, G. Smitherman, A. Ball and A.K. Spear (eds) *Black Linguistics: Language, Society and Politics in Africa and the Americas* (pp 132–153). New York: Routledge.

Makoni, S. and Meinhof, U. (2003) Introducing applied linguistics in Africa. *AILA Review* 16, 1–13.

Makoni, S., Spears, A.K., Smitherman, G. and Ball, A. (2003) Introduction. In S. Makoni, G. Smitherman, A. Ball and A.K. Spear (eds) *Black Linguistics: Language, Society and Politics in Africa and the Americas* (pp. 1–19). New York: Routledge.

Makoni, S. and Truddell, B. (2006) *Complimentary and Conflicting Discourses of Diversity in Language Planning*. Per Linguam (in press).

Mann, M. and Dalby, D. (1987) Online at www.geocities.com/athens/academy/8919/olmes/2htm. Accessed 01.06.06.

Masagara, N. (1997) Negotiating the truth through oath forms. *Journal of Multilingual and Multicultural Development* 18 (5), 385–400.

Mashiri, P. (2003) Managing face in urban public transport: Polite request strategies in Commuter Omnibus Discourse in Harare. *AILA Review* 16, 120–126.

Masolo, D.A. (1994) *African Philosophy in Search of Identity*. Bloomington, IN: Indiana University Press.

Mawadza, A. (2000) Harare Shona slang: A linguistic study. *Zambezia* 27 (1), 93–101.

Mazrui, A.A. and Mazrui, A.M. (1998) *The Power of Babel: Language & Governance in the African Experience*. Chicago: University of Chicago Press.

Mudimbe, V.Y. (1988) *The Invention of Africa: Gnosis, Philosophy, and the Order of Knowledge*. Bloomington, IN: Indiana University Press.

Mudimbe, V.Y. (1994) *The Idea of Africa*. Durham, NC: Duke University Press.

Mufwene, S. (2002) Colonisation, globalisation and the future of languages in the twenty-first century. *International Journal of Multicultural Societies* 4, 165–197

Mühlhäusler, P. (1996) *Linguistic Ecology: Language Change and Linguistic Imperialism in the Pacific Region*. New York: Routledge.

Mvula, E.T. (1992) Language policies in Africa: The case for chiChewa in Malawi. In R.K. Herbert (ed.) *Language and Society in Africa: The Theory and Practice of Sociolinguistics* (pp. 37–47). Johannesburg: Witwatersrand University Press.

Ngom, F. (2005) Linguistic and sociocultural hybridization in Senegalese urban spaces. In T. Falola and S. Salm (eds) *Urbanization and African Cultures* (pp. 279–295). Durham, NC: Carolina Academic Press.

Njoroge, K. (1986) Multilingualism and some of its implications for language policy and practices in Kenya. In A. Davies (ed.) *Language in Education in Africa* (pp. 327–353).

Prah, K. (1999) *African Languages for the Mass Education of Africans*. Cape Town: The Centre for the Advanced Studies of African Societies.

Phillipson, R. (2003) *English Only? Challenging Language Policy*. London: Routledge.

Prinsloo D.J and de Schruyer, (2000) *Sedipro 1.0: First Parallel Dictionary: Sepedi-English*. Pretoria: University of Pretoria.

Prinsloo, D. and de Schruyer, G-M. (2001) Corpus-based activities versus intuition-based compilations by lexicographers, the Sepedi-Lemma sign list as a case in point. *The Nordic Journal of African Languages* 10 (3), 374–398.

Prinsloo, D.J. and de Schruyver, G. (2003) Non-word error detection in current South African spell checkers. *Southern African Linguistics and Applied Language Studies* 21 (4), 307–326.

Ranger, T.O. (1989) *The Invention of Tribalism in Zimbabwe*. Gweru/Zimbabwe: Mambo Press.
Ranger, T.O. (1995) Are we not also men? *The Samkange Family and African Politics in Zimbabwe 1920–64*. London: James Currey.
Said, E. (1997) *Orientalism*. London: Penguin.
Said, E. (2003) Online document at http://www.zmaa.org/saidclash.htm. Accessed 01.06.06.
Salm, S.J. and Falola, T. (eds) (2005) *Urbanization and African Cultures*. Durham: Carolina Academic Press.
Sinclair, J. (1991) *Concordance and Collocation*. Oxford: Oxford University Press.
Skutnabb-Kangas, T. (2000) *Linguistic Genocide in Education – or Worldwide Diversity and Human Rights?* Mahwah, NJ: Lawrence Erlbaum.
Springer, J.M. (1909)*The Heart of Central Africa, Mineral Wealth and Missionary Opportunity*. Cincinnati: Jennings.
Stroud, C. (2000) Language and democracy: the notion of linguistic citizenship and mother tongue programs. In K. Legere and S. Ftchat (eds) *Talking Freedom: Language and Democratization in the SADC Region*. Windhoek: Gamsbey Macmillan.
Stroud, P. (2001) African mother tongues and the politics of language: Linguistic citizenship versus linguistic human rights. *Journal of Multilingual and Multicultural Development* 22 (4), 339–353.
Summers, C. (2002) *Colonial Lessons: Africans' Education in Southern Rhodesia, 1918–1940*. Cape Town: David Philip Publishers.
Webb, V. and Kembo-Sure, K. (2000) *African Voices: An Introduction to the Languages and Linguistics of Africa*. Cape Town: Oxford University Press.
Whiteley, S. (1974) *Language in Uganda*. Oxford University Press.
Widdowson, H. (2000) On the limitations of linguistics applied. *Applied Linguistics* 21 (1), 3–25.
Williams, G. (1992) *Sociolinguistics: A Sociological Critique*. New York: Routledge.
Yankah, K. (1999) African folk and the challenges of a global lore, *Africa Today*, 46 (2), 9–27.
Yngve, V. (1986) *Linguistics as a Science*. Bloomington, IN. Indiana University Press.
Yngve, V. (1996) *From Grammar to Science: New Foundations for General Linguistics*. Philadelphia: John Benjamins.
Yngve, V. and Wasik, Z. (eds) (2004) *Hard-science Linguistics*. New York: Continuum.

Chapter 4
The Myth of English as an International Language

ALASTAIR PENNYCOOK

Having striven for many years to come to grips with some of the hard questions that need to be asked about the role of English in the world – the cultural politics of English as an international language, implications of the global spread of English, colonial language policies and English and critical approaches to English language teaching – I here intend to address an issue that might seem contradictory when placed alongside these concerns. Although the effects of the global spread of English are of very real concern (we don't have to accept all of Phillipson's (1992) imperialistic claims to nevertheless acknowledge that there are widespread social, cultural, educational, economic and political effects), it is at the same time much less clear that English itself is equally real. While it is evident that vast resources are spent on learning and teaching something called English, and that English plays a key role in global affairs, it is less clear that all this activity operates around something that should be taken to exist in itself.

As Ndebele (1987) remarks, the 'very concept of an international, or world, language was an *invention* of Western imperialism' (1987: 3–4; my emphasis). Lurking behind such claims are sentiments similar to Phillipson's (1992) that English as an international language (EIL) has been created, promoted and sustained to the benefit of Western powers, global capitalism, the developed world, the centre over the periphery, or neoliberal ideology. Yet what if we take the notion of invention seriously here and question not only the underlying interests behind the global spread of English but also the ontological implications of its invention? To raise such a question is not merely to deal with the implications of a pluralisation of Englishes – though the very notion of the global spread of English is undeniably unsettled once we accept that the appropriation and development of different Englishes around the world divides English into a plurality of languages – since a pluralisation strategy falls short of posing the more crucial question: Why should we accord any particular ontological status to something called

English? As Reagan (2004: 42) puts it, 'there is, or at least there may well be, no such thing as English.'

Ontological and Empirical Arguments

Let us consider for a moment the grounds on which we might consider there to be such a thing as English. We might start with arguments based around reference and common sense: why would we have a term 'English' if it didn't refer to anything? But this doesn't take us very far: There are many terms (elves, fairies, democracy, freedom and so on) that don't refer to anything very real. A more likely argument, perhaps, is a 'common sense' one: Surely if people all over the world claim to use English, then we should accept that claim. This we have to take a bit more seriously, though to appeal to majority belief doesn't tell us anything much about the existence of what is believed in. The majority of Americans believe in a Christian god and the majority of people in the world believe in some god or another; this doesn't prove the existence of god. In fact, for any sceptical thinker, the contradictory nature of these beliefs and the fact that they are majority beliefs are reasons precisely to be suspicious.

It might be argued, again on the grounds of common sense, that since people around the world are apparently able to communicate with each other in English, then it's obvious that English exists. Or, from the other side of the coin, since people around the world can't understand each other, they must be speaking different languages. On the face of it, these might appear reasonable arguments, but on closer investigation, it becomes clear that, as with many of these lines of reasoning, they assume as premises what they set out to demonstrate. Thus, to claim that in order to communicate successfully we need a thing called a common language (assuming, therefore, both the successful effects of communication as well as the grounds for its effects), or to assert that if we don't understand each other, we must therefore be using different languages (assuming therefore both the unsuccessful effects of communication and the nature of the impediments to communication), is to have already presupposed that languages exist as distinct entities that facilitate or hinder communication.

Most arguments of this nature can be seen as rationalist ontological arguments, that is, arguments based on rational rather than empirical grounds. In this tradition of thinking, a version of St Anselm's ontological argument might be worth a try. If, by analogy with God, English is a language greater than which no language can be conceived, then, if such a language fails to exist, a greater language (which also exists) can be conceived. Yet, as the argument proceeds, this is absurd since nothing can be greater than a language greater than which nothing can be conceived. The conclusion must therefore be that a language (English) greater than which no language can be conceived must exist. Such arguments are notoriously hard to refute – though many attempts have been made, notably by Kant (1781/1998) in his *Critique of Pure Reason* – and have been reiterated in various forms throughout the rationalist tradition, from Descartes to Leibnitz (and, perhaps, on to the rationalist school of linguistics and its foremost exponent, Chomsky). While refutation in their own terms may be hard, they can nevertheless be rejected on the grounds that they are simply not *persuasive*, that is to say they do not provide a convincing argument for those who do not believe in the existence of God or English in the first place: they only provide a form of internal rational argument for the already faithful. Ontological arguments about English in the rationalist tradition are not going to take us very far.

A more obvious starting point, perhaps, is the empirical. Simply put, we might say that English exists in the words, grammar, lexicon, speech of all those books, dictionaries and grammars of English. Such a position, however, presents us with several problems. If we try to define the existence of a language according to its existence in such codifications, we are then left with an awkward argument as to the existence of all those languages that have not been thus codified. It is perhaps possible to argue that codified and standardised languages are the norm and that the proof of the existence of all languages awaits only their mass codification. Yet, as any basic understanding of literacy development will tell us (e.g. Mühlhäusler, 1996), the codification of languages is not so much a process of writing down what already exists as it is a process of *reducing* languages to writing. Thus, whatever may pre-exist dictionary and grammar writing, it cannot be defined on the basis of such texts. Most obviously, however, the process of writing dictionaries of languages is a process of invention par excellence. To argue that the vast materiality of the *Oxford English Dictionary* (OED), for example, attests to the size and existence of English is to overlook the point that this was yet another of those massive projects of Victorian invention.

Winchester's popular history of the OED, *The Meaning of Everything*, clearly locates the development of the dictionary in the context of 19th century empire building:

> Huge ships, immense palaces, bridges and roads and docks and railways of daunting scale, brave discoveries in science and medicine, scores of colonies seized, dozens of wars won and revolts suppressed, and missionaries and teachers fanning out into the darkest crannies of the planet – there seemed nothing that the Britain of the day could not

achieve. And now, to add to it all – a plan for a brand new dictionary. A brand new dictionary of what was, after all, the very language of all this greatness and moral suasion and muscularly Christian goodness, and a language that had been founded and nurtured in the Britain that was doing it – the idea seemed no more and no less than a natural successor to all of these other majestic ventures of iron and steam and fired brick. (Winchester, 2003: 43)

And yet, while Winchester thus eloquently depicts English as an imperial project, constructed like bridges, encouraged to spread like missionaries, colonising like armies, the implications of this construction are not taken up. Prior to this imperial project, English is still seen as a vast entity just waiting to be described:

No one had ever thought of making a list of all the words and noting down what they seemed to mean – even though from today's perspective, from a world that seems obsessed with a need to count and codify and define and make categories for everything, there seems no rational reason why this might have been so. (Winchester, 2003: 18)

English, in this view, pre-exists its description as a set of words that are already part of English. Yet this realist claim overlooks the obvious process by which English was produced by such activities, and to allege, as many do, on this basis that English has more words than other languages (see Pennycook, 1998) is akin to claiming that the British Empire included a vast number of territories prior to colonisation. Colonisation produced the empire as dictionary writing produced the language.

In his discussion of 'the myth of standard English,' Harris (1988: 1) points out that it is a 'self-fulfilling prophecy'. The view of standard English held by the creator of the *Oxford English Dictionary*, James Murray, was based on 'a myth which had been *invented* to serve the purposes of a typically Victorian brand of national idealism' (Harris, 1988: 26; my emphasis). As Willinsky (1994) has shown at length, the OED and other great Victorian projects of invented tradition 'retroactively assembled a historical foundation for a nation worthy of a global empire' (Willinsky, 1998: 120). Thus, the 'making of the OED provides its own lessons in how English was imagined as a civilising beacon, a light to guide lesser peoples out of their own dark ages' (Willinsky, 1998: 200). Any argument, therefore, that English can be taken to exist because of its representation in reference books fails to take into account either the process by which reference books invent languages or the circularity of any argument that proposes that, since something is 'in

English,' then English exists, and if English exists, then all these uses are clearly 'in English'.

Empirical linguists might sensibly eschew such arguments based on prior codings of the language and base a belief in languages instead on the ability of the scientific methodology of linguistics to determine the existence of the object. From this line of thinking, a line is drawn between subjective and objective, or political and scientific, approaches to understanding language. Thus Dixon (1997: 7) argues that 'Once political considerations are firmly discarded, it is generally not a difficult matter to decide whether one is dealing with one language or more than one in a given situation.' Here, then, linguistic positivism arrogates for itself the ability to distinguish languages as separate entities while disregarding the views of the speakers themselves. The conceit of such a view has of course been widely questioned, especially by linguistic anthropologists who draw our attention to language ideologies and regimes, and thus the need to understand language culturally (Blommaert, 1999; Kroskrity, 2000). Linguistics in this vein sets itself an impossible task here, both empirical and epistemological, since it is at least commonplace in most accounts of language variation to acknowledge that languages are political rather than ontological categories.

The epistemological impossibility of describing a language is also a major impediment for an empirical justification for the belief in the existence of English. If a real attempt were made to describe and identify all and every utterance produced under the name of English, the project would be both physically and temporally implausible (corpus linguistics only makes this marginally less so). Descriptive linguistics has of course never operated this way but has instead posited a core (grammar/ lexicon) from which deviations are deemed varieties. Yet the impossibility of accounting for English variation through a description of a supposed core, or of making the core a product of the variation renders this too an untenable proposition. Why should we believe that two utterances, mutually incomprehensible, spoken in different ways, with different meanings, by people on opposite sides of the world, with no connection to or knowledge of each other, should be considered to be part of the same thing, system, language, English, simply because this label is loosely applied to these moments of language use?

One other linguistic argument that might to be applied to explain the existence of English is a structuralist one. Languages are defined by their differences, and so English exists because of its relationship to all that it is not. Such an argument may suggest the relative existence of English, but obviously collapses if we question the hermetic systems of structuralism (all languages exist in relation to each other but not to anything else) or when we consider that it is not only English but all languages that are under question here. To argue that something is English because it is not French, Cornish or Greek is to be caught in a structuralist circularity. One might hold out hope for biological or neurological demonstrations of the representation of languages in the brain, yet these are much more effective at telling us about ways in which language in general operates than about the separability and identification of different languages. Research on bilingual aphasia (Paradis, 2004), for example, may in fact tell us more about the impossibility of distinguishing languages as discrete systems than the possibility of mapping separable neurological systems.

An alternative approach to this linguistic realism is to opt for the phenomenological argument that languages exist only to the extent that speakers perceive them to do so. By contrast with Dixon's rejection of what people say they speak, a phenomenological approach suggests that this may be the most important consideration, leading to the vast divergence between linguists' languages (6500) and peoples' languages (40,000) (see *Ethnologue*). Giving such absolute priority to the observing subject, as Foucault (1970) pointed out, however, is to oppose the impossible realism of structuralism with the impossible idealism of phenomenology. The phenomenological insights of 'native speaker intuition' have been a notoriously unreliable grounding for understanding language. Yet, while an argument that we can take English to be what people perceive it to be is probably unhelpful in terms of establishing claims to what English is, this may nevertheless provide some insights into the ways that English may be more usefully understood as a product of the will to certain goods and identities rather than as a linguistic system.

Constructions and Myths

What, then, if we take seriously the proposition that English does not exist? Surely this takes us into the rather difficult position of having to account for what it is that all those English users, English textbooks, English departments, are really doing. Here we need to explore further two important ways of talking about non-reality: construction and myth. Just as it is difficult to account for the existence of something called English, so it is also important to consider carefully what we might mean by its non-existence. Let us turn, then, to the notion of *myth*. A useful place to start is with Roland Barthes' (1957/1972: 142) classic *Mythologies*, in which he argues that myth 'has the task of giving an historical intention a natural justification, and making contingency appear eternal.' Barthes goes on,

Myth is constituted by the loss of the historical quality of things: in it, things lose the memory that they once were made. The world enters language as a dialectical relation between activities, between human activities, between human actions; it comes out of myth as a harmonious display of essences. A conjuring trick has taken place; it has turned reality inside out, it has emptied it of history and has filled it with nature, it has removed from things their human meaning so as to make them signify a human insignificance. (Barthes, 1957/1972: 142–3)

Myth, therefore, is 'depoliticised speech,' where the 'political' is understood as 'describing the whole of human relations in their real, social structure, in their power of making the world' (Barthes, 1957/1972: 143). Myth, he argues

... does not deny things, on the contrary, its function is to talk about them; simply, it purifies them, it makes them innocent, it gives them a natural and eternal justification, it gives them a clarity which is not that of an explanation but that of a statement of fact. (Barthes, 1957/1972: 143)

Barthes' understanding of myth raises a number of important points for an understanding of the construction of English. If we wish to argue that there is no such thing as English, we may be claiming, for example, that languages are constructions. Many would be happy to acknowledge that standard English was constructed in the sense that it was actively standardised or produced rather than having either immutable historical, or natural evolutionary, origins. On this view, languages are the products of social actors, and particular versions of languages, such as standard languages, are the very particular constructions of overt political activity. This version of construction potentially leaves languages as real entities while questioning any argument that suggests they have some status outside the social, cultural and political forces that make them. We might call this a general social constructionist position, a view common enough in the social sciences. Thus, while sociolinguists such as Trudgill (1999) can point to the historical process of standardisation that produced standard English, he is also happy to accord standard English a relatively unproblematic ontological status. Standard English, Trudgill (1999: 118) tells us, is a variety of English; it is the variety normally used in writing; it is the variety associated with education systems and therefore 'the variety spoken by those who are often referred to as "educated people".' It has no connection to accent, register or style, but rather is a dialect defined by various grammatical rules. From this perspective, then, although the processes by which a variety of English became standard English might be seen as a form of social construction, the object that resulted – standard English – is an objectively describable entity, a variety of English with a set of rules, used by a certain group of people.

A further step in this thinking, however, suggests that this construction itself produced a metalanguage rather than a language, or put another way, that the standardisation of English produced not so much standard English but rather discourses about standard English. Milroy (1999: 18), for example, suggests that 'standard languages are fixed and uniform-state idealisations' and that 'no one actually speaks a standard language' (Milroy, 1999: 27). As he points out, in addition to this idealisation, there is a standard language culture that inculcates and maintains a set of beliefs about standard English. He goes on to argue that 'language experts' have failed to appreciate either their role in supporting standard language ideologies or that 'what is involved is only superficially a debate about language and is more fundamentally a debate about ideologies' (Milroy, 1999: 23). Thus, from this point of view, the construction of standard English was a project that produced a set of beliefs about the supposed objects enshrined in dictionaries, grammars, and style manuals; it did not produce a 'real thing' called 'standard English'.

This understanding of construction adds an important dimension to the discussion so far: Like the first notion of construction, it draws our attention to the ways in which the supposedly natural (the existence of languages, of English, of standard English) has to be understood historically; it points to the ways in which myths work by constantly talking about things, by constantly assuming the existence of things; it highlights the idea of heroic stories that tell us about the origins or nature of various phenomena, or explain how something came to be. From this perspective, the question of reality is put on hold. As Watts (1999: 73) notes in his discussion of the myth of standard English, the notion of myth should not be taken to imply 'a false, unfounded or wrong-headed belief in the origin of a phenomenon' but rather as narratives that 'contain elements of reality in them since they derive from the past experiences of a group.' This position on myth is somewhat akin to the poststructuralist turn to discourse: if we cannot gain unmediated access to the real world, let us focus instead on the modes of representation (discourse) through which the world is constructed, on the naturalisations of language and the productions of metalanguage.

Construction and myth present us with several ways of addressing issues of reality. First, a social constructionist position aims to challenge views that suggest non-social origins to social phenomena: ideas, ideologies, research and knowledge all have their origins in social and cultural fields. Social constructionism is largely interested in challenging radical realist or foundationalist arguments that suggest an objective status outside human action. The notion of invention, viewed from this perspective, suggests that languages may exist, but they do so only as a product of human interests. This first meaning is linked to our basic concern about the very real invention of languages. Many languages were the products of specific processes of invention. While this position may usefully counter claims such as Dixon's (1997) that we can put aside political definitions of language and engage only with the scientific/linguistic, it does not necessarily challenge the ontological status of languages as social constructions, or the significance of the construction of metalanguages through which languages are made. Social constructionism, then, is useful only insofar as it dispels foundationalist myths of origin by showing how human action has produced current entities and beliefs about those entities.

A second position, which we might term ontological constructionism, is concerned with a more radical epistemology that suggests that the notion of 'language' does not refer to any real object. This position consequently goes further than merely suggesting that languages have been constructed: it suggests that the notions of languages themselves are constructions. Languages and the metalanguages that attend them are very particular cultural orientations towards understanding the world that produce what they purport to describe. Rather than suggesting therefore that different languages have been invented within particular contexts, this position argues that the very notion of languages themselves is an invention. Thus not only were languages invented but they were invented on invented terrain. There are no languages. And thus, the question of whether there is such a thing as English is not about a special case for English as a result of its widespread use or division into different varieties, but rather about English as the currently most significant invention amid all the other invented languages of our times.

To this position, however, it is important to add another dimension, which we might call historical constructionism, or the acknowledgement that the effects of repeated construction and reconstruction are very real. Although languages were invented on invented terrain, and although the dubious attempts to trace the linear linguistic origins of languages do so along invented genealogies, these inventions have a reality for the people who deal with them. In his discussion of Anderson's (1983) imagined communities, Žižek (1993: 202) argues that to emphasise:

> in a 'deconstructionist' mode that the Nation is not a biological or transhistorical fact but a contingent discursive construction, an overdetermined result of textual practices, is ... misleading; such an

emphasis overlooks the remainder of some *real*, nondiscursive kernel of enjoyment which must be present for the Nation qua discursive entity-effect to achieve its ontological consistency. (Žižek, 1993: 202)

The point here, then, is that it is not enough just to suggest that language is not a biological or transhistorical fact but a contingent discursive construction, since this fails to account for people's engagement with the concept of language, the pleasure that is to be had in the belief in the ontological consistency of language. This is not, it should be noted, another version of the old ideology-as-false-consciousness argument, which would suggest that people are ideologically duped into believing in language, but rather an argument that the historical construction of language creates realities that we need to deal with.

Finally, we also need to deal with discursive constructionism, or the realisation that languages are produced in different ways at different times. In the same way that Appadurai (1996) sees the modes of production of locality shifting under changing global conditions, so I would argue that the modes of production of language are at a very particular juncture. If the current understanding of languages was invented and maintained during an era of nation-building, modernity and a particular framing of identity, the global changes in recent years suggest new forms of construction. This is one reason why invention, disinvention and reconstruction of languages is so important at this current moment. It is also why a focus on English is of particular significance, since English is subject to a set of discursive formations that are quite different from those at different historical moments. And this is where the notion of myth is so important, since it draws our attention to the ways in which stories are constantly being told about English.

As Woolard (2004: 58) notes, 'the history of languages often function as Malinowskian charter myths, projecting from the present to an originary past a legitimation of contemporary power relations and interested positions'. Malinowski's insight here was to view myths in terms of the ways in which they validate current social customs and institutions. A typical myth about a people's origins not only 'conveys, expresses and strengthens the fundamental fact of local unity and of the kinship unity of the group of people' but also 'literally contains the legal charter of the community' (Malinowski, 1954: 116). Thus, myths justify social orders, institutions and languages; they define not only an imagined origin but also a current status, both orthodoxy and orthopraxy. And the charter myth of English, invoking certain origins, histories and lineages legitimates the current status of English, imagining into being a language that has spread from its insular origins into a world language. It is on this that I intend to focus in the next part of this chapter, looking briefly at the ways stories are told about English that constantly reconstruct it in particular ways.

English as Mythical Hero

Work such as Bailey's (1991) cultural history of English presents us with a broad picture of the cultural production of English. In light of both the focus of this book and this long history of producing myths around English, it is interesting to look at statements such as Read's (1849) not just as prescient and triumphalist but also as productive of the mythology of English.

> Ours is the language of the arts and sciences, of trade and commerce, of civilisation and religious liberty. ... It is a store-house of the varied knowledge which brings a nation within the pale of civilisation and Christianity. ... Already it is the language of the Bible ... So prevalent is this language already become, as to betoken that it may soon become the language of international communication for the world. (Read, 1849, cited in Bailey, 1991: 116)

I have already written extensively on myths about English as an international language, arguing for example that the myths of the global spread of English as natural (having evolved into the global language without overt political action), neutral (as disconnected to social, economic and political concerns) and beneficial (as being inherently beneficial to all that learn and use it) are untenable (Pennycook, 1994). I have also argued that the many myths about English as a 'marvellous tongue' need to be seen as 'cultural constructs of colonialism,' with a long history of colonial promotion and contemporary production (Pennycook, 1998).

The effect of the ongoing myth-making around English is not only to produce particular images about English, but also through their constant reiteration to incessantly invoke a thing called English. Myths about English put English into discourse. One of the casually insidious ways in which the notion of English as an international language (EIL) is employed is in the counts of English speakers/users around the globe (see for example Crystal, 1997; Kachru, 1986). Figures based on language policies, educational programs and estimates of use are added together to produce a figure of more than one billion users of English. But what sense does this make? Does this not have more to do with English myth-making than any useful description of global language use? Particularly salient today are claims that English is merely a 'language of international communication' rather than a language embedded in processes of globalisation; that

English holds out promise of social and economic development to all those who learn it (rather than a language tied to very particular class positions and possibilities of development); and that English is a language of equal opportunity (rather than a language that creates barriers as much as it presents possibilities). Although my central focus here is on the ways such myths put English into discourse rather than on debunking such myths, it is worth looking at each briefly in terms of the collusionary, delusionary and exclusionary effects of English. This thing called English colludes with many of the pernicious processes of globalisation, deludes many learners through the false promises it holds out for social and material gain, and excludes many people by operating as an exclusionary class dialect, favouring particular people, countries, cultures and forms of knowledge.

It would seem hard to deny that English, in a sense, colludes with globalisation. One of the problems in drawing these connections, however, has been the tendency to paint a simplistic version of globalisation. Thus, reviewing David Crystal's (1997) book on the global spread of English, Sir John Hanson, the former Director-General of the British Council, is able to proclaim: 'On it still strides: we can argue about what globalisation is till the cows come – but that globalisation exists is beyond question, with English its accompanist. The accompanist is indispensable to the performance' (Hanson, 1997: 22). Phillipson, by contrast, in his review of the same book, takes a more critical line, suggesting that 'Crystal's celebration of the growth of English' is tied to:

> an uncritical endorsement of capitalism, its science and technology, a modernisation ideology, monolingualism as a norm, ideological globalisation and internationalisation, transnationalisation, the Americanisation and homogenisation of world culture, linguistic, culture and media imperialism ... (Phillipson, 1999: 274)

If Hanson's and Crystal's position simply fails to engage with questions of globalisation and English, Phillipson's position rather problematically presents us only with an image of homogenisation within a neocolonial global polity (which I have elsewhere categorised as the 'homogeny' position on global English; see Pennycook, 2003b). Given that there is now a vast range of work looking at the complexities of globalisation (e.g. Appadurai, 1996; Hardt & Negri, 2000; Mignolo, 2000), studies of global English deserve better than this. At the very least, we need to understand how English is involved in global flows of culture and knowledge, how English is used and appropriated by users of English round the world, how English colludes with multiple domains of globalisation, from popular culture to unpopular politics, from international capital to local transaction, from ostensible diplomacy to purported peace-keeping, from religious proselytising to secular resistance. The incessant invocation of 'English as an international language' avoids the obligation to deal with the complexity of English in relation to globalisation while simultaneously reiterating the existence of English as being in the world.

With respect to English as a delusionary language, there are many myths that surround English as a language that will better people's lives. A common view, as expressed in an article in the *EL Gazette* (1999) a few years ago, suggests that the widespread introduction of English into primary sectors around the world should lead to the alleviation of poverty. Next to a picture of laughing children on the front page is the claim that 'English is key to a better life for the poor'. An editorial on the next page explains further that 'for many of the world's poorest people, *English can hold the key to escape from grinding poverty*' (emphasis in original). And finally on page 3 the article itself carries the title 'English language could be the key to a better life for the underprivileged', and the subtitle 'The benefits of primary English language teaching are finally being recognised'. But the key question we need to look at here is what the effects of English education might actually be. In order to understand this, we need to look at English in terms of class, and thus at poverty alleviation not in terms of individual escape from poverty but in terms of larger social and economic relations (Appleby *et al.*, 2002). We need to be clear about whether we are looking at individual rights to English or whether we are looking at how access to English can alleviate poverty across a broader domain. The question, then, is how English may be related to economic change. As Tollefson (2000: 8) warns, 'At a time when English is widely seen as a key to the economic success of nations and the economic well-being of individuals, the spread of English also contributes to significant social, political, and economic inequalities.' There is something rather bizarre in the belief that if everyone learned English, everyone would be better off.

Bruthiaux (2002: 292–3) argues convincingly that for many of the world's poor English language education is 'an outlandish irrelevance' and 'talk of a role for English language education in facilitating the process of poverty reduction and a major allocation of public resources to that end is likely to prove misguided and wasteful.' Grin (2001), one of the few to study the relationship between English and economic gain in any depth, argues that there is also an issue of diminishing returns here, since the more people learn English, the less the skill of knowing English will count. And bringing a sophisticated economic analysis to the question of global English, Lysandrou and Lysandrou (2003: 230) argue that 'the embrace of the English language is to the detriment of the majorities of communities the world over insofar as it contributes to their systematic dispossession.'[1] Thus we need to distinguish very clearly between individually-oriented access arguments about escape from poverty, and class-oriented arguments about large-scale poverty reduction. The challenge here is to get beyond liberal arguments for access, and look instead at the broad effects of educational provision in all their complexity. We need to ask what constellation of concerns comes to bear in the contextual relationships among what I call, following Janks (2000), dominion (the contingent and contextual effects of power), disparity (inequality and the need for access), difference (engaging with diversity) and desire (understanding how identity and agency are related). Without such analyses of English, the myth of English as a language of development and opportunity will continue to make English a delusionary language. And these constant calls for English as a solution to poverty not only hold out few prospects for change for the recipients of such policies but also reinforce a belief in the existence of English.

And finally, rather than offering opportunity for all, English operates as a deeply exclusionary language. Tollefson suggests that:

> For those who already speak English, the economic value of the language translates directly into greater opportunities in education, business and employment. For those who must learn English, however, particularly those who do not have access to high-quality English language education, the spread of English presents a formidable obstacle to education, employment, and other activities requiring English proficiency. (Tollefson, 2000: 9)

As Ramanathan's (2005) study of English medium (EM) and Vernacular education in India shows, English is a deeply divisive language: English and power circulate through the social system, 'producing a *selective tradition* that actively *dilutes* Vernaculars and Vernacular ways of knowing, learning and teaching' (Ramanathan, 2005: 38; emphasis in original). While Vernacular languages and cultures are thus denigrated and excluded, the education system 'dovetails with the values and aspirations of the elite Indian middle class: not only are all tertiary disciplines within their reach, they also bring with them cultural models that resonate with the thought structures of EM classrooms and institutions' (Ramanathan, 2005: 112). While English opens doors to some, it is simultaneously a barrier to learning, development and employment for others, and thus keeps out far more than it lets in. The myths that surround English as a language of opportunity, advancement and equality are beliefs that have profound effects for the (mis)education of many around the world. Addressing these collusionary, delusionary and exclusionary roles of English is only part of the story, however, since we also need to come to terms with the ways in which these stories mythologise English more generally. The concerns I have outlined here are part of a larger imperative to investigate the sociological functions of 'the Myth of English as an international language' (Krishnaswamy & Burde, 1998: 19).

English as Mythical Entity

To describe and refute such myths, therefore, is not a sufficient goal. Of greater significance are the ways in which such myths are incessant stories told about English, constantly putting English into discourses about education, development and poverty, chronicling English as a language of opportunity, equality and access. Such myths relentlessly construct the illusion of English, presenting the world with a view that there is an identifiable language called English. It might be assumed that the notion of a global entity called English is challenged by a World Englishes perspective, which suggests that English has now become a set of separable regional languages. From this perspective, at the very least, we have a plurality of Englishes. Yet the World Englishes perspective in fact does little more than pluralise the notion of English while at the same time positing a core entity that is English and excluding any other possibilities that destabilise this notion of global English in more fundamental ways. If we seek a more contextual and contingent understanding of language use, it becomes clear that both the monolithic presence of a language called English and the pluralistic belief in many Englishes are both myths. What we have instead are the 'language effects' of a particular set of claims about language and English.

The idea of World Englishes, then, seeks to challenge the notion of a monolithic English emanating from the central Anglo-institutions of global hegemony. While the homogeny position outlined above suggests that English is playing a role in world homogenisation, here we get the other side of the coin, the *heterogeny position*, focusing on the 'implications of pluricentricity ..., the new and emerging norms of performance, and the bilingual's creativity as a manifestation of the contextual and formal hybridity of Englishes' (Kachru, 1997: 66). Thus the World Englishes paradigm has focused on the ways in which English has become locally adapted and institutionalised to create different varieties of English (different Englishes) around the world. I have discussed many of the problems with World Englishes at greater length elsewhere (Pennycook, 2002, 2003a, 2003b), including the ubiquitous, insistent, unsubstantiated and unexplained 'pleas for the neutrality of English in the post-colonial contexts' (Parakrama, 1995: 22), and the inadequacy of the concentric circles model to capture the complexity of Englishes, since it fails, as Holborow (1999: 59–60) points out, 'to take adequate account of social factors and social differences *within* the circles,' and meanwhile continues problematically to locate native speakers and their norms in the centre, and non-native speakers elsewhere.

For the discussion here, however, of particular concern is the way in which these new Englishes are constructed along nationalist and exclusionary lines. As Krishnaswamy and Burde (1998: 30) observe, if Randolph Quirk represented 'the imperialistic attitude' to English, the World Englishes approach represents a 'a nationalistic point of view,' whereby nations and their varieties of English are conjured into existence: 'Like Indian nationalism, "Indian English" is "fundamentally insecure" since the notion "nation-India" is insecure' (Krishnaswamy & Burde,1998: 63). As Dasgupta (1993: 137) laments, ' ... seldom have so many talented men and women worked so long and so hard and achieved so little' since the linguistics on which it relies cannot capture the complexity of language use that it claims to investigate, a point emphasised by Krishnaswamy and Burde's (1998: 64) call for 'a reinvestigation of several concepts currently used by scholars.' By focusing centrally on the development of new national Englishes, the World Englishes approach reproduces precisely those linguistic paradigms that fell into the trap of believing the nationalist dream. Thus, not only does it fail to take into account Anderson's (1983) understanding of the process of imagining communities, but it also misses the point that languages were part of this dialectical co-imagining.

As Bruthiaux (2003: 161) points out, the descriptive and analytic inconsistency of the concentric circle model gives it little explanatory power. This 'superficially appealing and convenient model conceals more than it reveals' since it attempts to compare varieties of English, different speaker types and geographical locations all at once. Its use of inconsistent criteria to categorise so-called varieties of English is confounded by a 'primarily nation-based model.' Thus it overlooks difference within regions and ascribes variety based on postcolonial political history: where a nation state was created, so a variety emerged. Ultimately, concludes Bruthiaux (2003: 161), 'the Three Circles model is a 20th century construct that has outlived its usefulness'. By positing these new Englishes, it perpetuates the myth of national languages that the global spread of English allows us to start to rethink, and does so by focusing on a narrow selection of standardised forms in particular communities. As Parakrama (1995: 25–6) argues, 'The smoothing out of struggle within and without language is replicated in the homogenising of the varieties of English on the basis of "upper-class" forms. Kachru is thus able to theorise on the nature of a monolithic Indian

English.' While appearing, therefore, to work from an inclusionary political agenda in its attempt to have the new Englishes acknowledged as varieties of English, this approach to language is remorselessly exclusionary.

The process of constructing these new national varieties of English therefore involves a host of exclusions. Mufwene (1994, 1998) laments that the distinction between native and indigenised varieties of English 'excludes English creoles, most of which are spoken as native languages and vernaculars' (Mufwene, 1994: 24). This exclusion, he suggests, ultimately concerns the identity of creole speakers: 'the naming practices of new Englishes has to do more with the racial identity of those who speak them than with how these varieties developed and the extent of their structural deviations' (Mufwene, 2001: 107). The inclusion of creoles, furthermore, would profoundly challenge the notion of World Englishes: Not only would it challenge the racist exclusion of the wrong sorts of speakers, but it would also challenge what is understood by language in general, and English in particular. As Sebba (1997: 289) notes, following Mühlhäusler (1992), 'the study of pidgins and creoles forces us to stop conceptualising language as a *thing*, an *object* which can be captured and put under a microscope and dissected using a set of tools developed by linguists.' The dynamism of creoles, therefore, throws out a challenge to all study of languages as objects. This argument using the examples of creoles is not, it should be noted, an example of what Degraff (2005) calls 'linguists' most dangerous myth: the fallacy of creole exceptionalism,' which posits creoles as different from other languages. Rather, it is the opposite: It takes creoles as the norm (and not by the strategy of reducing them to 'real languages') and asks other theories of language to justify themselves.

The inclusion of creoles within an understanding of English questions not only the reification of English and World Englishes as objects on which linguists can do their work, but also how we think about languages. Although much debated (see e.g. Degraffe, 2005; Mufwene, 2001), a broad consensus on creoles is that rather than being debased or distorted versions of European (or other) languages, they are best conceived as mixed languages, possibly with a base in various grammatical systems from one set of languages, and a vocabulary drawn from one or more lexifying languages. An 'English creole' is therefore generally understood as a language with recognisably English words but a grammar derived form a range of sources including African languages, non-standard versions of English and other developmental processes. Such a notion immediately destabilises the concept of World Englishes, which by and large relies on a belief in a core, central grammar and lexicon of English (which is what makes new Englishes still English), with new Englishes characterised by a few grammatical shifts, new lexical items and different pragmatic and phonological features. In this view, divergences from the core are viewed as 'localisations' as long as the overarching system remains intact. English from a creole-inclusive point of view, however, not only embraces a wide variety of mutually incomprehensible uses of language but also potentially a wide variety of grammars. Creole languages have to be excluded from World Englishes, therefore, since they perforce destabilise the very definitions of language and grammar that underlie this version of a global language.

If it can be argued, furthermore, that African American English, for example, is a creole-based language derived from African languages with English lexifiers, which approaches standard American English at one end of the creole continuum (see Mufwene, 2001, for discussion; and similar arguments can be made for a host of other varieties of English such as Aboriginal English in Australia), then we clearly have not only the possibility of mutually incomprehensible versions of English with grammars from other languages, but also what may appear mutually comprehensible versions of the same language (American English) that are in fact languages with different histories that have come to take on the appearance of similarity. Once we accept this possibility, the argument that mutual comprehensibility may be a way of defining whether one is using the same language is challenged not only by the obvious difficulty that versions of some languages are not comprehensible to each other, but also by the notion that mutually comprehensible speakers may be using different languages. This is not the same as noting that speakers of politically divided language domains (say Swedish and Norwegian) may be able to understand each other; rather it raises the more interesting possibilities that speakers of apparently comprehensible versions of a language may be speaking very different languages. And once again, this suggests that the World Englishes paradigm, while supposedly emphasising diversity, in fact has at its core an underlying emphasis on the constraining similarities of English.

Pluralisation of English, therefore, does not take us far enough and remains an exclusionary paradigm. Just as Makoni (1998) has argued that the concept of multilingualism may do little more than pluralise monolingualism, so I am suggesting that the concept of World Englishes does little more than pluralise monolithic English. The notion of World Englishes leaves out all those Other Englishes that do not fit the paradigm of an emergent national standard, and in doing so, falls into the trap of mapping centre linguists' images of language and the world on to the periphery. As Parakrama argues, the World Englishes approach to diversity in English:

cannot do justice to those Other Englishes as long as they remain within the over-arching structures that these Englishes bring to crisis. To take these new/other Englishes seriously would require a fundamental revaluation of linguistic paradigms, and not merely a slight accommodation or adjustment. (Parakrama 1995: 17)

Similarly, Canagarajah argues that in Kachru's:

attempt to systematise the periphery variants, he has to standardise the language himself, leaving out many eccentric, hybrid forms of local Englishes as too unsystematic. In this, the Kachruvian paradigm follows the logic of the prescriptive and elitist tendencies of the center linguists. (Canagarajah, 1999: 180)

The irony here is that while looking like a pluralist, localised version of English, this paradigm reinforces both centrist views on language and dangerous myths about English.

We need, then, to ask some rather different questions that go beyond strategies of pluralisation. Let us return to Harris' (1990: 45) argument that 'linguistics does not need to postulate the existence of languages as part of its theoretical apparatus.' Surely at the heart of the problem of understanding English here is the continued belief in the existence of 'a language' called English. And this problem is not overcome simply by a strategy of pluralisation of Englishes since this does little more than reproduce the same normative linguistic paradigm. As Harris goes on to argue, the question here is whether

the concept of 'a language,' as defined by orthodox modern linguistics, corresponds to any determinate or determinable object of analysis at all, whether social or individual, whether institutional or psychological. If there is no such object, it is difficult to evade the conclusion that modern linguistics has been based upon a myth. (Harris, 1990: 45)

And given the scale of English and the scale of work on English, it is tempting to conclude that what we have here is the mother of all myths: English as an international language. Indeed one reason for focusing on English here is to avoid the suggestion that strategies of disinvention apply to so-called multilingual or minority contexts. Strategies of disinvention and reconstruction apply to all languages, and especially those on which so much effort at invention has been spent.

If we take a step back from this myth, it is indeed puzzling to observe the extraordinary continuation of the idea that something called English exists, a myth perpetuated by strategies of exclusion and circularity. It is assumed a priori that there is such a thing as English. This view is reinforced by excluding those types of English and, as Mufwene (2001) notes, those types of speakers, that don't fit what is deemed to be English, and then employing the circular argument that, if it doesn't fit, it isn't English. A core system of English is assumed, with deviations from this core that destabilise the notion of system discounted. The World Englishes paradigm, while attempting to achieve sociolinguistic equality for its varieties, is not epistemologically different from this model of core, variation and exclusion. For a world English to be such, it must adhere to the underlying grammar of central English, demonstrate enough variety to make it interestingly different, but not diverge to the extent that it undermines the myth of English. If we acknowledge creole languages, however, if we refuse to draw a line down the middle of a creole continuum (exclaiming that one end is English while the other is not), if we decide that those 'Other Englishes' may be part of English, then we are not dealing with a language held in place by a core structure but rather a notion of language status that is not definable by interior criteria.

Conclusion: Language Effects and Mobilisations

Returning to and rewriting Barthes for a moment, we can suggest that the myth (or myths) of English as an international language (EIL) can be understood as making the local contingencies of English appear to have broader ontological and temporal validity and a natural justification. The myth(s) of EIL erase the memory that English is a fabrication, that languages are inventions and that talk of English as an international language is a piece of intellectual slippage that replaces the history of this invention with a belief in its natural identity. The myth of EIL depoliticises English, and does so not by ignoring English but by constantly talking about it, making English innocent, giving it a natural and eternal justification, a clarity that is not that of a description but an assumption of fact. The myth of EIL deals not merely with the invention of English, but with the strategies that constantly keep that invention in place, with the relentless repetition of the stories and tales about this thing called English. We need to disinvent English, to demythologise it, and then to look at how a reinvention of English may help us understand more clearly what it is we are dealing with here.

Taking Hopper's (1998: 157) proposition seriously that 'there is no natural fixed structure to language,' the idea of a core that defines English seems hard to maintain. This takes us into rather different territory. Kandiah (1998: 100) points out that most approaches to the new Englishes miss the crucial point that these Englishes 'fundamentally involve a radical act of semiotic reconstruction and reconstitution which of itself confers native userhood on the subjects involved in the act.' Language use is centrally an agentive act, an act of reconstruction rather than act of reproduction, as an argument that languages have fixed structures that we repeat would suggest. Linking this notion to Le Page and Tabouret-Keller's (1985) proposition that linguistic and cultural identities are constituted through the performance of *acts of identity*, we can suggest that language use is not so much the repetition of prior grammatical structure but rather a semiotic restructuring as a claim to a particular identity.

Just as recent thinking (e.g. Butler, 1990; 1993) has focused on gendered and other identities in a non-foundational light, so may language itself be seen as a product of performative acts. It is instructive in this context to compare Butler's comments on gender with Hopper's discussion of *emergent grammar*: 'The subject is not *determined* by the rules through which it is generated because signification is *not a founding act, but rather a regulated process of repetition*' (Butler, 1990: 145; emphasis in original). For Hopper, the apparent structure or regularity of grammar is an emergent property that 'is shaped by discourse in an ongoing process. Grammar is, in this view, simply the name for certain categories of observed repetitions in discourse' (Hopper, 1998: 156). Thus, just as Butler (1999: 120) argues that identities are a product of ritualised social performatives calling the subject into being and 'sedimented through time,' so for Hopper (1998: 158). systematicity 'is an illusion produced by the partial settling or *sedimentation* of frequently used forms into temporary subsystems'. And by analogy English is an illusion of systematicity produced by ritualised social and linguistic activities that have become sedimented through time.

Where, then, does this leave us? English is a social, ideological, historical and discursive construction, the product of ritualised social performatives that become sedimented into temporary subsystems. These social performatives are acts of identity, investment and semiotic (re)construction. That is to say, the temporary sedimentation of English subsytems is a result of agentive acts, particular moves to identify, to use and adapt available semiotic resources for a variety of goals. And given the global status of the English myth, acts of English identification are used to perform, invent and (re)fashion identities across innumerable domains. English, like other languages, does not exist as a prior system but is produced and sedimented through acts of identity. Similar to the way that we perform identity with words (rather than reflect identities in language), we also perform languages with words. What we therefore have to understand is not this 'thing' 'English' that does or does not do things to and for people, but rather the multiple investments people bring to their acts, desires and performances in 'English'. English as an international language is not merely a set of social, cultural and political myths about what English can do, but is also based on the untenable myth that there is a real world object called English.

It might be asked what use all of this might be to teachers, users, or learners of English. Surely it is not helpful to teachers and learners to read that this activity we are engaged in – whether it is writing an e-mail to a friend in English, going over the meanings of vocabulary in an English comprehension passage, practising a dialogue in English, writing a poem in English, conducting a business meeting in English, calling air traffic control at an international airport in English – is in fact a myth, that while we have always reasonably believed that this thing we know, use, learn, teach, is something called English, we have in fact been deluded. The teacher is teaching nothing, the student is learning nothing, and the language users are fooling themselves in believing that they are communicating through English. This is of course not the point of the argument here. This project of disinvention is aimed neither to discredit the work of teachers, students, writers or poets, nor merely to engage in a form of linguistic deconstruction for its own sake. There is clearly a certain materiality to the products and processes of activities such as English language education; indeed, if we reflect for a moment on what people are currently doing around the world, after sleeping, eating and engaging in various forms of work, 'learning English' must surely account for quite a considerable part of current global human activity.

As Joseph (2002: 44) suggests, however, this activity might best be conceived in terms of a verb, of doing things with language, in terms, perhaps, of Englishing. This is different from the engagement with:

> the *institution* of the language, the noun-like thing that they ultimately cannot ignore, but must comprehend, grapple with, accept in some respects and resist in others, as they construct their own linguistic identities simultaneously within it and in opposition to it. (Joseph, 2002: 44)

It is clear that many people are engaged in activities such as 'teaching English,' 'learning English,' 'writing in English' and so forth, but much less clear what this implies about the institutional entity English. The argument here, then, is that once we grasp the implications of understanding languages as inventions, an alternative way forward presents itself for how we consider what it is we are doing. Thus, if we are concerned about the relation between English and lesser used languages, the way forward may be not so much in terms of language policies to support other languages over English but rather in terms of opposing language ideologies that construct English in particular ways.

Just as Butler (1993: 12) describes her project as 'a poststructuralist rewriting of discursive performativity as it operates in the materialisation of sex', so my interest here is in a poststructuralist rewriting of discursive performativity as it operates in the materialisation of language. If Foucault (eg 1980) was concerned with the 'truth effects' of discourse, and Butler (1993) with the 'body effects' of discourse, we are here concerned with the 'language effects' of discourse, the ways in which languages are materialised through discourse. By analogy, then, with Foucault's (1980) argument that we need to give up asking if something is true or false and instead focus on the truth effects of making different epistemological claims, so we would do better to go beyond asking whether English exists or not, and rather focus on the 'language effects' produced by language industries. A range of interested industries, from linguists to educationalists, from policy makers to publishers, constantly reproduce myths of English. This focus on language effects does not, I would argue, lessen the impact of something called the global spread of English but focuses our attention on the effects of the claims to the ontological status of English. While EIL may be a myth, the language effects of this myth are very real.

When we talk of English today we mean many things, and not many of them to do with some core notion of language. English is not so much a language as a discursive field: English *is* neoliberalism, English *is* globalisation, English *is* human capital. The question, then, is what is it that people do in their claims that something is English? Once we understand that languages are inventions and that we need to disinvent and reinvent what they are seen to be, we can start to work towards a quite different way of thinking about what English language teaching may be. The question then becomes not whether some monolithic thing called English is imperialistic or an escape from poverty, nor how many varieties there may be of this thing called English, but rather what kind of mobilisations underlie acts of English use or learning. In order to come to terms with such questions, we need a much more contextualised understanding of language as locally derived. Something called English is mobilised by English language industries with particular language effects. But something called English is also part of complex language chains, mobilised as part of multiple acts of identity; it is caught in a constant process of semiotic reconstruction.

Notes
1. Lysandrou and Lysandrou (2003) argue, however, that this does not mean that English should be opposed since (1) such dispossession occurs only in 'price

space' as opposed to 'physical space'; and (2) the solution to such a role for English is an economic one, not one of language policy.

References

Anderson, B. (1983) *Imagined Communities: Reflections on the Origin and Spread of Nationalism*. London: Verso.
Appadurai, A. (1996) *Modernity at Large: Cultural Dimensions of Globalization*. Minneapolis: University of Minnesota Press.
Appleby, R., Copley, K., Sithirajvongsa, S. and Pennycook, A. (2002) Language in development constrained: Three contexts. *TESOL Quarterly* 36 (3), 323–346.
Bailey, R. (1991) *Images of English: A Cultural History of the Language*. Ann Arbor: The University of Michigan Press.
Barthes, R. (1957/1972) *Mythologies* (A. Lavers, trans. from 1957 original). New York: Hill and Wang.
Blommaert, J. (ed.) (1999) *Language Ideological Debates*. Berlin: Mouton.
Bruthiaux, P. (2002) Hold your courses: Language education, language choice and economic development. *TESOL Quarterly* 36 (3), 275–296.
Bruthiaux, P. (2003) Squaring the circles: Issues in modeling English worldwide. *International Journal of Applied Linguistics* 13 (2), 159–177.
Butler, J. (1990) *Gender Trouble: Feminism and the Subversion of Identity*. London: Routledge.
Butler, J. (1993) *Bodies That Matter: On the Discursive Limits of 'Sex'*. London: Routledge.
Butler, J. (1999) Performativity's social magic. In R. Shusterman (ed.) *Bourdieu: A Critical Reader* (pp. 113–128). Oxford: Blackwell Publishers.
Canagarajah, S. (1999) *Resisting Linguistic Imperialism in English Teaching*. Oxford: Oxford University Press.
Crystal, D. (1997) *English as a Global Language*. Cambridge: Cambridge University Press.
Dasgupta, P. (1993) *The Otherness of English: India's Auntie Tongue Syndrome*. New Delhi: Sage Publications.
Degraff, M (2005) Linguists' most dangerous myth: The fallacy of Creole Exceptionalism. *Language in Society* 34, 533–591.
Dixon, R. (1997) *The Rise and Fall of Languages*. Cambridge: Cambridge University Press
EL Gazette (1999) English language could be the key to a better life for the underprivileged. Issue 237 (October), p. 3.
Ethnologue (2005). On WWW at http://www.ethnologue.com/ethno_docs/introduction.asp#language_id. Accessed 19.11.05.
Foucault, M (1970) *The Order of Things: An Archaeology of the Human Sciences*. London: Tavistock.
Foucault, M. (1980) *Power/Knowledge: Selected Interviews & Other Writings, 1972–1977*. New York: Pantheon Books.
Grin, F. (2001) English as economic value: Facts and fallacies. *World Englishes* 20 (1), 65–78.
Hanson, J. (1997) The mother of all tongues. Review of D. Crystal, *English as a Global Language. Times Higher Education Supplement* 1288 (July 11), 22.
Hardt, M. and Negri, A. (2000). *Empire*. Cambridge, MA: Harvard University Press.

Harris, R. (1988) Murray, Moore and the myth. In R. Harris (ed.) *Linguistic Thought in England, 1914–1945* (pp.1–26). London: Duckworth.

Harris, R. (1990) On redefining linguistics. In H. Davis and T. Taylor (eds) *Redefining Linguistics* (pp. 18–52). London: Routledge.

Holborow, M. (1999) *The Politics of English: A Marxist View of Language*. London: Sage Publications.

Hopper, P. (1998) Emergent grammar. In M. Tomasello (ed.) *The New Psychology of Language* (pp. 155–175). Mahwah, NJ: Lawrence Erlbaum.

Janks, H. (2000) Domination, access, diversity and design: A synthesis for critical literacy education. *Educational Review* 52 (2), 175–186.

Joseph, J. (2002) Is language a verb? Conceptual change in linguistics and language teaching. In H. Trappes-Lomax and G. Ferguson (eds) *Language in Language Teacher Education* (pp. 29–47). Amsterdam: John Benjamins.

Kachru, B. (1986) *The Alchemy of English: The Spread, Functions and Models of Non-native Englishes*. Oxford: Pergamon.

Kachru, B. (1997) World Englishes and English-using communities. *Annual Review of Applied Linguistics* 17, 66–87.

Kandiah, T (1998) Epiphanies of the deathless native users' manifold avatars: A post-colonial perspective on the native-speaker. In R. Singh (ed.) *The Native Speaker: Multilingual Perspectives* (pp. 79–110). New Delhi: Sage Publications.

Kant, I. (1781/1998) *The Critique of Pure Reason [Kritik der reinen Vernunft]* (P. Guyer and A. Wood, ed. and trans.). Cambridge: Cambridge University Press.

Krishnaswamy, N. and Burde, A. (1998) *The Politics of Indians' English: Linguistic Colonialism and The Expanding English Empire*. Delhi: Oxford University Press.

Kroskrity, P. (ed.) (2000) *Regimes of Language: Ideologies, Politics and Identities*. Santa Fe, NM: School of American Research Press.

Le Page, R. and Tabouret-Keller, A. (1985) *Acts of Identity*. Cambridge: Cambridge University Press.

Lysandrou, P. and Lysandrou, Y. (2003) Global English and proregression: Understanding English language spread in the contemporary era. *Economy and Society* 32 (2), 207–233.

Makoni, S. (1998) African languages as European scripts: The shaping of communal memory. In S. Nuttall and C. Coetzee (eds) *Negotiating the Past: The Making of Memory in South Africa* (pp. 242–248). Oxford: Oxford University Press.

Malinowski, B. (1954) *Magic, Science and Religion*. New York: Doubleday Anchor.

Mignolo, W. (2000) *Local Histories/Global Designs: Coloniality, Subaltern Knowledges and Border Thinking*. Princeton, NJ: Princeton University Press.

Milroy, J. (1999) The consequences of standardisation in descriptive linguistics. In T. Bex and R. Watts (eds) *Standard English: The Widening Debate* (pp. 16–39). London: Routledge.

Mufwene, S. (1994) New Englishes and criteria for naming them. *World Englishes* 13 (1), 21–31.

Mufwene, S. (1998) Native speaker, proficient speaker and norms. In R. Singh (ed.) *The Native Speaker: Multilingual Perspectives* (pp. 111–123). New Delhi: Sage Publications.

Mufwene, S. (2001) *The Ecology of Language Evolution*. Cambridge: Cambridge University Press.

Mühlhäusler, P. (1992) What is the use of studying pidgin and creole languages? *Language Sciences* 14 (3), 309–316

Mühlhäusler, P. (1996) *Linguistic Ecology: Language Change and Linguistic Imperialism in the Pacific Region*. London: Routledge.
Ndebele, N. S. (1987) The English language and social change in South Africa. *The English Academy Review* 4, 1–16
Paradis, M. (2004) *A Neurolinguistic Theory of Bilingualism*. Amsterdam: John Benjamins.
Parakrama, A. (1995) *De-hegemonizing Language Standards: Learning from (Post)colonial Englishes about 'English'*. Basingstoke: MacMillan.
Pennycook, A. (1994) *The Cultural Politics of English as an International Language*. London: Longman.
Pennycook, A. (1998) *English and the Discourses of Colonialism*. London: Routledge.
Pennycook, A. (2002) Turning English inside out. *Indian Journal of Applied Linguistics* 28 (2), 25–43.
Pennycook, A. (2003a) Global Englishes, Rip Slyme and performativity. *Journal of Sociolinguistics* 7 (4), 513–533.
Pennycook, A. (2003b) Beyond homogeny and heterogeny: English as a global and worldly language. In C. Mair (ed.) *The Cultural Politics of English* (pp. 3–17). Amsterdam: Rodopi.
Phillipson, R. (1992) *Linguistic Imperialism*. Oxford: Oxford University Press.
Phillipson, R. (1999) Voice in global English: Unheard chords in Crystal loud and clear. Review of D. Crystal's *English as a Global Language*. *Applied Linguistics* 20 (2), 265–276
Ramanathan, V. (2005) *The English-Vernacular divide: Postcolonial Language Politics and Practice*. Clevedon: Multilingual Matters.
Reagan, T. (2004) Objectification, positivism and language studies: A reconsideration. *Critical Inquiry in Language Studies: An International Journal* 1 (1), 41–60.
Sebba, M. (1997) *Contact Languages: Pidgins and Creoles*. Basingstoke: Palgrave.
Tollefson, J. (2000) Policy and ideology in the spread of English. In J.K. Hall and W. Eggington (eds) *The Sociopolitics of English Language Teaching* (pp. 7–21). Clevedon: Multilingual Matters.
Trudgill, P. (1999) Standard English: What it isn't. In T. Bex and R. Watts (eds) *Standard English: The Widening Debate* (pp. 117–128). London: Routledge.
Watts, R. (1999) The ideology of dialect in Switzerland. In J. Blommaert (ed.) *Language Ideological Debates* (pp. 67–103). Berlin: Mouton de Gruyter.
Willinsky, J. (1994) *Empire of Words: The Reign of the OED*. Princeton, NJ: Princeton University Press.
Willinsky, J. (1998) *Learning to Divide the World: Education at Empire's End*. Minneapolis, MN: University of Minnesota Press.
Winchester, S (2003) *The Meaning of Everything: The Story of the Oxford English Dictionary*. Oxford: Oxford University Press.
Woolard, K. (2004) Is the past a foreign country? Time, language origins and the nation in early modern Spain. *Journal of Linguistic Anthropology* 14 (1), 57–80
Žižek, S. (1993) *Tarrying with the Negative: Kant, Hegel and the Critique of Ideology*. Durham, NC: Duke University Press.

Chapter 5
Beyond 'Language': Linguistic Imperialism, Sign Languages and Linguistic Anthropology[1]

JAN BRANSON and DON MILLER

> The entire destiny of modern linguistics is in fact determined by Saussure's inaugural act through which he separates the 'external' elements of linguistics from the 'internal' elements, and, by reserving the title of linguistics for the latter, excludes from it all the investigations which establish a relationship between language and anthropology, the political history of those who speak it, or even the geography of the domain where it is spoken, because all of these things add nothing to a knowledge of the language taken in itself. (Bourdieu, 1991: 33)

Bourdieu's critique of conventional (Saussurean) linguistics strips it bare of its protective coating of assumed objectivity, and scientific rationality, and above all neutrality, placing it within the culturally and historically specific environment of the Western academy and the broader society. Safe within the walls of their universities, institutions 'which ha[ve] been socially licensed as entitled to operate an objectification which lays claim to objectivity and universality' (Bourdieu, 1988: xii), linguists distort the communicative environment to their academic ends, assuming themselves free to dissect the 'languages' they construct as a surgeon dissects a cadaver, a lifeless object of study, divested of all cultural, social, emotional and aesthetic identity and creativity. The link of the linguist to the surgeon is not simply metaphorical. As Foucault demonstrated, it was the development of a medical science based on the individuated, physical body, a medicine that focused its gaze 'upon the stable, visible, legible basis of death' (Foucault, 1975: 196), that laid the ground for the broader 'scientific' study of humanity. Through its focus on the individual cadaver, the importance of medicine 'in the constitution of the sciences of man ... is not only methodological, but ontological, in that it concerns man's being as object of positive knowledge' (Foucault, 1975: 197).

And so we move out of the laboratory into the real world where languages are living, changing, fluctuating processes of communication. In the process we will aim to 'trap *Homo Academicus*, supreme classifier among classifiers, in the net of his own classifications' (Bourdieu, 1988: xi) and show the linguist to be far from neutral, but rather an agent in the oppression of minorities within and beyond the Western world.

For the past 15 years we have been involved in the study of the linguistic oppression of deaf people in a range of social and cultural settings, namely Australia, Britain, Indonesia and Thailand. This has involved in part the documentation of languages of which there has been little or no linguistic record or analysis. In seeking to understand, record and analyse these languages and their social and cultural contexts, we have also sought to place ourselves in the picture, to understand the impact of our own research activities, of our presence among these communities and of the epistemological and cosmological traditions through which we seek to document and analyse. In the process we have been led to question the most fundamental of our linguistic concepts – 'language' and the 'linguistic community'. We have been particularly concerned with the intensely imperialist tendencies that dominate Western linguistic analyses of sign languages as they reshape the languages they study to fit their theories, their models of language, and their epistemologies, yet another form of 'epistemic violence', that unrecognised symbolic violence that 'effaces the subject ...' (Spivak, 1987), 'insidiously objectifying' the 'colonised' through a conceptual apparatus which robs people and their languages of their individual and cultural integrity, devaluing and distorting their differences.[2]

Here we explore this overtly academic and imperialist process.[3] A basic premise underlying this discussion is that linguistics is a cultural construct, that it is a way of thinking about communicative processes that is historically and culturally specific. If linguistics is as much a cultural construct as any other aspect of culture – kinship, religion, politics – then is its view of language tied to a distinctly Western cosmology? And if so, why should it apply unproblematically to languages in other cultures or even to the minority languages of subcultural groups in the West? Can linguists engage unproblematically in the formal linguistic analysis of any language? Indeed why do many linguists assume that they can engage in the formal linguistic analysis of any and every language? And what is the actual and potential impact of these assumptions? While most if not all academics will acknowledge the fact that cultural differences exist, that people from different cultures view the world and their place in it differently, Western academics have often seen their discipline-based activities as 'objective', as 'scientific', as 'rational', as neither culturally determined nor culturally specific. The categories and models they bring to both the data collection and analytical processes are regarded as scientific and beyond culture.

Language is culture, a product and manifestation of culture, but via Saussure is seen as separated from its cultural context to become an object in itself, to be examined as though it existed apart from its realisation in cultural practice. Linguists construct 'language' and its building blocks – morphemes, phonemes, nouns and verbs, words and clauses, classifiers and signifiers. The assumed arbitrariness of the sign ensures the assumed viability of studying language 'in itself'. Our particular focus is on sign languages, unwritten languages that run counter to most of the axiomatic assumptions that lie at the heart of Western conceptions of language and therefore of linguistics.

A Note on Sign Languages

Sign languages use the hands, face and body, space and time to construct the 'signs' through which language is expressed. Sign languages are multi-dimensional, fundamentally embodied, essentially located in time and space, generating meaning through the strategic manipulation of time. Space and the body, and the associated problems involved in representing sign languages in a 'written' form, stand in contrast to the *assumed* qualities of spoken/written languages. Spoken languages are assumed to be, especially to enable them to be analysed linguistically, disembodied in sound and writing, and easily extracted from space and time through the two-dimensional and linear medium of writing. Whatever angle we take on the impact of writing on language, it has had the impact of reducing the communicative process in all its complexity to a two-dimensional linear process. The difficulties faced by sign language linguists, not only in representing sign languages' units of meaning as arbitrary but also in representing signing in written form, has highlighted the violent impact that linguists, the definers of language, have had on language in general.

Both iconicity and mimesis are present in sign languages in varying degrees, varying from language to language and impacted upon by the social and cultural environments in which they exist. Whatever role iconicity and mimesis play, the signs themselves must not be understood as a bundle of unchanging signifiers, each 'sign' the equivalent of a written 'word', which are simply arranged in grammatical order. While some signs are what are referred to as a 'frozen sign' (i.e. a fixed lexical item), much of the lexicon is a productive lexicon – signs change and develop in response to the meaning being generated, utilising a range of conventions of transformation based on handshapes, the use of space, movement, the face and body. The historical and linguistic links between gesture and the development and nature of sign languages is complex and controversial, and will be further discussed below.

The orientation of hearing communities towards sign languages has varied markedly from time to time and from culture to culture. In the West, the orientation towards sign languages by hearing intellectuals over the last couple of centuries has been in the main derogatory and/or dismissive. While a few educators embarked on the linguistic analysis of natural sign languages in the 19th century, the systematic linguistic analysis of sign languages began in the early 1960s. The central aim was to establish that sign languages were bona fide languages in their own right, to grant them linguistic legitimacy. Only very recently have a few linguists considered the possibility that the study of sign languages might in fact be of importance to our understanding of spoken languages. They have shown that the multi-dimensional nature of spoken language – its strategic use of time, of space through gesture and body language, and of tone – can be rediscovered through the examination of sign languages.

In order to explore the impact of formal linguistics on sign languages and their users it is necessary to understand that the devaluation of sign language has a very long history. Long before Saussure stressed the importance of the arbitrary nature of the sign, the signing of deaf people was frequently seen simply as gesture, as mimicry, not as language. Indeed, the Abbé de l'Epée, who started a school for poor deaf children in Paris in 1755, was in his time, and is often even today, credited with having, through his system of methodological signs, given language to the Deaf (rather than having learnt sign language from them). These hearing educators were seen as arousing abilities that had lain dormant in the Deaf until the hearing educators came along and released them through the gift of language. Walter Ong went so far as to claim that:

> Until the pedagogical techniques for introducing deaf-mutes more thoroughly, if always indirectly, into the oral–aural world were perfected in the past few generations, deaf-mutes always grew up intellectually subnormal. Left unattended, the congenitally deaf are more intellectually retarded than the congenitally blind. (Ong, 1967: 142)

This devaluation of natural sign languages and the conviction among hearing educators that the only viable media for education were Western national written languages, resulted in the development of artificial signed versions of these written languages. When the Abbé de l'Epée moved away from speech training as central to the education of the deaf towards the use of signing as a means for teaching the deaf pupils to read and write, he did not use the two-handed alphabet in use among the Parisian Deaf communities and did not, as indicated above, use the existing sign language with its distinctive syntax as the language of instruction. Rather he used the one-handed alphabet and developed a system of signed French. The die had been cast. While other educators in other times and places – Casteberg in Denmark, Bébian in France later – used natural sign languages to a greater or lesser degree and did not necessarily develop manually-coded versions of the written language, hearing educators constantly tampered with the signing traditions of their pupils, subordinating and severely restricting its lexicon to the demands of spoken and written languages, some insisting on the possibility of signing and speaking at the same time. Then in the 1960s, led by an American teacher of the deaf, David Anthony, educators again developed formal, manually-coded versions of spoken and written languages. In the development of these manually-coded systems, we encounter a particularly intense linguistic imperialism, not only a denial of linguistic identity, not simply the denial of the right to use a language, but the final colonial possession – the transformation of one language to conform to the form and content of the dominant language. In the process, language is destroyed, and all we are left with is semi-language and semi-lingualism.

The devaluation of these languages was of course linked not only to their gestural qualities but also to their association with a group of people who were seen as lacking access to real language, a group of people who were to be labelled 'disabled'.[4] In addition, linking these orientations towards sign language to the linguistic devaluations discussed below, is a view of language associated with the separation of mind and body. In the 'Preface' to his book *The Language Makers*, Roy Harris (1980) describes a picture of the messenger of the gods in Greek mythology, the god Hermes, the god of communication, of language:

> [The] engraved frontispiece ... depicts a statue of the god, in the form of a head wearing a winged helmet, placed upon a quadrilateral base bearing the letters of 'some old Alphabet'. The author explains why the god of language is represented as having no body: 'No other part of the human figure but the Head ... was deemed requisite to rational Communication.' (Harris, 1980: i)

The mind was seen as the source of learning through language. The head dominated the body. With the development of modern science, the intellectuals saw the body as limited and the mind as the source of endless creativity. Language is seen as coming from the mind and the mouth.

Writing is assumed to be simply a representation of disembodied sound. So even as late as 1982, Ong wrote: 'The basic orality of language is permanent' (Ong, 1982: 7); he continued:

> Wherever human beings exist they have a language, and in every instance a language that exists basically as spoken and heard, in the world of sound (...). Despite the richness of gesture, elaborated sign languages are substitutes for speech and dependent on oral speech systems, even when used by the congenitally deaf. (Ong, 1982: 7)

The dismissal of sign languages by this Jesuit philosopher of language is frequent and clothed in ignorance, but is by no means an isolated incident. Siertsema, in her critical survey of glossematics (1965), not only claimed that sound was an essential element of language per se, and that 'all other possible substances of expression besides sound are only secondary and only try to represent in a more or less successful way spoken language' (Siertsema, 1965: 10), but reinterpreted Saussure to support her view. Much more recently, Umberto Eco, in his book *The Search for the Perfect Language* (Eco, 1995), completely ignored the existence of sign languages, referring instead to the language of Deaf communities as 'the common, dactylogical form of deaf-mute speak, which then [in the mid 18th-century] as now, was the common method of signing with fingers the letters of the alphabet', thus assuming communication among the Deaf to be via fingerspelling of sound-based 'words'.[5] But, as Stokoe, the grand old man of sign linguistics, wrote of the impact of the Cartesian separation of mind and body on the analysis of language, 'Descartes thought wrong' (Stokoe, 2001: 78ff).

The devaluation of sign languages has therefore been linked to the absence of sound, to the apparent reliance on gesture, and to the evaluation of the users of these natural sign languages as pathological, as 'disabled'. Also important has been the fact that all natural sign languages are unwritten languages. Linguistics has commonly required that a language be written down before it can be effectively analysed. The linguistic evaluation and indeed denigration of sign languages has therefore been directly linked to 'the core intention of linguistics, namely, the *intellectualist philosophy* that treats language as an object of contemplation rather than as an instrument of action and power' (Bourdieu, 1991: 37, emphasis in original).

Sign Languages and the Tyranny of the Arbitrary Sign

At least since Ferdinand de Saussure (1974) put forward his structural model of language, a range of premises have become doxic in relation to the way language is understood and defined. Of particular importance has been his assertion that the units of meaning in language, its signs, are arbitrary, that these signs, usually words, have no intrinsic meaning and are not linked to their referents in any necessary way. The arbitrariness of the sign thus becomes the definiens of language. Where, in a sign language, mime is particularly prominent, the meaning may be apparent even to someone who has no knowledge of sign language at all. In other cases where there is an iconic element, the iconicity may not be apparent until the meaning is known. Here the arbitrary element is certainly present, but it is mitigated by the visual iconicity of the sign. How then are these iconic and mimetic aspects of sign language affected by doxic assumptions about the arbitrariness of 'signs' (used in the Saussurean sense)?

A frequent response to the use of mime in particular is to respond with the idea that mime is not language because it is not arbitrary. The same is true of the iconic aspects of sign language. Because mime and iconicity are virtually impossible in sound-based languages in their oral form, apart from onomatopoeia, and absent from most but not all written forms (hieroglyphics and ancient forms of Chinese writing are picture images and thus either direct visual representations or strongly iconic forms), the mimetic aspects of the sign language are often regarded as apart from the language itself, rather than integral to it. To acknowledge that mime was language would somehow devalue its linguistic status. In more extreme cases, because mimesis is integral to sign language, sign language has frequently been defined as not really language, but 'gesture', lacking the arbitrariness intrinsic to the concept of language, an attitude clearly evident in Eco's ill-informed dismissal of any form of gestures as capable of constituting a language since they must, according to Eco 'depend (parasitically) on the semantic universe of the verbal language' (Eco, 1995: 174), that the gestures must be 'anchored', to use his term, through association with the words of a verbal language.

Western linguistics, in its analysis of sign languages, mostly Western sign languages, has assumed that sign languages are made up, like spoken and written languages, of a lexicon of arbitrary signs – both frozen signs and a productive lexicon – which are combined syntactically through a process at least akin to word order, to produce meaning. The fight by linguists to have sign languages recognised as bona fide languages hinged on the demonstration of the arbitrariness of the sign and on the arbitrariness of the grammatical structure of sign languages. The current development of sign language linguistics continues to be based in these fundamental linguistic assumptions. As Armstrong has recently written,

... in a linguistics based on spoken languages, iconicity is seen as somehow primitive, and it has been given short shrift by the scientific linguists of signed languages. In fact, one could almost say there has been a taboo against discussing it. (Armstrong, 1999: 75)

While the tide has not turned and the tyranny, indeed the hegemony, of the arbitrary sign remains, research demonstrating that conventional linguistic assumptions about the nature of language do not necessarily apply in relation to sign languages has seriously challenged these assumptions. Indeed it is Bill Stokoe, the very linguist credited with demonstrating that sign languages were bona fide languages, who has led the move to recognise and understand the limitations of conventional linguistics, especially in relation to the linguistics of sign languages. In the year of his death he addressed the International Conference in Sign Linguistics with a challenge to all there to recognise and understand the differences between signed and spoken languages, to move beyond the tyranny of the arbitrary sign and understand the nature and importance of gesture, and to explore the way that a radical linguistics of sign languages can enliven and reform the linguistics of spoken languages (see Stokoe, 2001). He wrote in his last book, published posthumously, of 'a difference that makes a difference' (Stokoe, 2001: 193ff). The work of Armstrong et al. (1995), Bouvet (1997), Armstrong (1999) and Stokoe (2001), all attempts to move beyond conventional linguistic paradigms, point to the inappropriate and indeed the crippling impact of conventional linguistics. They propose alternative models and theories, some focusing on the origins of language, others on the development of a more effective linguistic analysis.

The subordination of sign linguistics to the linguistics of spoken languages, written and unwritten, provided no challenge to the linguistics of spoken/written languages. But to acknowledge the special qualities of sign languages, particularly the role and nature of gesture, to refuse to fit sign languages and their linguistic analysis into moulds linked to the assumed nature of sound-based languages, is to acknowledge a 'difference that makes a difference' not only to the linguistics of sign languages, but also to the linguistics of sound-based languages. Attention is drawn to languages as practice, to language as a dynamic event involving a whole range of elements, including gesture, that have hitherto been ignored. But there has been little sociolinguistic analysis of the symbolic violence wrought upon these sign languages and their users by the hegemony of conventional linguistics, a symbolic violence made all the more potent when that conventional analysis is applied to non-Western sign languages.

Analysing a Balinese Sign Language

In order to explore the potential symbolic violence of conventional Western linguistics, we turn to our analysis of the use of classifiers in a Balinese sign language, the Kata Kolok.[6] Our analysis of the use of classifiers in the sign language of the village – especially in relation to traditional aspects of village life associated with agriculture, home life and ritual – revealed an integral link between the use of the object and its representation in sign language. Indeed what emerged was that there was, in fact, no identifiable abstract sign for most objects. There was no word order involved, for there was in many cases no identifiable subject, verb or object. For example, when shown a frangipani flower and asked to produce the sign for it, women showed how the flower was placed in offerings to the spirits and gods, and men demonstrated how it was placed behind the ear. When asked to instruct a child to go and get a frangipani flower, the woman mimicked the placing of the frangipani in the offering and then signed for the child to go and bring the flower back. The child returned with a frangipani flower. The same was true of all village plants with a particular focus on their use in cooking or as animal fodder, demonstrating how they were prepared. Were the respondents responding to our questions by describing how the plants were used? No. To guard against this we asked our respondents to instruct others to collect the plants involved, and also recorded their use in natural conversation.

Must all 'sentences' or 'phrases' have a noun and a verb? Let us turn briefly from sign language use in Bali to sign language use in Australia. The use of classifiers in Auslan (Australian Sign Language), in many situations does not involve the use of separate signs for the subject or object – the classifier is used as a morpheme of the verb (Branson & Miller, 1995; Branson *et al.*, 1995). We require the use of nouns and verbs etc. in translating into English but this does not mean that they are present/required in the original. So in the Kata Kolok, the frangipani is placed behind the ear or in the offering. How it is done and in what context will determine whether the signing is an explanation or an instruction.

The Kata Kolok is a language used in face-to-face situations among an active and known community – often within the confines of extended kinship networks and localised religious communities. It therefore focuses on fulfilling what McMahon sees as the basic requirements of a language:

> ... speakers must learn their native language(s) in such a way as to allow communications with the generations above and below them: since language is a vehicle of communication, it would be failing in its

primary function if it did not allow parents to be understood by their children, or grandchildren by their grandparents. (McMahon, 1994: 5)

The language has evolved within this communal context and has not been influenced by educational environments or written language. In such a known environment, the specific contexts within which objects feature in people's lives are experienced by all. Few clues are required. The development of abstract concepts is on the whole unnecessary. The problem of referring to the flower apart from its ritual context does not arise since all know its ritual context and it is precisely the ritual context that is, at least for women, of prime concern. Gender based differences in language use are also immediately understood and taken for granted. The people with whom a person communicates are known for all their idiosyncrasies – personal, cultural and linguistic. The communal face-to-face circumstances in which the language has developed and is used do not require more formalised or complex processes.

The Kata Kolok therefore operates in a known, face-to-face communal environment that:

- has high levels of redundancy;
- demands low levels of formalisation;
- rarely demands the use of abstractions;
- allows for constant adaptation to the particular qualities and needs of specific individuals.

The on-going analysis of the Kata Kolok is also revealing a complex and creative relationship between the Kata Kolok and spoken Balinese. The links between the two languages relate particularly to the gestural aspects of spoken Balinese. Clear links between the languages have been established at the phonological, morphological and syntactical levels. Not only do these findings help us to understand the on-going development of the Kata Kolok in active communication, they also demonstrate clearly the need to look at the gestural aspects of spoken languages to understand the complexities of the communicative process: to acknowledge and explore 'the communicative function of visible gesture and, in particular, the habitual use by human beings of coordinated streams of speech and visible gesture in the normal course of interaction' (Armstrong, 1999: 123). The impact of the Kata Kolok on the communicative processes among hearing people in Desa Kolok is also under examination, revealing aspects of the communicative process based in speech which also do not conform neatly to the assumptions of conventional linguistics.

The Kata Kolok is therefore an entirely natural sign language, a language that has evolved as a communicative process, not as an educational tool. While all fully-fledged sign languages are 'natural' to some degree, sign linguists have conventionally dealt with sign languages in Western developed countries where the use and development of signing has not only been integrally linked to educational processes in which the dominant language of education has been the dominant written language, and the dominant individuals, the teachers, have been predominantly hearing, but also where fingerspelling and aspects of the syntax of the written language have become an integral part of the signing process.

With regard to the grammatical features of the Kata Kolok, research is revealing regularities in the signing used, but there is also evidence of a high level of freedom (Branson & Miller, 1998). Clearly a model of language as a process governed by rules, of language in the singular with a distinct grammar, does not apply to the Kata Kolok. Far more appropriate is to do as Bourdieu suggested for the study of culture and 'substitute strategy for the rule', to recognise the participants in linguistic activity as strategically using the language and its possible conventions to their own ends. As Bourdieu also indicates,

> To substitute strategy for the rule is to reintroduce time, with its rhythm, its orientation, its irreversibility. Science has a time which is not that of practice. For the analyst, time no longer counts ... (Bourdieu, 1977: 9)

The Kata Kolok exists only as a practice and therefore its analysis must not be bound by the atemporal nature of conventional linguistics:

> To restore to practice its practical truth, we must therefore reintroduce time into the theoretical representation of a practice which, being temporally structured, is intrinsically defined by its tempo. (Bourdieu, 1977: 8)

It is also clear, again following Bourdieu but this time with regard to his critiques of conventional linguistics, that the users of the Kata Kolok are:

> ... endowed with the diacritical dispositions which enable them to make *distinctions* between different *ways of saying*, distinctive manners of speaking. It follows that style, whether it be a matter of poetry as compared with prose or of the diction of a particular (social, sexual or generational) class compared with that of another class, exists only in relation to agents endowed with schemes of perception and appreciation that enable them to constitute it as a set of systematic differences, apprehended syncretically. What circulates on the linguistic market is not 'language' as such, but rather discourses that are stylistically marked both in their production, in so far as each speaker fashions an idiolect

from the common language, and in their reception, in so far as each recipient helps to produce the message which he perceives and appreciates by bringing to it everything that makes up his singular and collective experience. (Bourdieu, 1991: 38–9)

This last point is particularly important with regard to Kata Kolok, as indeed it was in our analysis of Auslan: 'What circulates on the linguistic market is not 'language' as such, but rather discourses that are stylistically marked' (Bourdieu, 1991: 39). Yet this view of 'language' still focuses on the strategic use of what is considered proper or improper, where the overtly ungrammatical can be a strategic possibility. The very existence of a sense of what is linguistically proper, however, of a distinctly grammatical way of signing, is itself associated with the formalisation of language by literate people within a complex and often faceless society. Need there even be a sense of what is proper, a sense of linguistic rules, in the use of a language such as the Kata Kolok? There are conventions associated with hand shapes which allow for a productive lexicon and a complex range of relatively frozen signs linked directly to experience where the people, animals, plants and man-made structures – temples, houses, shrines, cow byres etc. – used in discursive processes are specifically known and named. Conventions also exist for levels of abstraction such as signs for 'man', 'woman', 'child', 'flower', 'fire', 'water' and so on. But the way these are used is very free. One is reminded of the ethnographic source of Bourdieu's theory of practice, the theory that sought answers beyond a search for rules – his study of the acephalous Kabyle of Algeria, where he experienced the maintenance of order etc. without laws or overt leadership, and sought to explain how this was possible (see Bourdieu, 1977).

Which brings us back again to the Saussurean theory that the arbitrariness of the sign is the definiens of language. Linguists spent decades proving that sign languages were bona fide languages – a necessary political process in which they stressed the arbitrariness of the sign and the complexities of grammatical construction. But need language be arbitrary? Are sign languages less dependent on the arbitrariness of the sign than spoken language? Now that sign languages have been recognised as languages, can we begin to concentrate on differences between speech and sign? As far as Stokoe and his colleagues are concerned, the answer is an emphatic 'yes!'. But there is more to it than that. If language is culture and if languages are culturally specific, then need the culturally and historically specific theories of Saussure and his followers, or indeed of Descartes and his heritage, apply to other cultures and other times?

The process of studying and recording a language is fraught with the same problems as those faced by anthropologists studying 'other' cultures. The cosmology of the researchers, the epistemology through which they operate, and the specific paradigms of their discipline, all influence what is seen and what is recorded, let alone how it is analysed. The danger is that:

- we find what in Western and academic terms makes sense, in particular lexical and syntactical qualities that conform to the conventions that a sound-based linguistics and a culture of communication based on a spoken, literate language regard as the norm;
- we state that this is the case, representing the language to others in these terms;
- we are in a dominant power situation – bestowing legitimacy;
- our model of the language is assumed correct because of the apparently scientific nature of the recording process;
- the model is taken on board by those studied as theirs, the authority of the linguist becoming the basis for the evaluation of linguistic correctness;
- rules therefore become established;
- the language becomes formalised;
- the language is fundamentally transformed.

All linguistic research is therefore potentially linguistic imperialism – imperialism via linguists and linguistics. In the case of the Kata Kolok, all these dangers (Spivak, 1987), especially the potential 'epistemic violence' that 'insidiously objectifies' the language through a conceptual apparatus which robs the language of its individual and cultural integrity, devaluing and distorting its 'differences', are particularly apparent. As we move to consider how we attempted to avoid such linguistic imperialism we need to clarify further the role of literacy in the traditional Balinese linguistic and broader cultural environment, for here we encounter differences that increase the threat of epistemic violence.

As we indicated above, The language has evolved within its communal context and has not been influenced by educational environments or written language. While everyday Balinese is now taught in schools, transcribed into Roman script, Balinese was not traditionally a written language. Traditionally, written language was learnt and accessed only by elites and priests. Few learnt the languages involved, let alone the literary skills to read them. While there are literary texts, particularly poetic forms, which were and still are read or sung aloud in secular contexts, access was and remains very restricted, the activity of a leisured elite. Other texts are much more restricted and much further removed from the spoken word:

Unlike narrative texts, *there are no contexts in which speculative 'metaphysical' texts* – texts recounting offerings and mantras to cure illness, invoke a deity, or liberate the soul; those narrating mystical connections between divinities and categories of persons; or those concerning the structure and origins of the cosmos – *are voiced;* some say they cannot even be discussed ... (Wiener, 1995: 83, emphasis added)

Even further removed are the priestly texts which are regarded as sacred, dangerous and having magical powers, and which can only be studied by those trained and consecrated. In Desa Kolok, the bronze plates recording the origins of the village and its population, the village's *prasasti*, are sacred, stored in the village temple and the subject of important village ritual. No villagers can read them, nor do they expect to be able to do so. That is the business of elites far removed from the everyday life of the village. Today, while the narrative, 'metaphysical' and sacred texts remain the province of cultured and sacred elites, most secular written language is in the national language Indonesian, again a language quite distinct from local spoken languages.

Beyond 'Language'

So how do we deal with the sociolinguistics of the Kata Kolok and its surrounding linguistic environment? We have already moved beyond conventional views of 'language' via Bourdieu's statement that 'what circulates on the linguistic market is not 'language' as such, but rather discourses that are stylistically marked' (Bourdieu, 1991: 39). In seeking to analyse these 'stylistically marked' discourses (see Branson, *et al.*, 1999), we have treated the linguistic environment as a linguistic ecology, indeed a fragile ecological environment[7] and followed Mühlhäusler (1996) in eschewing approaches that focus on the 'given languages' of a region, because of the problem of separating languages from other forms of communication. Whether or not the 'ways of communicating' we are seeking to analyse qualify as 'languages' has in fact been put to one side, for two main reasons:

(1) because, as Mühlhäusler stresses, the linguistic ecology is not just made up of 'languages';
(2) because for the majority people of north Bali whom we are dealing with, the question 'when is a way of communicating a language?' is not an issue.

We have focused therefore on communicative action rather than on 'languages' as distinct entities. We are concerned with the ways that the people of north Bali communicate with each other. At the same time we are concerned with current pressures for change, pressures that threaten the complex discursive environments of north Bali, pressures that are associated with economic and political processes often seen to be outside the field of linguistics, but in fact integral to the communicative processes at work. To quote Mühlhäusler again:

> The ecological metaphor in my view is action oriented. It shifts the attention from linguists being players of academic language games to becoming shop stewards for linguistic diversity, and to addressing moral economic and other 'non-linguistic' issues. (Mühlhäusler, 1996: 2)

Again we are faced, in conventional linguistics, with aspects of its Saussurean heritage that transform, indeed deform, through the epistemic violence of its ethnocentric assumptions, the communicative environment it seeks to understand.

In the linguistic environments of north Bali, people strategically manipulate their linguistic skills to satisfy their linguistic needs. They do so in terms of their linguistic habitus,[8] habituses that are dynamic and changing, influenced by shifting linguistic, cultural, economic and political conditions of existence. We are faced in the region with a complex linguistic ecology, a polylingualism that also involves different forms of communication. It is also an ecology under threat, an ecology experiencing an all-too-familiar decline in the face of national and international pressures for linguistic and cultural conformity and uniformity. In this changing environment, the hegemony of Western views of language is being felt (see Heryanto, 1995; this volume). Through the formal education system and local administrative personnel the linguistic environment is being redefined, with those in positions of power and influence beginning to question the nature and status of various ways of communicating. The flexible linguistic mosaic that accommodated a range of 'ways of communicating' is challenged by official views of language that question the legitimacy of the signing mode.

> ... one must not forget that the relations of communication par excellence – linguistic exchanges – are also relations of symbolic power in which the power relations between speakers or their respective groups are actualised. (Bourdieu, 1991: 37)

In this process, linguists are unwitting agents of linguistic oppression.

Concluding Remarks

This brief comment on the relationship between conventional linguistics and the study of sign languages, Western and non-Western, in the context of both literate and oral cultures, is but a case study of a broader process of linguistic and cultural oppression. The work of Bourdieu and Mühlhäusler that we have drawn on relates after all to spoken languages, not sign languages. But when we seek to deal with languages that defy most of the assumptions of what constitutes a 'language', the symbolic violence of conventional linguistic analysis becomes starkly apparent, despite the attempts by most sign linguistics to fit sign languages into conventional moulds. The concepts of 'language' and 'linguistics' are not culture free. They do not exist in a space beyond place and time. They have emerged, like the concept of rationality itself, in response to particular economic, political and religious conditions and have become integral to the reproduction and transformation of particular kinds of social structures and processes. As surely as the concept of rationality served to construct the contemporary diagnosis of madness, insanity and mental illness (see Foucault, 1965), and the concept of normality provided for the cultural construction of pathological humanity, 'the disabled' (see Canguilhem, 1988; Branson & Miller, 2002), so too have the concepts of 'language' and then 'linguistics' been integral to both the conceptual and actual transformation of communicative environments throughout the world in a way that promotes particular languages at the expense of others, serves the interests of powerful elites, and in the process creates linguistic minorities.

As we approach the study of sign languages internationally, we must not take our ethnocentric assumptions about language and its academic investigation with us. Sign language studies must be informed by sociolinguistics, and by a sociolinguistics that is anthropologically sophisticated, prepared for and capable of dealing analytically with the cultural diversity of humanity and its ways of communicating. We must not exclude from our linguistic analyses 'all the investigations which establish a relationship between language and anthropology, the political history of those who speak it, or even the geography of the domain where it is spoken ... ' (Bourdieu, 1991: 33). And above all, we must learn from and work through the conceptual environments of the linguistic communities that we seek to understand.

Notes

1. An earlier version of this paper appeared in a volume to celebrate the 60th birthday of Tove Skutnabb-Kangas, renowned linguist, campaigner for linguistic human rights and recipient of the linguapax prize for 2003. That paper focused in

particular on our analysis of the sign language of a village in north Bali, Indonesia. In this version of that paper we expand on the impact of linguistics on the analysis of sign languages in general.
2. For further discussion, see Branson & Miller (1989).
3. Thompson notes with regard to the imperialist aspects of this process:
   The misadventures of structuralism alerted Bourdieu at an early stage both to the inherent limitations of Saussurian linguistics and to the dangers of a certain kind of intellectual imperialism, whereby a particular model of language could assume a paradigmatic status in the social sciences as a whole. (Thompson, 1991: 3-4)
4. For a discussion of the history of the cultural construction of deaf people as 'disabled' see Branson & Miller (2002).
5. Eco also completely misinterprets the Abbé de l'Epée's orientation towards the development of his system of methodological signs (Eco, 1995: 173–4).
6. The research referred to here has been conducted in a Region of north Bali in Indonesia, the Region of Buleleng. A particular focus of the research has been the documentation of the sign language used in a village with a large hereditary deaf population. The village, which we here call Desa Kolok, has always had a population of deaf people, according to local folklore. These deaf people, referred to as kolok, are scattered through many households with both deaf and hearing people fluent in the sign language that has developed in the village (see Branson et al., 1996 and 1999 for more detailed descriptions of the village and the region). The village sign language is referred to as the Kata Kolok, deaf talking. This analysis of classifiers was first presented at the International Conference on Sign Linguistics at Gallaudet University in 1998 and was published in the volume in honour of Tove Skutnabb-Kangas (Phillipson, 2000).
7. As we have examined the dynamics of change in the village and its region, we have revealed an ecology in danger. That danger arises from the impact of political forces exerting effective dominance through a drive for linguistic uniformity and control. These forces serve not only to transform a complex linguistic ecology but to isolate and disable a group of people who were formerly a part of the ecological diversity (see Branson, et al., 1999, Branson & Miller, in press).
8. Bourdieu defines the 'habitus' as:
   systems of durable, transposable dispositions, structured structures predisposed to act as structuring structures, that is, as principles of the generation and structuring of practices and representations. (Bourdieu, 1977: 72)
   A linguistic 'habitus' is therefore the bundle of linguistic dispositions, a bundle of dispositions that in large part we share with those who share our social and cultural lot in life, a bundle of linguistic dispositions that is structured by our social environment.

References

Armstrong, D.F. (1999) *Original Signs: Gesture, Sign, and the Sources of Language*. Washington, DC: Gallaudet University Press.
Armstrong, D.F., Stokoe, W.C. and Wilcox, S.E. (1995) *Gesture and the Nature of Language*. Cambridge: Cambridge University Press.

Bourdieu, P. (1977) *Outline of a Theory of Practice*. London: Cambridge University Press.
Bourdieu, P. (1988) *Homo Academicus*. London: Polity Press.
Bourdieu, P. (1991) *Language and Symbolic Power*. London: Polity Press.
Bouvet, D. (1997) *Le corps et la métaphore dans les langues gestuelles: A la recherche des modes de production des signes*. Paris: L'Harmattan,
Branson, J. and Miller, D. (1989) Beyond integration policy: The deconstruction of disability. In L. Barton (ed.) *Integration: Myth or Reality?* London: Falmer Press.
Branson, J. and Miller, D. (1995) *Understanding Classifiers in Auslan*. Melbourne: NID/DEET.
Branson, J. and Miller, D. (1998) The ethnography of classifiers in a village in Northern Bali, Indonesia. International Conference in Sign Linguistics, Gallaudet University, Washington, DC, November.
Branson, J. and Miller, D. (2002) *Damned for their Difference: The Cultural Construction of Deaf People as 'Disabled*. Washington, DC: Gallaudet University Press.
Branson, J. and Miller, D. (in press) The cultural construction of linguistic incompetence through schooling: Deaf education and the transformation of the linguistic environment in Bali, Indonesia. *Sign Language Studies*.
Branson, J., Miller, D. and Marsaja, G. (1996) Everyone here speaks sign language too: A deaf village in Bali, Indonesia. In C. Lucas (ed.) *Multicultural Aspects of Sociolinguistics in Deaf Communities* (pp. 39–57). Washington, DC: Gallaudet University Press.
Branson, J., Miller, D. and Marsaja, G. (1999) Sign languages as a natural part of the linguistic mosaic: The impact of Deaf people on discourse forms in North Bali, Indonesia. In E. Watson (ed.) *Storytelling and Conversation: Discourse in Deaf Communities. The Sociolinguistics in Deaf Communities Series*. Washington, DC: Gallaudet University Press.
Branson, J., Miller, D., Toms, J. and Bernal, B. (1995) Understanding the use of classifiers in Auslan. 18th International Congress on Education of the Deaf, Tel Aviv, August.
Canguilhem, G. (1988) *The Normal and the Pathological*. Cambridge: MIT Press.
Eco, U. (1995) *The Search for the Perfect Language*. Oxford: Blackwell.
Foucault, M. (1965) *Madness and Civilization: A History of Insanity in the Age of Reason*. New York: Random House.
Foucault, M. (1975) *The Birth of the Clinic*. New York: Vintage Books.
Harris, R. (1980) *The Language Makers*. London: Duckworth.
Heryanto, A. (1995) *Language Development and Development of Language: The Case of Indonesia. Pacific Linguistics Series D*, no. 86. Canberra: The Australian National University Department of Linguistics, Research School of Pacific and Asian Studies.
McMahon, A.M.S. (1994) *Understanding Language Change*. Cambridge: Cambridge University Press.
Mühlhäusler, P. (1996) *Linguistic Ecology: Language Change and Linguistic Imperialism in the Pacific Region*. London: Routledge.
Ong, Walter. (1967) *The Presence of the Word: Some Proglemena for Cultural and Religious History*. New Haven: Yale University Press.
Ong, W. (1982) *Orality and Literacy*. London: Methuen.
Phillipson, R. (ed.) (2000) *Rights to Language: Equity, Power and Education*. Mahwah, NJ: Lawrence Erlbaum Associates.

Saussure, F. (1974) *Course in General Linguistics* (W. Baskin, trans. and with an introduction by J. Culler). London: Peter Own.
Siertsema, B. (1965) *A Study of Glossematics: Critical Survey of its Fundamental Concepts*. The Hague: Martinus Nijhoff.
Spivak, G.C. (1987) *In Other Worlds: Essays in Cultural Politics*. New York: Methuen
Stokoe, W.C. (2001) *Language in Hand: Why Sign Came before Speech*. Washington, DC: Gallaudet University Press.
Thompson, J.B. (1991) Editor's introduction. P. Bourdieu *Language and Symbolic Power*. Oxford: Polity Press.
Wiener, M.J. (1995) *Visible and Invisible Realms: Power, Magic and Colonial Conquest in Bali*. Chicago: The University of Chicago Press.

Chapter 6
Entering a Culture Quietly: Writing and Cultural Survival in Indigenous Education in Brazil

LYNN MARIO T. MENEZES DE SOUZA

> ... *a new duty arises*. ...*We must see to it that the hard task of subordinating the love of traditional lore to clear thinking be shared with us by the larger and larger masses of our people. We must do our share in trying to spread the art, and to engender the habit of clear thinking.*
> Franz Boas (1945: 1–2)

In critical analyses of the power/knowledge collusion in colonial and post colonial discourses from the perspective of 'Third World' critics, both Chakrabarty (2000) and Mignolo (2000) emphasize a problem that haunts knowledge production in such situations. Whereas Eurocentric analysts, academics and theoreticians see no reason to, and as a matter of course do not refer to, 'Third World' knowledges and theories, 'Third World' analysts, academics and theoreticians feel constantly obliged to refer to Eurocentric knowledges. Mignolo suggests that a way out of this dilemma is to locate knowledge within 'coloniality'; that is, knowledge production should be read against the historical and discursive background of the European colonization of these regions from which such 'Third World' intellectuals, like himself, write; in such contexts, knowledge, culture and languages are unequally and hierarchically distributed (generating 'colonial difference') in favor of the former colonizing powers and to the detriment of the colonized regions. This gives rise to the prevailing concept that, whereas the former colonizing cultures *produce* knowledge, the formerly colonized cultures merely *consume* this knowledge and continue to supply the raw materials based on which the former colonizing cultures produce their new knowledges.[1]

Mignolo (2000: 204) locates as a possible origin of this dilemma, the preference in colonial discourses for 'narratives of transition' which tend to locate the difference between the colonizing and the colonized cultures, knowledges and languages along an evolutionary, linear and progressive concept of time, based in its turn on the concept of Europe as the location and origin of modernity. The corollary of this is that all difference to Europe is explained in terms of 'pastness' and the colonized cultures are seen as 'pre-modern' or 'primitive' (and hence in the shadow of Modernity), engaged in a process of *transition* to the Modernity that has already been purportedly attained by the colonizing cultures. As Paranjape (2002:13) puts it: ' Seeing its own history in terms of a progression from the premodern to the modern, to the post-modern, the West has relegated other societies to a space equivalent to its own irrational past, thereby turning geography into history'.

Embedded in such 'narratives of transition' is what Mignolo calls, after Fabian (1983), the 'denial of coevalness' through which the knowledges, cultures and languages of the colonized are seen either as not worthy of consideration or as totally invisible.

Mignolo (2000: 205) suggests, as a way out of this dilemma, the need to first of all, 'spatialize time' which means negating or abandoning the 'narratives of transition'; instead of locating difference from a Eurocentric perspective on a linear concept of time, this should itself be replaced by a concept of time as space. On this view, difference would then be located (time-wise) as *co-existent* and *simultaneous*, as existing *elsewhere* in another space, *at the same time* and no longer in pastness or anteriority. In this way, post-colonial intellectuals may overcome the Eurocentric idea that 'History begins in Greece' and may show that diverse histories co-exist and depend on different *loci* of enunciation (Bhabha, 1994: 117).

Chakrabarty (2000) similarly suggests that one way out of this dilemma is to 'provincialize' the West. This is to locate the West's claims for the universality, objectivity or scientificity of its (Western) knowledge within the sociohistoric context of the recent history of colonization and the attendant collusion between power and knowledge. From this perspective, Western scholarship would then be seen as knowledge produced within a particular geographic, historical and ideological context. As a result of the conjunctural configuration of this context (i.e. of the so-called project of Modernity), Western knowledge, through the power exercised by colonization, ceased to see itself and to be seen as 'local' or 'ethno' (i.e. culturally marked) and became 'universal'. 'Provincializing' the West would then be to attribute the qualifiers 'ethno' or 'local' to its cultural and scientific products. Both Mignolo and Dirlik (1996) state that this should not be seen as an outright dichotomical us/them rejection of modernity, liberal values, universals and reason, nor as a plea for post-modern relativism, but as a quest for re-contextualization and de-standardization and for a greater relevance for and of knowledge in specific local communities.

In the current sociopolitical context where the purportedly homogenizing processes of globalization threaten local conceptions of culture, language and knowledge, this need becomes evermore urgent. Based on the premise of the inseparability of knowledge and power, and on the undesirability of decontextualized, disembodied knowledge, this stance for a defense of local knowledges has its own problems. The greatest of these, as Dirlik rightly points out, are the risks of an insistence on purity, atavistic essentialism and a celebration of pre-modern pasts. Dirlik (1996: 38), however, argues for a 'critical localism' that 'even as it subjects the present to the critical evaluation from past perspectives, retains in the evaluation of the past the critical perspectives afforded by modernity'.

This again calls for a clearer understanding of the relationship between temporality and spatiality within coloniality. From a contemporary globalized perspective, culture, knowledge and language have to cease being seen as reified, homogenous, decontextualized concepts and should be seen in the context of a daily confrontation between different cultures, knowledges and languages, where reification and reproduction are replaced by dynamic ongoing production and reconstruction; where, in Dirlik's (1996: 39) words, 'That culture is thus constructed does not imply that the present is therefore immune to the burden of the past; only that the burden itself is restructured in the course of present activity. [...] Culture is no less cultural for being subject to change'.

In his turn, also in a counter-modern anti-colonial strategy, the postcolonial critic, Bhabha (1994) offers an alternative to the standard anti-colonial strategy that generally consisted of simply negating colonial discourse (which invariably represented the colonized as inferior or negative) and tries to replace it with an 'authentic' and truer representation of the colonized. As an alternative to this standard strategy, Bhabha shows how all representations, colonial or anti-colonial, are discursive products 'enunciated' from within specific socially, ideologically and historically located discursive 'loci of enunciation'; as such, an *agent* or speaker, located within an ideologically loaded socio-historical discursive locus of enunciation, formulates a particular enunciated representation, moved and motivated by the factors present in that locus.

According to this view, considering that different representations (enunciateds) emanate from different discursive ideological loci (enunciations), and considering that in these contexts different regimes of distribution of power/knowledge prevail, it is politically naive to simply seek to replace one representation (enunciated) with another without addressing the inequality of power and the ideological differences that permeate the very discursive contexts (loci) that produced such representations. Bhabha therefore suggests that emphasis should be placed instead on identifying representations with the historical and ideological contexts within which they are produced; in this way rather than being simply 'false', certain colonial representations of the colonized may be seen to be products of colonial ideology and discourse, and not 'reflections' of 'true' characteristics pertaining to the colonized.

Following Bhabha's reasoning, in order to effectively counter these representations, the anti- or post-colonial critic should seek to usurp the *locus of enunciation* and critically occupy an ideologically and discursively different discursive context from which new and different representations (enunciated) may be formulated. Mignolo (2000: 119) refers to this proposal as a move from *representation* to *agency*, whereby, as *agent*, no longer an *object* or product of the knowledge produced by colonizing discourses, the post-colonial critic is now the *subject* or producer of alternative, conflicting knowledges. A consequence of this usurpation of the locus of enunciation from the hands of colonial discourse producers is that the power/knowledge collusion may become clearer, and knowledge may cease to be seen as neutral, scientific and universal; it may now be seen (on both sides of the divide) as the 'local' product of a particular ideological and discursive community and its sociohistorical context. Therefore, rather than persisting within a colonizer/colonized dichotomy, Bhabha's move from representation to *agency* introduces the 'antagonistic and agonistic' dimension of the power/knowledge collusion in post-colonial cultures; as a result, the previous dichotomies – 'either/or', 'them/us', 'true/false', 'myth/history', 'science/mysticism' – are now replaced by *hybridities* arising from the complex sites of colonized spaces, traversed by ideologies, languages and cultures both native and colonial.[2]

Besides the colonial representation of linear progressive time that denied coevalness to the difference between the colonizing and the colonized cultures and languages, the colonial conception of *representations* of the colonized as being synonymous with the colonized themselves was also another instance of the same denial of coevalness. Thus, in order to counterpose or 'deny the denial of coevalness' (Mignolo, 2000:121), one has to adopt the tactics[3] of *spatializing time* (Mignolo), *provincializing knowledge* (Chakrabarty) and moving from *representation to agency* (Bhabha). It is against the backdrop of these proposals that I would like, in this chaper, to focus my attention on the case of the role of language in indigenous education in Brazil and more specifically, in the dissemination of literacy and writing. As such, my objects of analysis in what follows are the linguistic and educational policies and practices elaborated by linguists, anthropologists and other 'care-takers' of indigenous communities such as official government agencies and non-governmental organizations.

In these policies and practices of the uses of language and literacy in indigenous education, the colonial difference and the power/knowledge collusion is largely maintained. Writing, its necessity and its forms of dissemination in indigenous education tend to be anchored in a non-indigenous locus of enunciation, which, however, is unaware of the localness of its own concepts. This is apparent in the total lack of appreciation or understanding of indigenous oral tradition and orality, and the presupposition that the role of orality and writing is universal, i.e. similar if not identical to the roles they play in Western culture. More serious is the uncritical unawareness of Western phonocentrism. All in all, these ethnocentric ideas of writing and literacy, which attribute deficiencies of knowledge and value to indigenous oral cultures based on their lack of writing are not dissimilar to the ideas held in the 16th century by the Jesuit missionaries, who also had immense difficulties in understanding and valuing indigenous oral culture. Though writing, language study and indigenous education have been supposedly cleansed of their colonial, missionary and assimilationist hues in Brazil, in practice the epistemologies and ideologies in which they were inscribed continue to rear their ugly heads. In spite of the advances in linguistics, education and identity politics, which have in recent years promoted the respect for difference, old prejudices, which may have diminished in quantity, qualitatively still resist the march of time. With this I hope to contribute towards reducing the harmful effects such policies and concepts may have on education in indigenous communities in Brazil.

The *tactic of disinvention* that I undertake in this is to locate both sociohistorically and ideologically the process of invention of the conceptual categories of language prevalent in indigenous education in Brazil, especially those pertaining to the historically reified and ideologically loaded concepts of grammatization, writing and literacy. Given their historical, cultural and ideological contexts, the invention of these concepts contributed to what I have been calling the 'denial of coevalness'. Once understood as no longer objective universal categories, but as 'inventions' or constructions of clearly marked ideological contexts, it is easier to counterpose or deny the 'denial of coevalness' implicit in them, taking recourse to the tactics proposed by Mignolo, Chakrabarty and Bhabha. Far from claims to proposing a *truer* picture of *reality*, given my own postcolonial locus of enunciation, I am myself deeply implicated in my own strategy of disinvention, which here consists of re-contextualizing ('provincializing') concepts of colonial linguistics once clothed in objectivity, decontextualization and universalization. In doing so, I hope not only to implement my own agency, but also to contribute towards creating conditions for indigenous agency to reveal itself.

Linguistic Descriptions, Missionaries and the Elimination Of Difference

Linguistic and educational policies pertaining to indigenous communities in Brazil have long used linguistic descriptions and grammars of indigenous languages as weapons wielded in the effort to dominate indigenous communities in Brazil. Among the first missionaries in Brazil in the 16th century, the concept of educating the indigenous populations was inseparable from the process of converting them to Christianity. Based both on a logic of Christian faith, and on the fundaments of what would later become the logic of Modernity, the early missionaries sought to fit the new reality they encountered in the 'Fourth World' into the cultural, linguistic and religious codes they brought with them from Europe. This colonial attempt to 'fit' the strangeness of the new reality encountered into the codes known to the European, is described by Greenblatt (1991: 88) as an attempt to render transparent what was seen as opaque, or to reduce the profusion of unknown signs into known codes, thereby imposing sense and control over what was seen as lacking both of these. Greenblatt calls this process the 'kidnapping' of language.

Also analyzing this moment of contact, Pompa (2002: 85) shows how these codes suggested that language was synonymous with culture and that conversion would only be possible through prior communication with the indigenous population; hence the need to learn the native language. These European missionaries were convinced that, like the Apostles before them, they would be blessed with the gift of mastering different tongues. This in turn was reinforced by the idea that the 'savages', with no Laws, God or King, would have difficulty in comprehending the sacred Word and it would thus have to be adapted to their level of comprehensibility. Moreover, by mastering the language of the natives, the missionaries believed they would gain access to the native way of thinking and, once the natives perceived this, they were expected to be more appreciative of the way of thinking of the missionaries. Complementing this Christian logic, even at this early stage, was what Bauman and Briggs (2003) call the 'logic of Modernity', which claimed rationality and consciousness for itself and denied it to others, generating what, as we have seen, Mignolo called the 'colonial difference', or the 'denial of coevalness'.

The first grammars and linguistic descriptions of the language of the natives in Brazil were written by the Jesuits José de Anchieta in 1595 and Luis Figueira in 1621[4] (Ferreira da Silva, 1994). As to be expected, these grammars of the indigenous language (Tupi) were based on the known categories and structures of Latin, the language of education used by the

Jesuits in Europe at the time (Freire & Rosa, 2003). Based on these grammars, various catechisms were written in the indigenous language and used to educate/convert the native population, still acting on the presupposition that they had no culture, religion or language of repute. Inscribed thus in a narrative of transition, supposedly marking the exit of primitive culture from obscurity into the march of time, grammars thus began their long career in Brazil, not only 'kidnapping' indigenous languages, but seeing themselves as true representations (in Bhabha´s terms) of indigenous knowledge. As such they were seen to justify the presence of the European outsider, without whom indigenous knowledge would never be represented, registered and systematized. Therefore, as tools of an insidious modernity and the politics of inequality and exclusion, grammars inaugurated on local soil the power/knowledge collusion of coloniality.

Obsessed with the denial of coevalness, the early bloody colonial strategy of negating difference through the outright massacring of the natives was paralleled by the later, alternative, discursive strategy of assimilation and integration; in this, conversion to Christianity was still seen to be synonymous with the process of civilization; hence the continuing inseparability of education and conversion. Thus, in the middle of the 20th century, linguistic descriptions continued to be used as evidence of Eurocentric modernity/superiority and instruments at the service of the elimination of difference in indigenous education in Brazil. The earlier undisguised move to eliminate difference was now replaced by more subtle attempts to domesticate it.

Still counting on the persistent collusion between colonial ideology, education, religion and language, the ultimate objectives of civilizing and converting the natives remained unchanged. This newer strategy, disseminated largely by the Summer Institute of Linguistics (SIL) gave linguistic descriptions and grammars of indigenous languages the limelight they still enjoy in the field of indigenous education in Brazil by introducing the notion of scientificity into linguistic descriptions. According to Barros (1994) this was accomplished by the simultaneous missionary/linguistic/educational role of the SIL in Brazil, and the cornerstone of its strategy was the *phoneme* used to develop standardized orthographies and subsequent grammars. By introducing the notion of the scientificity of linguistics and linguistic descriptions, the SIL located itself squarely within the Eurocentric project of rationalistic modernity; seeing itself as the harbinger of 'true knowledge', once more like the Jesuits three centuries before, the SIL reiterated a narrative of transition. By emphasizing the fundamental role of 'scientific' linguistic descriptions in the dissemination of literacy and hence, education, the SIL succeeded in downplaying and masquerading its essentially missionary role in converting the indigenous populations to Christianity. Grammars had now been transformed from the language 'Arts' as the Jesuits called them[5] in the 16th century, to linguistic 'science' as characterized by the SIL.

However, once more the role of grammars in the service of a purportedly progressive modernity was reiterated, sustaining their instrumentality in a politics of inequality. The work of the SIL received official support in Brazil at that time for its contributions towards the assimilation of the indigenous populations into the folds of the Brazilian nation, confirming its use of narratives of transition and bringing the indigenous out of obscurity into the modern nation. Curiously, this was marked by the apparently ambiguous role of grammars and linguistic descriptions as tools for *both* the preservation/valorization of indigenous languages *and* their simultaneous elimination. By 'registering' indigenous languages in written form and by making their speakers literate in their native tongues, grammars as benevolent instruments for the preservation of indigenous knowledge were allegedly used by the SIL to *deny* the denial of coevalness and to *preserve* difference in an apparent politics of equality and inclusion. Below the surface, however, given the simultaneous Christianizing role of the SIL, these same grammars of indigenous languages were used to translate Christian scripture into the indigenous languages, revealing a fundamental rejection of indigenous knowledge and culture as heathen and lacking, i.e. in need of substitution, conversion and civilization.

Auroux (1992) calls attention to the fact that grammars are products of writing and a literate culture. As such they presuppose the superiority of knowledge represented in writing in relation to the knowledge of orality, and this superiority is seen to be due to the decontextualized nature of written knowledge which, once removed from its locus of origin, permits rational and abstract scrutiny. The linguistic knowledge represented in a written grammar is defined by Auroux as *metalinguistic* (i.e. rationally and abstractly categorized) and radically different from the *epilinguistic* (intuitive, unconscious) knowledge possessed by any native speaker. Auroux also significantly notes the fact that, historically, even in Europe grammars were not mere descriptions but also used as pedagogic instruments of teaching and learning languages. Used as the basis for acquiring the knowledge of a foreign language, grammars were seen as unquestioned representations of the same linguistic knowledge held by native speakers, and thus were instrumental in confusing the difference between epilinguistic and metalinguistic knowledge. Moreover, given the superiority ideologically attributed to written grammars as products of a literate culture, they were also curiously instrumental in marginalizing epilinguistic knowledge as the knowledge of 'illiterates' (and therefore deficient) even when the original objective of a grammar as a description of linguistic knowledge was purportedly to attempt to reproduce the very same epilinguistic knowledge of the native speaker.

The interconnections between the use of grammars as representations of knowledge, pedagogical instruments and literate ideologies of writing become apparent when Barros (1994, 33) critically emphasizes the connection between Christian cosmology and the introduction of bilingual education in indigenous schools in Brazil:

> The missionary, as the principal agent of the process of introducing the bilingual school in Latin America, has directed indigenous writing towards the reading of the New testament. [...] being Christian has to do with having access to writing. God revealed himself to Man through writing, and conversion depends on its mastery. (Barros, 1994, my translation)

In this sense, the apparent ambiguity of the role of grammars disappears when they are clearly and unambiguously seen to have been used at various levels to eliminate indigenous knowledge and culture. Their sinuous role in eliminating indigenous languages was accomplished by the practice, disseminated by the SIL, of *transitional bilingualism*, whereby in indigenous schools learners were made literate first in their indigenous languages only for the initial stages of the school system. After this they were taught and made literate in Portuguese, the language of the Brazilian nation. Rather than literacy in the indigenous language serving the declared purpose of preserving and valorizing that community language, its more insidious role transpired to be in the valorization of the language of the nation. Thus literacy in the indigenous language was a mere stepping-stone or facilitator for assimilation into the national culture and language. Once more, like the Jesuits in the centuries preceding them, the SIL used linguistic descriptions and grammars as narratives of transition to be used as tools for the elimination of difference and the perpetuation of the denial of coevalness.

Linguistic Descriptions and the Domestication of Difference: 'Differential Education'

In present-day Brazil, under the rubric of propagating 'differential education' for indigenous schools, official discourse appears to have replaced the previous accent on the elimination or domestication of difference with a newer emphasis on the preservation of and respect for difference. The Brazilian federal constitution of 1988 officially recognized the existence and the linguistic, cultural and political rights of all indigenous peoples in Brazil. A significant aspect of this was the constitutional provision allowing indigenous communities to have their own official schools, in their own languages, with their own cultural contents, allocating to each indigenous community the right to make its own decisions as to its choice of language(s) and content. Following suit, and with the objective of implementing the new Constitution, the Brazilian Ministry of Education published in 1998 the official curricular proposals[6] for indigenous schools; these proposals clearly declare themselves to be merely non-regulatory guidelines. In these, the basic tenets are the 'preservation and valorization' of indigenous languages and cultures under the aegis of an official indigenous educational policy which is now deemed 'differential', 'intercultural' and 'bilingual'. However, in spite of these new proposals aiming at preserving linguistic and cultural difference (as opposed to the previous missionary attempts to eliminate it), the linguistic ideologies that underlie them largely remain unchanged and unquestioned and may, as we shall see below, run the risk of accomplishing exactly the opposite.

Given the officially declared 'bilingual' and 'intercultural' nature of these recent policies, the predominant orality of indigenous cultures and the continuing importance attributed to literacy in indigenous education, the role of linguists and linguistic descriptions continues to be deemed officially necessary. However, because of the sociohistoric circumstances of indigenous cultures, the linguists involved in indigenous education for the most part come from the non-indigenous Eurocentric urban centers of a very different Brazil, and this tends to exacerbate the problematic role of linguistic descriptions in the field.

As previously mentioned, denounced by Barros (1994) for their historically insidious role in colonial history and detrimental to indigenous languages and cultures, linguistic descriptions and grammars of indigenous languages have come a long way from their early characterization as 'language arts' and their use as instruments of religious conversion in the 16th century. Also as already mentioned, with the work of the SIL in the mid-20th century, linguistic descriptions of indigenous languages acquired 'scientific' status, though they persisted in their religious connections. In fact, it is this very missionary underbelly of linguistic descriptions that provides a clue to their persisting ideological basis in the myths of modernity, narratives of transition and the perpetuation of the colonial difference.

The purportedly scientific nature of linguistic theory inherited from the SIL in indigenous education gave linguists and linguistics the aura of rationality, objectivity and universality that they still enjoy. Many linguists seem to be unaware that much of this aura has its origin and basis in the same persistent myths of modernity and its attendant power/knowledge collusion in place since the early colonial period and whose function was to deny coevalness and eliminate difference. Though at this moment in time, at the beginning of the 21st century, the previous connection between religion (i.e. conversion to Christianity), assimilation into the dominant national culture and linguistic descriptions is no longer openly tolerated in the field of indigenous education in Brazil, important resonances of previous linguistic ideologies persist as 'enunciateds' disconnected from their original loci of enunciation. As Mignolo (2000) and Bhabha (1994) have both warned, when 'enunciateds' are disconnected from their loci of enunciation, they acquire the status of naturalized 'universal' truths and are unavailable for criticism and change. Such seems to be the case today for many linguistic practices in the field of indigenous education in Brazil.

For instance, the eminent Brazilian linguist Leite (2003) recently repudiated the criticism leveled at the 16th-century Jesuit Anchieta for using Latin categories to describe the linguistic structure of Tupi in his 16th century grammar of this indigenous language. Leite (2003: 22, my translation) justifies her stance as follows: 'Each epoch and each theory will have its own way of saying things; what is important is the record of the fact. Anchieta could not help using Latin as a model as it was the model of his day'. In the same text, Leite laments the history of exploitation and massacres that assailed the indigenous populations whose language Anchieta's grammar sought to describe. However, by defending Anchieta's option to model his grammar on Latin as a mere 'academic option', Leite (2003: 23) decontextualizes and disconnects science from ideology and knowledge from power. She seems to be unaware of the contribution of Anchieta's grammar to the colonial 'kidnapping' of indigenous languages (as an instrument of control, reduction of diversity and transformation of 'opacity' into 'transparency') and seems unaware therefore of its probable role in the very same exploitation and massacre of the natives that she laments.

A similar posture is that of Monserrat (1994), another eminent Brazilian specialist of indigenous linguistics. Explaining the necessity of the role of linguists in indigenous education as specialist assistants (*assessores*) to indigenous learners and teachers, and declaredly aware of the political aim of indigenous education, Monserrat sees the role of the linguist as a 'neutral' judge or referee in issues pertaining to the description of indigenous languages. For Monserrat, linguistic studies of indigenous languages should aim at 'modernizing' and 'normatizing' them. Thus, by establishing orthographies for these languages, the task of the linguist is to objectively eliminate the linguistic 'discrepancies' committed by the speakers of the indigenous languages in their agonizing battle over the phoneme:

The linguist coordinates the linguistic tasks in the [indigenous teacher training] course [...] This is followed by a collective discussion [...] The linguist takes note of the orthographic discrepancies observed. [...] Then the linguist comments on the discrepancies observed in their writing and promotes a collective analysis of the issues, so that the final decision may be the product of a real consensus.' (Monserrat,1994: 16)

As such, the non-indigenous linguist, in an effort towards modernizing and normatizing the language, should merely and 'neutrally' register the 'consensus' of the decisions taken by the indigenous participants as to the choice between one letter or another to represent a particular phoneme. In practice, in such a context of non-linguists, it is unlikely that the very concept of the phoneme and its role in the orthographic representation of speech in writing, can come from anyone other than the linguist who is present; such an apparently democratic discussion can therefore hardly be 'consensual'. Consensus here appears to suggest a commonsensical decision, when clearly the presence of the linguist presupposes that the decision is expected to be more technical than consensual. Therefore, if there is a discrepancy in this situation, it is between the knowledge of the linguist and that of the native-speakers of the indigenous language. However, the discrepancy to which Monserrat seems to refer is the conflict between the various native speakers present as to the grapheme to be considered most adequate to represent the sounds of their language.

Once again, it is the scientific, neutral, modernizing role of linguistics that is emphasized. There are two problems in this recommended practice of the *assessores*. First, as we have seen, Auroux (1992) points to the confusion as to the kind of knowledge represented in linguistic descriptions, i.e. whether it is epilinguistic or metalinguistic knowledge. For Auroux, a linguistic description such as a grammar or phonemic analysis is essentially metalinguistic and does not necessarily overlap with or represent epilinguistic knowledge. As we have seen, metalinguistic knowledge and representations, as the product of a written literate culture are, as such, a different type of knowledge. Linguistics as the disciplinary knowledge of a literate culture privileges metalinguistic knowledge, and the power/ knowledge collusion in which such a posture is ideologically inscribed remains un-thought.

Similar to what occurred in the practices of the SIL, in the cases just mentioned the 'knowledge' of outsider linguists is also inscribed in an asymmetrical position of power in the name of a neutral objective modern science and a putatively superior literate culture. As a result, these linguist *assessores* who do not possess epilinguistic knowledge of the indigenous languages they are helping to describe are still the specialists who are required to legitimate and authorize the metalinguistic representations of these languages. This is once again reminiscent of 'the fundamental modernist move of claiming consciousness and rationality for oneself and one's followers and denying it to others' (Bauman & Briggs, 2003: 298). This is not surprising, considering that most of the linguists and *assessores* are non-indigenous and come from the Eurocentric, literate, national culture, with little knowledge of oral indigenous cultures and languages. The 'modernist move' mentioned, implicit in the posture of these linguist *assessores* is a re-enactment of the same posture as that which justified the colonial onslaught of previous epochs. In spite of the apparently profound changes in attitudes to indigenous education and the distancing from the missionary stance, the colonial ideology seems not to have disappeared but to have been forced below the surface only to resurge during activities pertaining to the linguistic description of indigenous languages.

Boas, Sil and the Americanist Linguistic Stance

The ambiguity of the modernist attitude among linguists involved in indigenous education whereby coevalness is promoted at the same time as it is in practice denied, may have its roots in the Americanist linguistic tradition, championed by Franz Boas and later brought to Brazil via the work of the SIL (Barros, 1994:18). Boas saw linguistic theory as propitiating a general scientific method of analysis which, when applied to the analysis of culture, would eliminate racist ideas such as a lack of coevalness between cultures and languages, or even between written and oral languages. However, as Bauman and Briggs (2003) show in their analysis of Boas' work, his very notion of culture is traversed by profound ideological ambiguities.

Boas believed that, like language, culture consisted of the internalizing of shared patterns and categories, which remain unconscious to its members, and therefore inaccessible for critical scrutiny. As such, native speakers of a language, like the members of a native culture, are incapable of critically accessing, and hence, of changing these patterns. Boas believed that the traditions that produced these cultural or linguistic patterns or categories served as limitations: 'Habitual speech causes conformity of our actions and thought' (1962: 149). Moreover, because the patterns or categories are unconscious and not accessible to the conscious mind of the native speakers/members, attempts to access them (as occur when these members/native speakers attempt to explain phenomena of their own languages or cultures) can only be emotional and irrational and therefore partial, in both senses of the word. For Boas, this partial access could only result in ethnocentrism, whereby these speakers of a language or members of a culture believe that their patterns or categories are universal.

A combination of the unconscious, ethnocentric, emotional and irrational nature of these patterns and categories can, according to Boas, be extremely dangerous:

> The unscrupulous demagogue who arouses slumbering hatreds and designedly invents reasons that give to the gullible mass a plausible excuse to yield to the excited passions make use of the desire of man to give a rational excuse for actions that are fundamentally based on unconscious emotion. (Boas, 1965: 210)

According to Boas, it is only the anthropologist with a scientific methodology, inspired by linguistics, who can have critical access to and describe cultural patterns and categories, and who can hence promote change in these cultures. Clearly, Boas's concept of culture falls again within the 'modernist move' mentioned previously, attributing greater power and value to the rational knowledge of himself and other anthropologists as opposed to the lesser, partial, emotional knowledge of the members of the culture under analysis:

> Culture becomes an object of knowledge for anthropologists and their means of developing epistemological and political freedom at the same time that it constitutes the principal obstacle to objective knowledge, rationality and freedom from traditional dogma for all others. (Boas, 1965: 287)

For Boas (1911), this occurs through the use of an analytical method borrowed from linguistic analysis, which permits the anthropologist to be rationally and critically aware of his own cultural categories, and to seek, in his analysis of the indigenous culture, the categories used by the very members of the culture; for this to occur, the analysis had to be done from the point of view of the native.

In Auroux's terms, Boas separates epilinguistic knowledge from metalinguistic knowledge and, as we have seen above, he seems to consider epilinguistic knowledge on its own as insufficient and dangerous. The curious paradox in Boas' posture is that, at the same time that he considers metalinguistic knowledge to be more desirable (because it is rational), his methodology (by emphasizing the native's point of view) seems to require metalinguistic knowledge to approximate itself as much as possible to (and therefore to represent) epilinguistic knowledge. Boas thus seems to propose that epilinguistic knowledge is safer in the hands of an outsider, when it has been transformed into metalinguistic knowledge. This seems to echo the same strategy mentioned by Greenblatt of reducing opacity to transparency or a proliferations of signs to a previously known fixed code. All this in spite of Boas' declared objectives to preserve indigenous languages and cultures.

In relation to his concept of culture, the ambiguity or paradox in Boas' posture was that at the same time that he sought to study the threatened 'primitive' indigenous cultures of North America, in order to preserve them (or a knowledge of them), by believing in a culture's traditions as 'fetters' and hence as an obstacle to modernity or progress, Boas simultaneously desired to see these cultures undergo change. Boas' linguistic analytical method, which he claimed to be objective and rational (and against discriminations between oral/written and indigenous/European cultures and languages) is similarly wrought with contradiction. By positing the anthropologist/analyst as immune to the fetters of his own culture, Boas attributed greater value to the knowledge of the anthropologist and hence to the culture of the anthropologist. Besides being inscribed in a narrative of transition and temporalizing space (where indigenous difference is seen as pre-modern) Bauman and Briggs (2003: 298) also call attention to the fact that it is the politics of inequality embedded in Boas's notion of culture that restricts its role in contributing to change.

If, as Barros says, Americanist linguistics, influenced by Boas, was brought to Brazil by the SIL and established a tradition of Americanist linguistics in indigenous education which persists until today, then this same double-bind which valorizes and denies coevalness in Boas' work may be visible in the present work of linguists in this field in Brazil, as we have seen above. This certainly seems to have been the case of the SIL and its forays in Brazil, where the complicity between anthropology, education, linguistics and religion becomes clear; this is especially so in the words of one of the SIL's foremost linguists, Kenneth Pike, President of SIL:

> The missionary must learn that a moral system, present in every culture, can not be smashed without breaking a control system [...] to preserve tribes from chaos. [...] Christianity, as a moral system, should operate like yeast, entering a culture quietly, transforming its institutions, changing their forms to contribute more effectively to the culture. [...] Just as a person unified with and transformed by Christ still lives, so should a culture be infused with the fruits of the Spirit to change by the power of God harshness to kindness, and dirtiness to cleanliness. (Pike, 1962, cited in Hvalkov & Aaby, 1981: 37)

Clearly embedded in these words is a narrative of transition and a politics of inequality, accompanied by a repetition of the 'modernist move' (Bauman & Briggs, 2003: 285). The double-bind inscribed in Pike's words is also clear: in the name of 'preservation', destruction and transformation must be perpetrated, where the destruction is seen as positive, removing a detrimental 'control system' to bring order to chaos and 'dirtiness to cleanliness', all with 'the power of God'. What remains unquestioned, or unconscious, is the religion-bound and culture-bound nature of the values of the missionary-cum-educator-cum-linguist-cum-anthropologist. Like Boas' anthropologists, Pike seems to be convinced that the missionary is himself free from the fetters of his own culture, and that therefore his reading of the indigenous religion and its detrimental nature is a truer (scientific?) representation of reality than that of a member of the culture concerned.

Like Boas, who sought to speak *for* culture and to preserve and interpret it, but at the same time sought to contribute to its transformation, Pike and the SIL claimed to preserve indigenous knowledge, but in fact contributed to its destruction. Considering that Brazilian indigenous linguistics in the field of indigenous education may have inherited the Americanist linguistic tradition descending from Boas and Pike, there are serious risks involved if this tradition continues to be uncritically or unconsciously applied, even if it has divested itself of its previous missionary clothing.

It seems that the most pernicious aspects of this linguistic/cultural ideology are its attitude that, because the methodology used is 'scientific', objective and rational, the linguist/analyst is above criticism; this in turn is based on the conviction that the linguist/ analyst is 'informed' and aware, and therefore carries out his analysis from the native's point of view, without, however, succumbing to the fetters that impede the native from being critically aware of his own limitations; the corollary of this is that the linguist/analyst is not aware of the fetters and differences of his own culture or ideology and the fact that these may interfere in his interpretations of the language under analysis, even when he believes he is analyzing from the 'native's point of view'; the drastic result of this unawareness is the perpetuation of the colonial difference.

Language, Writing and Indigenous Education

As we have seen, the recent proposals for indigenous education in Brazil favor the 'differential', intercultural and bilingual community school, as described by the official guidelines of the Ministry of Education in 1998. With the objective of 'preserving' and 'rescuing' indigenous languages and cultures from disappearance, these proposals claim to be different from the previous missionary proposals in that they do not aim at the assimilation of the indigenous populations into the national Brazilian culture; they do aim however, at politically integrating the same populations into an awareness of citizenship and their political rights.

Considering their declared valorization of difference and the need to preserve indigenous languages and cultures, the main strategy of the official proposals is the promotion of indigenous teacher education courses. The Brazilian Federal Law 10.172 of 1 September 2001 established the National Education Plan,[7] which set the following guidelines for these courses:

> The education intended should prepare teachers for: the elaboration of curricula and specific syllabi for indigenous schools; bilingual education, in terms of second language teaching methodology and the creation and use of orthographic systems for the mother tongues; the carrying out of anthropological research aiming at the systematization and incorporation of indigenous knowledges, and the writing of teaching materials, bilingual or not, to be used in the schools in the teacher's community.[8]

It is clear here how the need for both linguistic and anthropological knowledges intertwine in these proposals.

A great number of these courses are given by linguists and anthropologists, and the logic often given for continuing this situation is in the exact terms of the legislation as shown above, which would require these specialists to educate indigenous teachers in their areas of knowledge. However, it is more likely that the reality of the situation is the opposite; that is, it is probably *because* the initial proposals for indigenous education in 1998 were drawn up by teams of anthropologists and linguists, that the legislation of 2001 establishes the need for the presence of these specialists. Whatever the reality may be, indigenous education in Brazil (at least in its mid-20th century format) was not only a product of, but is still inseparable (though now legally) from linguistics and anthropology; and therefore still probably implicated in the epistemologies and ideologies of these disciplines.

The cornerstone of indigenous education still continues to be literacy, even though the educational ideologies associated with literacy have changed; apparently long gone is the missionary project that sought to teach literacy in order to read the Scriptures. Literacy is now associated with the two basic objectives of the acquisition of citizenship and cultural preservation. The former is to be attained by acquiring the skills and the capacity to enter into and participate in the 'white-man's world', for example by acquiring a knowledge of written arithmetic and being able to read and interact with official documents, such as contracts, receipts and legislation. Cultural preservation is to be achieved by putting into writing the knowledge available in the oral traditions. This may generally be done in two different ways: in the indigenous language, to 'preserve' the oral tradition from disappearance, or in the national language, Portuguese, when the objective is to display or portray indigenous knowledge to the national, non-indigenous community.

In the field of indigenous literacy, two main conflicts arise with linguistics, both based on different conceptions of writing, and hence of literacy; these may be termed loosely (a) the fetishization of the phoneme and (b) writing as communication.

The fetishization of the phoneme

Barros (1994) has written extensively about the fetishization of the phoneme view in indigenous linguistics in Brazil, a stance inherited from the SIL and its tradition of scientific linguistics. This view essentially saw writing as a technology or code, and had its origins in Christian proselytism, where written scriptures were seen as a register of the sacred spoken word; the function of writing was considered to be to register speech. In order to develop the technology of writing, speech – to which primacy was attributed – had to be codified; writing was then developed as a second-order code or system for the representation of speech. This is the product of the well-known history of the modern Americanist linguistics of Sapir and Bloomfield and the development of the concept of the phoneme. As is known, this linguistics historically appeared in North America as a means of registering the local indigenous languages that were threatened with extinction; its main concern, therefore, was descriptive. As it saw writing as a second-order form of representation (a concept inherited from Saussurean linguistics), the registering of speech involved a prior syntactic and morphological analysis of the spoken language that then yielded the concept of the phoneme. As Barros (1994: 30) emphasizes, the methodology involved was considered to be rational, precise and scientific, and the role of the linguist involved in the transposition of speech into writing was considered to be neutral. As such, the conventional or arbitrary aspect of Saussurean linguistics was not considered to interfere in this scientific representation of speech in writing. With this possibility of faithfully registering speech in writing, it was considered to be an efficient instrument for registering the knowledge of the oral traditions of threatened indigenous communities.

As we have seen, this practice of phonemically describing indigenous languages necessarily involved their prior normatization (Barros, 1994: 32) and this produced not only writing systems but also linguistic descriptions. It is important to remember that, as a descriptive and 'pure science' tradition, it was not necessarily involved in indigenous education, which would have called for an 'applied' form of this descriptive linguistics. This applied form would subsequently transform, as described by Auroux, linguistic descriptions into pedagogic grammars and writing systems into orthographies.

In present-day indigenous linguistics in the field of indigenous education, in many cases there seems to be a confusion between the 'pure' form of this linguistics, with its emphasis on description, and its 'applied' form in teaching, which generates what I have called the 'fetishization of the phoneme'; I refer here to the reification of the phoneme and its isolation from its context of communicative use. This reification resulting from a purportedly disinterested and objective description, besides blurring epilinguistic and metalinguistic knowledges, is a resurfacing of the colonial strategy of reducing opacity to transparency and the missionary strategy of reducing chaos to order.

Thus, much classroom time is spent in indigenous teacher education courses, given by linguists of this bent, discussing the adequacy and correctness of orthographic systems, on a wild goose chase for the perfect phoneme and the perfect grapheme (Silva & Salanova, 2001), when the main objectives of writing in the indigenous language are lost. As Camargo (2001: 364) shows, phonological representation in orthography is essentially conventional and ultimately arbitrary, and a native speaker, when reading even an 'imperfect' phonemic orthographic representation of his language 'will never make a mistake in reading or pronunciation'. D'Angelis (2003: 39) warns against simply repeating – in indigenous teacher education courses – the methods and practices of theoretical linguists and their emphasis on linguistic abstraction and correction. He suggests, as an alternative, activities that can contribute towards more positive attitudes of speakers in relation to their indigenous mother tongues, such as a reflection on how their languages extend their lexicons and create new words, developing their oral and communicative skills in the language.

Writing as communication

This second main area of conflict with linguistics in indigenous literacy involves a concept of writing radically different from that implicit in the 'fetishization of the phoneme' approach. According to this view, the origins of writing lie not in descriptive theoretical linguistics and its fixation with abstract codes, but in the classroom practices of Applied Linguistics, especially the Applied Linguistics of second- and foreign-language teaching.

This view draws more specifically on the recent history and experiences of this area of linguistics, with knowledge from needs analysis and skills-based teaching, especially the communicative teaching of reading and writing skills. Rather than seeing writing as a technique or code, this view sees writing as a series of social practices and discourses (Barton, 1994), and therefore as more conventional and cultural than scientific. It does not waste much time with establishing orthographies, and works on the basis that, if they are conventional, and if writing is a social practice, then each community of practice, over time, will attain its own conventional orthography. Makeshift orthographies, based on the orthography of Portuguese, are proposed and discussed with the native speaker teachers at the outset of the teacher education courses, and it is the community of practice that will adapt them in and through communicative use.

This view of writing has produced interesting and innovative materials in indigenous education, such as those used in the Acre region of northwest Brazil. Units of this material teach how to write narrative and descriptive compositions, fill out forms, give information etc. The criticism leveled at this view (D'Angelis 2003) is based on the fact that it has its origins in second-language and foreign-language teaching, and that it therefore does not apply to the complex situation of indigenous languages and indigenous education in Brazil. Though this is indeed true in terms of the status of indigenous languages in Brazil, and their relationship to the national language, much of the methodology used in foreign language teaching may also be used with due adaptations in contexts of mother-tongue or second-language teaching. There are problems, however; like the view that fetishizes the phoneme, the problems are based on gross conceptual reductions, which are in turn related to cultural perceptions and the locus of enunciation of those involved.

These perceptions are related to the age-old orality/literacy conflict discussed by Ong (1982), Goody (1986), Street (1984) and Harris (1980) in that the wealth and complexity of orality remain invisible to a literate eye. Given that indigenous cultures are primarily cultures of oral traditions (that is, different from written cultures), almost the totality of their cultural traditions are expressed orally; not to perceive this wealth inevitably leads to a perception of these cultures as lacking value and complexity (Menezes de Souza, 2003a). Whereas the first view – the fetishization of the phoneme – tends to reduce writing to 'speech written down' (Barton, 2001), the second 'communication' view of writing, tends to reduce speech to 'writing spoken'. In other words, the first view primarily reduces writing through phonemes to a representation of sounds. In contrast, the second view, with a complex view of writing as skills and rhetorical structures, tends to assume that speech has similar categories and structures, and works in a way similar to writing, rather than being a wholly different set of communicative skills with totally different characteristics.

Both of these views remain largely ignorant of the dynamic performative and synaesthetic characteristics of orality in the indigenous oral traditions. Kress (1997) shows how meaning-making in orality involves several different and complex modes of bodily engagements with the world, involving all the human senses. In terms of performativity, Turner (1988) and Carneiro da Cunha (1999) have shown how in the indigenous cultures of Brazil orality cannot be separated from the other material, ritual and organizational aspects of these cultures, and orality, rather than mere dialogue or narrative, involves the *enactment* and *embodiment* of various cultural beliefs and values. Given the high degree of shared knowledge and the ritualistic aspect of much of the oral tradition, its performative quality, unlike writing, must be enacted in a contextualized manner in order to be communicatively effective.

Moreover, both reductions of orality are ultimately based on the same Western tradition of phonocentrism (Derrida, 1974) whereby writing is considered to be a second-order representation of meaning. According to Derrida, meaning in this tradition is generally associated with presence and voice, where presence indicates the existence of the thinking subject and where voice is the means of expression of the ideas of this subject. Speech, as voice, is therefore the first-order representation of the meanings of the thinking subject, and writing, as a representation of speech, becomes a second-order representation of meaning. It is the phonocentric belief, which sees writing as the repository of meaning and hence, knowledge, that leads Western culture to value writing and literacy as the *sine qua non* condition for education and culture. However, as we shall see below, in the case of the oral traditions of Brazilian indigenous cultures the Eurocentric phonocentric belief does not apply.

Hence, in contradiction to its purported valorization of communities of practice and communicative needs, the uncritical phonocentric beliefs of this posture lead to the effective valorization of the communicative needs of the indigenous learner but not of indigenous knowledge. Like the fetishization of the phoneme and its valorization of abstraction and rationalization over communicative practice, this phonocentric view of writing also temporalizes space. It does so by situating oral indigenous knowledge and culture as pre-modern or pre-literate, thus inscribing them in narratives of transition, and as such, contributes to perpetuating the colonial difference.

In spite of the differences in the three moments of the study of language in indigenous education that we have looked at – the 16th century Jesuits, the mid-20th century SIL and the present day practices, all three embarked on varying attempts to access the native point of view. The Jesuits learned the language, as did the SIL, and the present policymakers seem to have reached the maximum point in the process, envisaging, facilitating and providing for an indigenous school run by indigenous teachers who define their own curricula and write their own materials in their own languages. Unfortunately, like Boas's anthropologist who is above criticism and authorized to criticize, and like Pike's missionary-cum-linguist-cum-educator, who desperately wants to replace chaos with reason and salvation, the problem lies, as we have seen, in what Bauman & Briggs (2003) have called the 'modernist move', which claims rationality and consciousness for oneself and denies it to the other. This is done by uncritically and unconsciously using one's own categories and patterns to classify the other, and subsequently denying that one has done so (even to oneself). Even one's so-called access to the native's point of view is unselfconsciously obstructed by the carrying over of one's own categories to the Other's point of view, which thus remains inaccessible, because it can never be more than a mere abstraction and, at the most, a bad translation but never a fixed, pristine accessible locus.

What we have seen so far, in this part of our tactic of disinvention, has been to clarify the socio-historic context of the practices of linguistic descriptions and writing. Our perspective has been post-colonial in that it has sought to critically locate these descriptions and practices in terms of the beliefs and practices prevalent in what Mignolo (2000: 52) called coloniality. In the next section we shall embark more closely on the tactic suggested by Bhabha (1994: 185), i.e. the move from representation to agency, and the tactic suggested by Mignolo (2000: 205), the spatialization of time. These should hopefully contribute to ending narratives of transition and the denial of the denial of coevalness.

The Indigenous Perspective: Writing

The indigenous population of Brazil is estimated at around 400,000 (part of a total population of 160 million), distributed into 210 indigenous 'peoples' or 'nations', speaking an estimated 180 indigenous languages (Lopes da Silva, 2003). For the purposes of this analysis, my focus in this section will be on aspects of indigenous knowledge and how they affect practices of language and writing. Given the well-known diversity of indigenous cultures in Brazil, for my present purpose I consciously choose to avoid the specificity of an ethnographic perspective and focus on general similarities in order to contribute to the diminishing of the colonial difference, if not to its elimination.

Bhabha (1996) shows how, even in societies that purport to attribute *equal respect* to the cultures of minority communities within a nation, the fact that these cultures are limited in extent in comparison with the national culture (i.e. by virtue of their 'localness') causes them to be granted equal respect, but not *equal worth*. In spite of the 'indigenous turn' in recent Brazilian policy, this appears to be very much the case. As mentioned above, the recent bilingual and intercultural indigenous education policies in Brazil tend to occur under the tutelage of monolingual, non-indigenous specialists, generally linguists or anthropologists, well-meaningly conscious of the objectives of the new policy to preserve and protect indigenous languages and cultures. With this in mind, these specialists are keen to see as much indigenous knowledge and language as possible written down for posterity and disseminated in the indigenous schools. As we have seen, in general, writing is at present considered an innocuous, transparent technology and an essential instrument for the preservation and dissemination of indigenous knowledge. However, conflicts arise in the different perceptions of writing held by the indigenous cultures and by their non-indigenous tutors, and this becomes especially apparent in the multimodal texts produced as a result of this intercultural contact.

These multimodal texts are written alphabetic texts with a highly visual component, and tend to be seen by the non-indigenous tutors as pictographs or a primitive stage of alphabetic literacy – primitive because, as the Eurocentric phonocentric theories of writing go (Elkins, 1999), pictographs are supposedly merely mnemonic. Seen as mere *aide-memoires*, pictographs supposedly require completion by oral explanation, are dependent on previous knowledge and are therefore incomplete, context- bound and lack independence; in contrast, alphabetic texts are supposedly self contained, context-free and independent. Embedded in this view of the primitiveness of pictographs is the Eurocentric belief that previously-spoken ephemeral thoughts now registered and fixed on paper, and distanced from the immediacy of their context of occurrence, may become the object of sophisticated contemplation. Because of this, responsibility is attributed to alphabetic writing for the development of abstract, rational decontextualized thought.

Continuing from the non-indigenous perspective of seeing the pictograph as a primitive form of proto-writing, it is believed that this visual form of writing should have progressively disappeared once alphabetic writing as a technology and a skill was fully acquired. This, however, has not occurred. The indigenous communities that are taught alphabetic writing continue to produce in varying degrees multimodal writing on paper and, like the alphabetic writing in Portuguese (rather than in indigenous languages) that accompanies it, it contradicts all expectations, apart from the standard historical (now unvoiced) preconception that a propensity for drawing may be a sign of the inherent infantility of the indigenous.

However, from the perspective of indigenous knowledge, the same multimodal texts are given a different significance. For example, in both Kashinawa and Kali'na, two Amazonian languages, the same word is used to refer both to 'drawing' and to 'writing', so, from the perspective of indigenous writers from these communities (Renault-Lescure, 2002), one writes when one draws and vice versa. Moreover, in Kali'na, a neologism had to be created to signify 'reading', given that to 'read' an alphabetic text (that is, to recuperate sound and knowledge from it) is seen to be radically different from 'reading' a visual text, from which one 'recuperates' knowledge, but not sound. As we have seen above in the discussion of Eurocentric phonocentrism, what is at stake here is the concept of *writing* in indigenous knowledge; rather than a mere technique or instrument for registering knowledge, for these indigenous communities writing itself is an inseparable part of what constitutes knowledge.

Several Amazonian cultures, like Kashinawa, are cultures of *vision* (Guss, 1989; Lagrou, 1996; Keifenheim, 1999; Albert, 2000); visions occur in dreams or else a ritual drink is consumed to bring them on whenever there is need for acquiring information or knowledge. Knowledge is thus gained from vision. If, as they learn from their non-indigenous tutors, the function of writing is the registration of knowledge, then from the indigenous perspective, writing has to register vision. In this sense, far from being a neutral technology or skill, a mere instrument of progress, alphabetic writing is strongly implicated, as we have seen above, in Eurocentric concepts of knowledge and its phonocentric source (Derrida, 1974) which sees writing as a second-order form of representing speech and hence knowledge.

Given the purpose of writing to represent knowledge and not merely speech, from the perspective of Kashinawa writers, for example, alphabetic writing that merely registers speech needs to be complemented by the drawing of a visual text to guarantee the registration of knowledge. Besides being a source of knowledge, *vision* for indigenous cultures (such as the Kashinawa) is always contextualized and situated. Considering that one knows what one sees, what one speaker knows/sees may not be what one's interlocutor knows/sees, because both see from different locations and hence different perspectives; these changes in perspective are linguistically marked by evidential suffixes. This has been called 'indigenous perspectivism' (Castro, 2000), a philosophy that does not privilege any single viewpoint, but considers all viewpoints, like all the elements of nature, as being inter-related and mutually implicated. There is thus no separation of subject from object; the seer is also the seen. Truth-value in indigenous perspectivism is *social*: what I see/know as an individual is qualitatively different, socially, from what you and I see/know; what the collective community sees/knows has the greatest social value. These perspectives are linguistically marked by suffixes. Personal narratives or opinions, as the product of personal views or perspectives (personal knowledge) are therefore marked differently from communal narratives or knowledge shared by the community (for example, the knowledge defined as 'myths' in Eurocentric anthropological tradition). In their analysis of indigenous discourse, Beier *et al.* (2002: 133) are intrigued by this feature: 'a prominent concern with epistemological matters is an areal cultural feature, which in some cases becomes grammaticalized as part of the morphological system of the language and in other cases manifests as a discursive evidential system'.

In this process of knowledge formulation in indigenous perspectivism, *contextualization* is highly significant and necessary in order to establish the inter-relationship between interlocutors in a given social context (and hence establish the truth-values implicated in the given inter-relationship). Considering that alphabetic writing registers speech but not the speaker, by separating and distancing 'speech' from the speaker it therefore decontextualizes the information or knowledge it purports to represent. For members of indigenous cultures such as the Kashinawa, alphabetic writing, being incapable of marking differences of perspective in information or knowledge, is seen to be deeply lacking, given that knowledge registered alphabetically has no means of indicating its truth-value. From the point of view of indigenous perspectivism, decontextualized information cannot be knowledge. If it does not indicate its context, perspective or inter-relationship of the interlocutors, decontextualized information cannot distinguish between 'fact' and 'fiction', between narratives of communal historiographic value and those of the creative imagination. Thus alphabetic knowledge, from this indigenous perspective cannot function independently and needs to be contextualized; and this contextualization, lacking in alphabetic writing, needs to be provided by visual indications ('pictographs') of perspective and context. Similar to the primitiveness of the pictograph from the Eurocentric perspective (because of its need for complementation, and its context-bound nature), for indigenous cultures such as the Kashinawa, as we have seen, it is alphabetic writing that is lacking and needs complementation. This is no different to the reading habits of many in the literary field in Western academies in whose practices there reigns the belief that texts *need* to be complemented (by literary critics), because alphabetic text is not as self-contained as imagined, even when it purports to be non-fictional.

Writing and the Change of Tongue

A second, related, aspect of Brazilian indigenous writing also indicative of how writing may be seen as a map of intercultural contact and conflict, is the fact that much of it is written in Portuguese and not in indigenous languages, in spite of the official commitment to preserve the indigenous languages and cultures. As we have seen, from the perspective of modern (Eurocentric) linguistics, putting a language into writing, and registering sounds in alphabets, requires an accompanying process of normatization. Based on the hypothesis that all languages consist in their natural states, as 'bundles' of multiple social and contextual variants, the process of normatization requires that a single form of 'the' language be chosen as 'the' norm and then have its sound system translated into letters. This institutional, ideological and conventional process is based on the need for a grammar as a register and guardian of the norm, used then to accompany the teaching of writing. From this Eurocentric stance, this process of normatization seems natural, transparent, logical, rational and harmless enough. Not so for indigenous perspectivism.

As an explanation for the 16th century Jesuit idea mentioned above that indigenous cultures had no Law, God or King, modern anthropology has shown that indigenous cultures are generally *non-normative* cultures. They are not *pre-state* social formations as many believed (following a logic of narratives of transition) but, as Clastres (1977) emphasizes, *anti-state* social formations, connected to the indigenous philosophy of perspectivism. As a consequence of this philosophy, these cultures see all forms of nature as inter-related in a non-hierarchical fashion. Difference is qualitative and not quantitative, contextual and never decontextualized; these are societies of spokes-persons and not chiefs or headmen; and obligations are learnt non-coercively and non-normatively and not imposed. Non-hierarchical and non-normative does not mean that signification or appropriateness are absent from these cultures; on the contrary, both of these are contextually and not inherently defined. Learning is done implicitly by participating in and watching the actions of others and listening to narratives; subjecthood is constructed through inter-relationships, and the greatest punishment is banishment from the community, seen as a fate equivalent to death (given that by severing all inter-connections with the community, subjecthood will cease to exist).

An important corollary of this indigenous philosophy of perspectivism and inter-relatedness, is the tradition of *predation* and *domestication* (Fausto, 1999), through which a given social unit sees itself as vitally dependent on a real or symbolic relation with alterity and difference, based on a 'logic of predation and domestication'. This social mechanism requires the periodic appropriation (often physically or symbolically violent) of difference, rather than the peaceful exchange of identities. Given the epistemological concerns of these cultures, the violence in the appropriation of difference is not to possess difference as reified substance but, from the perspectival, interrelated stance, it is the perceived need to gain access to the perspective of the other, to see as the other sees, to have access to the vision of the other. This does not imply a sense of loss of one's own vision, as vision is always un-fixed, shifting and dependent on locus and perspective.

The exogenous difference that is thus appropriated (symbols, knowledge, persons, artifacts, tools) from external communities is then subjected to a process of domestication or transformation before it is consumed. In order to satisfy this logic of predation and the need for difference, the desired exogenous difference (the novelty or newness) must be seen as qualitatively equal or superior to a related existent endogenous aspect of the culture, before it is appropriated and transformed.

In a similar sense, to say these cultures and their languages are non-normative does not mean that for them there are no norms or rules; it does mean the rejection of a concept of a *fixed, static, decontextualized* norm (such as that exemplified by a grammar). As Bourdieu (1997) has shown, norms are mutually constitutive with everyday practice, they orientate practice, and changes in practice modify norms. Bourdieu further shows how the 'fallacy of the rule' establishes a rule based on practice and then pre-poses the rule to practice, forgetting that the origins of rules lie in practice and not in idealized abstraction.

In a similar vein, Bruner (2002) has shown how narratives have embedded in them cognitive-maps and function very much like grammars in the sense of acting as a repository for rule-governed behavior. Like grammars, then, narratives consist of abstract 'reality constructs' or rules for constructing experience in terms of events and meanings, where these rules originated in practice. For Bruner, it is through these reality constructs that one learns to distance oneself from and organize the here and now of the input flux of lived experience. Narratives therefore imply distancing, organization and abstraction: 'we distance ourselves from the immediacy of events by converting what we've encountered into story form' (Bruner, 2002: 89). As in the communally-shared mythical narratives of indigenous cultures, the story form, as a communally-shared narrative, acquires a standing of its own, representing a form of knowledge not unlike that embedded in communally-shared abstract sets of rules, such as grammars. However, whereas narrative structures can and are actualized and updated, grammars tend to be less flexible. The Eurocentric linguistic tradition of grammatization may then be seen as a typical product of a hierarchical tradition and its predilection for the 'fallacy of the rule'. It is this that lies at the basis of the Eurocentric view that indigenous languages without written grammars, like indigenous cultures without philosophies or writing, are lesser forms of language and culture.

Against this background of knowledges and traditions, the indigenous reluctance to write in indigenous languages may be understood in the following terms: as members of perspectival, non-normative cultures, they cannot recognize their own indigenous languages in fixed, static, decontextualized written grammars which (as we have seen above) besides being incapable of indicating a particular perspective (and hence unable to accommodate contextual shifts in perspective and truth value) propose to privilege one single form of language (a 'norm') over several possible and qualitatively equivalent others.

On the other hand, from the indigenous perspective, Portuguese in Brazil as the language of colonial hierarchy and imposition, as an instrument of a tradition of rejection of difference (and imposed truth values), should lend itself easily to normatization and a single fixed perspective, and hence to alphabetic writing. From the indigenous perspective, if one has to write alphabetically, with all the linguistic and ideological implications embedded in alphabetic literacy, it seems more logical that this be done in Portuguese. Given the characteristics of indigenous knowledge, these two aspects of indigenous writing in Brazil – the use of visual texts and the preference for writing in Portuguese, portray no essentialistic anti-colonial reaction, no outright rejection of writing as *theirs and not ours*; no essentialistic quest for even 'strategic' authenticity (Razack, 2004).

They reflect, rather, what I have mentioned above as the capacity of these indigenous communities to appropriate and transform (predation and domestication) Eurocentric knowledge, adapt it and recontextualize it for their own purposes. This complex process of cultural and linguistic appropriation has not been done in any complicated rationalistic metalanguage. As is customary, thinking is done in practice, in action, as in listening to narratives, and watching the actions of others; it is not abstracted or separated from practice and decontextualized, as is characteristic of Eurocentric thinking. Thus, in blatant contrast to the Eurocentric misconceptions we have seen above, the apparent absence of indigenous metalinguistic categories and abstract and decontextualized thinking in these cultures (seen as the result of the absence of alphabetic writing) does not mean the absence of critical thinking per se. And there is nothing that portrays this more than multimodal indigenous writing in Portuguese.

Symbolically, in its recent official commitment to indigenous education and the valorization of indigenous languages and knowledges, the Brazilian State sees writing as part of a process of mutual recognition, as an exchange between equals. Bhabha (1996) shows how, even in societies that purport to attribute *equal respect* to the cultures of minority communities within a nation, the fact that these cultures are limited in extent, in comparison with the national culture (i.e. by virtue of their 'localness') causes them to be granted equal respect, but not *equal worth*. In spite of the official predisposition to attribute equal respect to indigenous knowledge, this posture towards indigenous knowledge present in the practice of many of those working with indigenous language and linguistics reveals, as Bhabha warned, a propensity to attribute *equal cultural respect* but not *equal cultural worth*. Without sufficient consideration of indigenous knowledges and their characteristics (knowledge as vision, perspectivism, inter-relatedness, the need for difference and alterity, the logic of predation and domestication) the linguistic and educational policies involved tend to patronizingly seek to 'preserve' what they in fact do not seem to understand.

The very concept of preservation and the need for it in relation to these indigenous cultures implies the presupposed existence of a prior homogeneous cultural and linguistic essence or authenticity which was then corrupted, transformed or destroyed by the vicissitudes of colonial history, which the new official commitment now seeks to terminate and compensate. Inscribed in a narrative of transition, the lack of critical awareness of the culture-bound nature of concepts such as writing, grammar, reading and most of all, knowledge, makes their use as instruments in a purported process of cultural and linguistic preservation, lethal and self-defeating.

From the indigenous perspective discussed here, the impossibility of equal exchange, the need for newness, difference and change will lead, not to the preservation of an authentic static cultural substance or essence, but to the preservation of abstract cultural relationships and mechanisms such as perspectivism, knowledge as vision, predation/domestication and inter-relatedness, all of these visible in their uses of language and their production of multimodal writing. As such, the object of, and the process of preservation may most likely continue to be the source of conflict between the indigenous cultures and the State. What is called for is a de-provincializing of prevalent non-indigenous views of language and writing and their accompanying ethno-belief that the mere registration of indigenous knowledge on paper will contribute to its preservation. The non-indigenous academy that ultimately supplies the linguists and the anthropologists who become instrumental in implementing these policies, ironically has to learn to interrupt the act of teaching *to write* (where they themselves and all their cultural concepts may uncritically offer themselves as the models of decontextualized authors of decontextualized written texts), and learn *to read* what is written by their indigenous students. The irony lies in the fact that these non-indigenous *assessores*/collaborators play an active role in teacher-education courses, where their indigenous students are learning to be teachers, and where, as student teachers, they are critically aware of the fine line between teaching and learning. This same awareness appears to be lacking on the part of many non-indigenous teacher *assessores*, who tend to assume the role of specialists, de-provincialize their knowledge, and as such become immune to a process of learning from their students.

In his innovative ethnography of indigenous education in central Brazil, Cavalcanti (1999) offers an inkling into what may be a new sensitivity towards indigenous knowledge among some *assessores*. He questions the standard logic that automatizes the connection between writing, education, the school and the transmission of knowledge. Cavalcanti shows how, contrary to the standard views in the field, writing in some indigenous communities is not seen as a universal technology or a practice to be applied to one's own language, but is seen as someone else's language. Like a language with its own words and meanings, writing, on this view, has to be learnt part and parcel with the language it carries (i.e. if writing is seen to 'belong' to the official national language, it cannot be innocuously detached from it and re-attached to an indigenous language – see below how this leads to the rejection of mother tongue literacy).

In terms of the indigenous school, Cavalcanti claims many indigenous communities see the school not as a place for the transmission of knowledge, but as a place of contact with the external world, a place of intermediation between the indigenous world and the privileged and powerful 'white-man's world'. Rather than a place for the transmission of knowledge, the school is seen as the place where writing is located; as writing is seen as someone else's language – the white-man's language – the school is where this language is spoken. Hence the attraction of writing and the school for indigenous communities, and the consequent common rejection of officially prescribed schooling in the mother tongue. But what of education and the transmission of knowledge? These are taken care of by the oral tradition, outside and in spite of the school, as they have always been even before the Jesuits arrived, and probably always will be.

By Way of Conclusion ...

In my tactic of disinvention I have looked, in the first part of this analysis, at how concepts of language and writing in indigenous education in Brazil have been deeply implicated in colonial ideologies of conversion and civilization, where they became instruments of a politics of inequality and the negation of difference. I have done this from the perspectives suggested by the postcolonial critics Mignolo, Chakrabarty and Bhabha who seek to show how the power–knowledge collusion is an important aspect of colonial discourse. I have sought to show how this collusion has historically permeated much of the work carried out in linguistics in the field of indigenous education in Brazil. Most of all, I have tried to emphasize the continuity of this collusion in the use of present-day linguistic concepts such as linguistic descriptions and language teaching in indigenous education. In the second part of the analysis, where the perspective changes from Eurocentric to indigenous knowledge, I have tried to show the radical differences from Eurocentric concepts of knowledge and the world.

As a postcolonial tactic, I have tried hard to avoid the dichotomous us/them frame, and to spatialize time, juxtaposing two contemporaneous co-existing radically different sets of languages, cultures and knowledges, as an alternative to their customary location (in a typical colonial strategy of temporalizing space, where spatially distant difference becomes temporal difference) of linear precedence as one being archaic or primitive and the other modern. Considering that colonization is an undeniable fact and an unending process, the reality of which has been to bring disparate languages, cultures and knowledges into contact with each other, I have also tried to show that neither of the parties involved in the contact escape unscathed. The results of the contact for either party have depended on their knowledge systems, more specifically, on how they conceive of difference. From the Eurocentric modernist perspective, difference, conceived as negative, is to be eliminated at all costs. I have shown how this has been done in Brazil following varying strategies, from radical outright elimination through conversion, to the Pikean strategy of 'entering a culture quietly'. The consciousness (or malice?) of these previous strategies helped to construct and select the tools and instruments used, such as grammars, linguistic descriptions, and policies of literacy, translation and language learning.

What is lacking in the policies of today is exactly the malice of the policies of yesteryear, which helped in the selection of tools and instruments (even though these did not, at the end of the day, guarantee success). This lack of malice or *naïveté* in indigenous education in Brazil today curiously leads to the uncritical choice of instruments, which are selected simply because they are there as residues and remnants from the past. This has meant that most of the same instruments used by the more malicious strategists of the past continue to be used today, such as abstract decontextualized linguistic descriptions, metalanguages inherited from Eurocentric traditions, and phonocentric concepts of literacy. Ironically, the persistent use of these residual instruments of the past are today capable of wreaking more damage on indigenous languages and cultures, exactly because they are used naively (formerly instruments of eradicating difference, they are now used innocently to valorize difference), and are unaccompanied by an awareness of the damage they are capable of. In other words, the usefulness of disinvention here is to understand how such instruments of eradicating linguistic and cultural difference were invented in order to decide whether they should be discarded, maintained or reinvented for present purposes.

On the other hand, the other, indigenous, party involved in the contact, rather than investing in the elimination of difference, culturally valorizes the appropriation of difference; this begs the question why the colonial strategy of eliminating difference has not fully worked? The answer lies in the very concept of difference (or identity). From the Eurocentric colonial perspective, difference or identity is seen statically as a substance, a set of values, beliefs or contents, or as a point of arrival in which one may supposedly, finally and victoriously proclaim the elimination of difference or the imposition of identity. From the indigenous perspective, however, identity or difference are relationships and processes, spaces to be constantly filled and not substances or contents. And this is what frustrated the colonial attempts at conversion and education. At the basis of the indigenous tactic of receptivity to exogenous inputs, lies something similar to the Pikean tactic of 'entering a culture quietly'. The difference is that the indigenous tactic is to 'enter quietly' the other culture, yes, but not to remain, or to stay put (for 'entering quietly' is an ongoing process), but to appropriate and transform, *in order to preserve* one's own (indigenous) culture. From the indigenous perspective, and reminiscent of Dirlik's (1996: 39) words quoted above, 'Culture is no less cultural for being subject to change'.

Notes

1. For a similar recent stance in anthropology, see the comment by Sahlins (1999: v) denouncing anthropologists for 'using other societies as an alibi for redressing what has been troubling us lately [...] It is as if other peoples had constructed their lives for our purposes'.
2. Note here that, like Bhabha, Sahlins (1999: xi) also sees cultural hybridity as 'geological' rather than structural: cultures are generally 'foreign in origin and local in pattern'.

3. I use here de Certeau´s (1998) concept of *tactic* as opposed to *strategy*. Where strategies are openly declarable actions taken by those in legitimate dominant positions, tactics are almost illegitimate, invisible measures taken by those not in socially dominant or authorized positions.
4. Curiously and symbolically, Figueira was later devoured in an indigenous cannibalistic ritual.
5. The Jesuit Jose de Anchieta's 1595 grammar was called *Arte de gramática da lingua mais usada na costa do Brasil* (*Art of Grammar of the Most Used Language on the Coast of Brazil*).
6. Ministério da Educação e do Desporto (1998) *Referencial Curricular Nacional para as Escolas Indígenas*, Brasília, MEC.
7. For further information on these policies, see Grupioni (2003: 6).
8. As Leis e a Educação Escolar Indígena, Ministério da Educação, Brasília (2002). On WWW at http://www.mec.gov.br/sef/indigena/materiais/Legisla caom iolo.pdf (my translation).

References

Albert, B. (2000) O Ouro canibal e a queda do ceu: Uma critica xamanica da economia politica da natureza. In B. Albert and A. Ramos (eds) *Pacificando o Branco: Cosmogonias do contato no norte-amazonico*. Sao Paulo: Editora Unesp.
Auroux, S. (1992) *A Revolução Tecnológica da Gramatização*. Campinas: Editora da Unicamp.
Barros, M.C. (1994) Educação bilíngüe, lingüística e missionários. *Em Aberto* 63.
Barton, D. (1994) *Literacy: An Introduction to the Ecology of Written Language*. Oxford: Blackwell.
Barton, D. (2001) Directions for literacy research. *Language and Education* 15, 2 and 3
Bauman, R. and Briggs, C.L. (2003) *Voices of Modernity: Language Ideologies and the Politics of Inequality*. Cambridge: Cambridge University Press.
Beier, C., Michael, L. and Shrezer, J. (2002) Discourse forms and processes in indigenous lowland South America: An areal-typological perspective. *Annual Review of Anthropology* 31, 121–45.
Bhabha, H. (1994) *The Location of Culture*. London: Routledge.
Bhabha, H. (1996) Culture's in-between. In S. Hall and P. du Gay (eds) *Questions of Cultural Identity*. London: Sage.
Boas, F. (ed.) (1911) Introduction to *Handbook of American Indian Languages*. Washington: Government Printing Office.
Boas, F. (1945) *Race and Democratic Society*. New York: J.J. Augustin.
Boas, F. (1962) *Anthropology and Modern Life*. New York: W.W.Norton.
Boas, F. (1965) *The Mind of Primitive Man*. New York: Free Press.
Bourdieu. P. (1997) *Outline of a Theory of Practice*. Cambridge: Cambridge University Press.
Bruner, J. (2002) Narrative distancing: A foundation of literacy. In J. Brockmeier, M. Wang and D. Olson (eds) *Literacy, Narrative and Culture*. London: Curzon Press.
Camargo, E. (2001) Grafando o agrafo: Um ponto de vista lingüístico a partir do caxinaua. In A.L Silva and M.K.L. Ferreira (eds) *Antropologia, História e Educação*. São Paulo: Global.
Carneiro da Cunha, M. (1999) Xamanismo e Tradução. In A. Novaes (ed.) *A Outra Margem do Ocidente*. São Paulo: Companhia das Letras.

Castro, E.V. (2000) Cosmological deixis and Amerindian perspectivism. In M. Lambek (ed.) *Anthropology of Religion*. Oxford: Blackwell.
Cavalcanti, R.A.S. (1999) Presente de branco, presente de grego? Escola e escrita em comunidades indigenas do Brasil Central. Unpublished MA dissertation, Museu Nacional, Rio De Janeiro.
Chakrabarty, D. (2000) *Provincializing Europe: Postcolonial Thought and Historical Difference*. Princeton: Princeton University Press.
Clastres. P. (1977) *Society Against the State*. New York: Urizen.
D'Angelis, W. (2003) Propostas para a formação de Professores Indígenas no Brasil. *Em Aberto 76*.
De Certeau, M. (1998) From the practice of everyday life. In N. Mirzoeff (ed.) *The Visual Culture Reader*. London: Routledge.
Derrida, J. (1974) *Of Grammatology*. Baltimore: Johns Hopkins University Press.
Dirlik, A. (1996) The global in the local. In R. Wilson and W. Dissanayake (eds) *Global/Local: Cultural Production and the Transnational Imaginary* (pp. 21–43). Durham: Duke University Press.
Elkins, J. (1999) *The Domain of Images*. Ithaca: Cornell University Press.
Fabian, J. (1983) *Time and the Other: How Anthropology Makes its Object*. New York: Columbia University Press.
Fausto, C. (1999) Da inimizade: forma e simbolismo da guerra indígena. In A. Novaes (ed.) *A Outra Margem do Ocidente*. Sao Paulo: Companhia das Letras.
Ferreira da Silva, M. (1994) A conquista da escola: Educação escolar e movimento de professores indígenas no Brasil. *Em Aberto 63*.
Freire, J.R. and Rosa, M.C. (2003) *Línguas Gerais: Políticas Lingüísticas e Catequese na América do Sul no Período Colonial*. Rio: EDUERJ.
Goody, J. (1986) *The Logic of Writing and the Organization of Society*. Cambridge: Cambridge University Press.
Greenblatt, S. (1991) *Marvellous Possesions: The Wonder of the New World*. Chicago: Chicago University Press.
Grupioni, L.D. (2003) Experiências e desafios na formação de professores indígenas no Brasil. *Em Aberto 76*.
Guss, D. (1989) *To Weave and Sing: Art, Symbol and Narrative in the South American Rain Forest*. Berkeley: University of California Press.
Harris, R. (1980) *The Language Makers*. London: Duckworth.
Hvalkof, S. and Aaby, P. (eds) (1981) *Is God an American? An Anthropological Perspective on the Missionary Work of the Summer Institute of Linguistics*. Copenhagen, International Work Group for Indigenous Affairs (IWGIA): Survival International.
Keifenheim, B. (1999) Concepts of perception, visual perception and pattern art among the Cashinahua indians (Peruvian Amazon area). *Visual Anthropology* 12, 27–48.
Kress, G. (1997) *Before Writing: Rethinking the Paths to Literacy*. London: Routledge.
Lagrou, E.M. (1996) Xamanismo e Representação entre os Kaxinawá. In E.J.M. Langdon (ed.) *Xamanismo no Brasil: Novas Perspectivas*. Florianópolis: Editora da UFSC.
Leite, Y. (2003) A arte de gramática da língua mais usada na costa do Brasil e as línguas indígenas brasileiras. In J.R. Freire and M.C. Rosa *Línguas Gerais: Políticas Lingüísticas e Catequese na América Do Sul no Período Colonial*. Rio: EDUERJ.
Lopes da Silva, A. (2003) A educacao de adultos e os povos Indigenas no Brasil. *Em Aberto 76*, 89–129.

Menezes de Souza, L.M. (2003a) Literacy and dreamspace: Multimodal texts in a Brazilian indigenous community. In S. Goodman, T. Lillis, J. Maybin (eds) *Language, Literacy and Education: A Reader*. Stoke on Trent: Trentham Books.
Menezes de Souza, L.M. (2003b) Voices on paper: Multimodal texts and indigenous literacy in Brazil. *Social Semiotics* 13 (1).
Mignolo, W. (2000) *Local Histories/Global Designs: Coloniality, Subaltern Knowledges and Border Thinking*. Princeton: Princeton University Press.
Monserrat, R. (1994) O que é ensino bilíngüe: A metodologia da gramática contrastiva. *Em Aberto* 63.
Ong, W. (1982) *Orality and Literacy*. London: Methuen.
Paranjape, M. (2002) The third eye and two ways of (un) knowing: Gnosis, alternative modernities and postcolonial futures. Paper presented at the Infinity Colloquium, New York, 24–29 July. On WWW at http://www.tamilnation.org / aurobindo/paranjape.htm. Accessed 25.5.06
Pompa, C. (2002) *Religião como Tradução: Missionário, Tupi, Tapuia no Brasil Colonial*. Bauru: EDUSC.
Razack, S. (2004) To essentialize or not to essentialize, is this the question? In C. Sugars (ed.) *Unhomely States: Theorizing English–Canadian Postcolonialism*. Toronto: Broadview Press.
Renault-Lescure, O. (2002) As palavras e as coisas do contato: Os neologismos Kali'na. In B. Albert and A. Ramos (eds) *Pacificando o Branco: Cosmogonias do contato no norte-amazonico*. Sao Paulo: Editora Unesp.
Sahlins, M. (1999) What is anthropological enlightenment? Some lessons of the twentieth century. *Annual Review of Anthropology* 28, I–xxiii.
Silva, M.A.R. and Salanova, A.P. (2001) A assessoria lingüística nos projetos escolares indígenas: o caso da formação de professores mebengokre. In A.L. Silva and M.K.L. Ferreira (eds) *Antropologia, Historia e Educação*. São Paulo: Global.
Street, B (1984) *Literacy in Theory and Practice*. Cambridge: Cambridge University Press.
Turner, T. (1988) Ethno-history: Myth and history in native South American representations of contact with Western society. In J.D. Hill and R. Wright (eds) *Rethinking History and Myth: Indigenous South American Perspectives on the Past*. Urbana: University of Illinois Press.

Chapter 7
A Linguistics of Communicative Activity

STEVEN L. THORNE and JAMES P. LANTOLF

> *A definition of language is always, implicitly or explicitly, a definition of human beings in the world.*
> Raymond Williams (1977: 21)

Introduction

To admittedly essentialize the complex field of modern linguistics as it developed over the 20th century, we can speak of two basic approaches to language: a formalist tradition concerned with language-as-system and a relational–contextual tradition that has focused on issues of meaning, communication and the co-weaving of language, cognition, person and the world. For a specific camp of language-as-system theorists, language acquisition involves the triggering of genetically available a priori principles of grammar (e.g. Chomsky, 2000; Pinker, 1991). From a distinctly different vantage point, the Hallidayan tradition attempts to unite systematicity with usage by invoking a non-dualistic two-perspective framework. Language seen as a system describes the meaning-making potential of a set of social-semiotic resources, while instantiation refers to specific inscriptions of that system in concrete communicative practice. The metaphor used by Halliday and Matthiesen is that of the relation between climate and weather – they are not two different phenomena:

> rather, they are the same phenomenon seen from different standpoints of the observer. What we call 'climate' is weather seen from a greater depth of time – it is what is instantiated in the form of weather. ... The climate is the *theory* of the weather. ... Similarly with the system of language: this is language as a virtual thing; it is not the sum of all possible texts but a theoretical entity to which we can assign certain properties and which we can invest with considerable explanatory power. (Halliday & Matthiesen, 2004: 26–7, italics in the original)

Yet other orientations to language research have focused on the performance of human communicative activity. From this latter vantage point, communicative practice (both speech and writing) is construed as recurrent patterns of functional-pragmatic units that are understood to be 'shaped by interactional considerations' (Schegloff, 1996: 55; see also Becker, 1982). The anthropological linguist William Hanks (1996) notes that linguistic analysis has always been beset by contradictions; that language can be seen as both an abstract system and an aspect of everyday practice, a generalizable form and a temporally local action, a social fact as well as an individual's utterance. Inarguably, human language has radically systematic features, but we will argue that these features are 'locked into the kinds of activities that speakers carry out with speech' (Hanks, 1996: 9).

This chapter describes an approach we are calling a linguistics of communicative activity (LCA). LCA is rooted in, and attempts also to augment, the Vygotskian cultural-historical tradition. The motivation for developing the LCA framework is to disinvent language understood as an object and to reinvent language as *activity*, where the term activity describes a specific form of human societal existence that consists of purposeful changes to, and transformations of, natural, social and mental realities (Davydov, 1999: 39). Language use and development are at the core of this characterization of activity and span from local interaction (i.e. interpersonal communication) to that of society and the modern nation state in arenas such as language policies, language ideologies and public education as mass social intervention. This perspective implies that human languaging activity structures, and is structured by, enduring conceptual properties of the social, political and material world.

The contribution of cultural-historical approaches, broadly construed, to the theorization of language has been significant (e.g. Bakhtin, 1986; Vygotsky, 1986; Wells, 2002) and in some cases has explicitly articulated Marxian criticality (e.g. Bakhurst, 1997; Collins, 1999; Jones, 1999; Thorne, 2005; Vološinov, 1973). However, Vygotsky-inspired cultural-historical psychology does not currently draw upon the philosophical, linguistic and communication theory research that could significantly contribute to its power as an analytic and activist framework. The purpose of this chapter, therefore, is two-fold: the first is to briefly describe the historical antecedents that strongly shaped what we interpret to be a debilitating and ongoing construction of language as a natural object independent of lived communicative activity (e.g. Saussure, Bloomfield, Chomsky); the second purpose is to provide a synoptic exegesis of models of language that provide usage-based and meaning-centered characterizations of linguistically mediated human activity – what we are terming the LCA framework.

The latter effort, comprising the majority of the chapter, attempts to selectively recover key insights from earlier work by Peirce (1897/1955), Wittgenstein (1953), Whorf (1956) and Garfinkel (1967), and bring them into contact with current scholarship by linguists and communication theorists such as Rommetveit (1974, 1992), Hopper (1998), Hanks (1996) and Tomasello (2003), among others. We will begin by providing a selective overview of problematic consequences of the development of certain linguistic theories over the 20th century. The discussion then moves toward outlining the LCA framework, beginning with philosophy of communication and then narrowing to address precise questions about the nature of language structure and processes of language development. The concluding sections integrate the LCA framework with Vygotskian developmental theory.

Problems with Privileging Structure

It has become something of a truism, at least across the social sciences and humanities, that the specificities of a discipline's methods, object(s) of study and gate-keeping mechanisms are built from historically developed ideologies, professional cultures and philosophical traditions (Latour, 1999; Bourdieu, 1988; Foucault, 1972). History is a defining element in cultural–historical approaches (e.g. Scribner, 1985) that both affords the 'ratcheting up' of human performance through the inheritance of accumulated knowledge (Tomasello, 1999) while at the same time producing an accepted and naturalized arena of habitual activity, of epistemology and disciplinary particularity, that is difficult to challenge and see beyond.[1] In particular, the construction of dominant paradigms and subfields of linguistic inquiry, as described by Joseph, Love and Taylor, have shown extremes of 'disciplinary territoriality' that in many cases have become 'inseparable from the inquiry itself' (Joseph et al., 2001: viii; see also Joseph & Taylor, 1990). That is, theoretical frameworks have shown a tendency to become treated as co-equivalent with the phenomena they attempt to document and explain. Makoni and Pennycook (2005 and Chapter 1 of this volume) describe the highly consequential implications of this confusion of static model with living cultural-communicative practices and argue that so-called languages are epiphenomena of 'invention', a term that describes the historical and political processes that reify mutable, local and contingent communicative repertoires into categorical linguistic varieties. As Vološinov (1973: 98) describes it, language as a system of normative forms is a scientific abstraction. It is 'solely through the utterance [or use] that language makes contact with communication, is imbued with its vital power, and becomes a reality' (Vološinov, 1973: 123). A number of the paradigms developed by 20th century linguists have supported the invention of language as an object that is independent of human communicative activity and meaning making – important exceptions include Boas (1911/1983) and the Sapir–Whorf tradition of linguistic anthropology (Bright, 1990).

Fauconnier and Turner (2002: 3) remark that 'we live in an age of the triumph of form' in which knowledge has been reduced to 'a matter of essential formal structures and their transformation.' Arguably, the two scholars most responsible for the triumph of form in linguistics, and with it the ostensible conversion of linguistics into a scientific discipline, are Ferdinand de Saussure and Leonard Bloomfield (Agar, 1994). Saussure succeeded in constructing language as a scientific object by first distinguishing language (*langue*) from speech (*parole*) and subsequently arguing that because speech is 'many-sided and heterogeneous' and belongs simultaneously to 'the individual and to society', it cannot be 'put into any category of human facts'; in contrast, language (*langue*) 'is a self-contained whole and a principle of classification ... [a]s soon as we give langue first place among the facts of language, we introduce a natural order into a mass that lends itself to no other classification' (Saussure, 1959: 9; see Timpanaro, 1975, for discussion). As Agar (1994: 37) succinctly puts it, 'speech is a mess' (see also Becker, 1982). As a consequence of Saussure's distinction between language and speech, considerable linguistic analysis and theory building over the 20th century focused on *langue* and the search for a governing system of rules that could plausibly underlie the variable speech activity of everyday communication.

The problem confronting Saussure (1959) (and a similar problem presented itself to Wihlem Wundt as he tried to formulate a scientific psychology; see Cole, 1996) was how to build linguistics into a legitimate science on a par with other physical sciences. To do this, he had to find a way to conceive of language as a natural, a priori and immutable object that could then be subjected to the rigors of scientific analysis. He achieved this by making two critical moves: the first was to background the importance of time (i.e. history) and the second was to assign language the ontological status of stable thing rather than mutable process (Crowley, 1996: 18). Once language was thus reified, it could be studied through the lens of the scientific method. At the same time, however, the centrality of human communicative activity in shaping language was removed from the interest of linguistics and in the extreme, as in the case of performance in Chomsky's theory, was assigned the status of 'mystery' and thus not open to scientific investigation (Chomsky, 1992). Another consequence of Saussure's move was to preserve the Cartesian mind/body (langue/parole, competence/performance) dualism, which effectively took human meaning-making activity out of the picture, resulting in the belief that meaning resides within language – that is, meaning is transparently encoded and transmitted in linguistic signs themselves rather than in concrete material human activity. As Saussure described it, 'language presupposes the exclusion of everything that is outside its organism or system – in a word, of everything known as "external linguistics"' (Saussure, 1959: 22). In essence Saussure drew a circle around language (Agar, 1994: 41) and proposed that linguistic science be restricted to the study of form and 'the part of meaning that can be characterized formally and truth-conditionally' (Fauconnier & Turner, 2002: 15). Bloomfield drew the Saussurian circle yet tighter and to a large extent even dictionary meaning was expunged, pushing his influential variety of linguistic inquiry toward the exclusive study of 'the sound system and the grammar' (Agar, 1994: 55).

As the structuralist perspective became entrenched, linguists and soon anthropologists (e.g. Levi-Strauss 1979, 1987) began to assert that abstract structural relationships regulated phenomena as diverse as grammar, kinship patterns, myth and economics (see Timpanaro, 1975: 135–220). Across disciplines, the dominance of the structuralist tradition throughout the 1950s and 60s produced a counter-productive consequence in the form of the 'gradual megalomania of the signifier' (Anderson, 1984: 45), where language and its structure formed the lens through which other phenomena were described and understood. Marxian theorist Perry Anderson critiques this impulse to posit underlying structure to all human activity as an anti-humanist enterprise, and proposes further that it is a failed intellectual enterprise for, as he states, 'if structures alone obtain in a world beyond all subjects, what secures their objectivity?' (Anderson, 1984: 52). Put another way, when the focus of inquiry is exclusively on signs and their relations, where is communication? Where is intent? Where is meaning and the motive driving the communicative activity in question? In essence, where is social action and where are people?

Structuralist, and in particular specific nativist arguments (e.g. Chomsky, 2002), suffer from the disconnection between lived communicative activity and the purported underlying mechanisms that are posited to account for it (see, for example, corpus-based research that problematizes Universal Grammar principles and parameters, e.g. Carter & McCarthy, 1995). These traditions have yielded contentious if interesting findings, but they have come at the significant cost of furthering the anti-humanist enterprise of a focus that includes only language form and structure. The gist of language from a user's perspective is far removed from such concerns (see van Lier,

2004). As Vološinov has remarked, what is 'important for the speaker about a linguistic form is not that it is a stable and always self-equivalent signal, but that it is an always changeable and adaptable sign. That is the speaker's point of view' (Vološinov, 1973: 68). The LCA framework we describe below addresses the historical-contextual dynamics of the adaptability of the sign as it mediates communication, meaning and thinking.

Russian Psycholinguistics and Cultural-Historical Psychology

Working within the framework of Vygotsky-inspired cultural-historical psychology, Soviet psycholinguist A.A. Leontiev (1981) described the field of psycholinguistics as having three stages since its inception in the 1950s. The first generation, based on descriptive linguistics and behaviorist psychology, had as its goal to understand how individuals acquire and master discrete linguistic elements. The problem with the assumptions of this first generation, according to Leontiev (1981: 92), is that 'it is a speech theory about the behaviour of the individual, isolated not only from society but also from any real process of communication, as such communication is reduced to the most elementary model of information transfer from speaker to listener'. The second generation, represented in the research of Noam Chomsky (1957, 1965) and George Miller (1951, 1962), overcame the atomism of the first generation in its claim that what is acquired and what underlies linguistic performance is a system of rules. In Leontiev's (1981: 93) view, however, the second generation maintains the individualism of the first generation. and the social environment serves only to trigger innately specified linguistic principles. Moreover, the second generation is primarily linguistic rather than psychological in scope, despite claims to the contrary (e.g. Chomsky, 2002). In other words, psychological processes are reduced 'to mere speech manifestation of linguistic structures' using a unit of analysis – the sentence – that has no concrete reality outside of graphical literacy (Leontiev, 1981: 93).

Leontiev argues that the emerging third generation of psycholinguistics is characterized by its concern with the complex relationships that link participation in semiotically-mediated communicative activity and psychological processes. This effort is informed by the Vygotskian cultural-historical lineage and seeks to forge explicit linkages between an individual's ontogenesis and the social–material conditions of their everyday practice (e.g. Engeström, 1999; Chaiklin, 2001; Stetsenko & Arievitch, 2004a; Vygotsky, 1997; and in second language research, Lantolf, 2000; Lantolf & Thorne, 2006; Swain, 2000; Thorne, 2000a, 2005; van Lier, 2004). Innate, biological endowments certainly exist and serve an indispensable function in human cognition (see Luria, 1976), but emphasis is placed on the historical and societal constitution of higher-order thinking. In this respect, Vygotsky was influenced by the Marxist arguments for the primacy of economic and social structures, over and above human biology, as the generative catalysts for the development of human societies and cultures (Timpanaro, 1975: 29–54). Hence for Vygotsky, higher order cognitive functions, including intentional memory, planning, voluntary attention, interpretive strategies and rationality, were understood to develop out of participation in social practices such as schooling, interaction with care givers, the learning and use of a wide array of semiotic systems such as spoken languages, textual and digital literacies, mathematics and music. Within this framework, development involves gaining voluntary control of thinking and behavior through the use of cultural artifacts that mediate, and allow humans to regulate, their biological and behavioral activity (Frawley, 1997). Vygotsky made his position clear in the following comment:

> Lower or elementary functions, being processes that are ... earlier, simpler and independent of concepts in genetic, functional and structural relations, are reconstructed on a new basis when influenced by thinking in concepts ... they are included as component parts, as subordinate stages, into new, complex combinations created by thinking on the basis of concepts, and finally under the influence of thinking, foundations of the personality and world view ... are laid down. (Vygotsky, 1998: 81)

This view is evocative of the Sapir-Whorf hypothesis of linguistic relativity (e.g. Gumperz & Levinson, 1996; Gentner & Goldin-Meadow, 2003; Whorf, 1956). That the obligatory semantic distinctions of a linguistic variety correspond to habitual forms of thought has been robustly documented (e.g. for spatial cognition, see Levinson, 2003; Bowerman & Choi, 2003). This suggests that the organization of communicative activity at the levels of grammaticization and lexicalization form a primary carrier of historically developed systems of meaning – what can be termed more simply as culture – into the process ontology of unfolding activity (for a review, see Lucy, 1996). Levinson (2003: 41–42) sums up the cognition–language–culture connections of this position as follows: '(1) languages vary in their semantics just as they do in their form; (2) semantic differences are bound to engender cognitive differences; (3) these cognitive correlates of semantic differences can be empirically found on a widespread basis.' From within the cultural-historical tradition, Vološinov makes a parallel formulation concerning the relationship between signs and consciousness:

Consciousness takes shape and being in the material of signs created by an organized group in the process of its social intercourse. The individual consciousness is nurtured on signs; it derives growth from them; it reflects their logic and laws. The logic of consciousness is the logic of ideological communication, of the semiotic interaction of a social group. (Vološinov, 1973: 13)

The third generation of Vygotskian psycholinguistics, to which our efforts to develop a LCA framework contributes, investigates the linguistic means people deploy in the service of specific real-world activity, whether oriented toward the negotiation of collective action or to regulate one's own cognitive activity. The third generation eschews interest in the psycholinguistics of the sentence and focuses instead on the functional elements of communication, where the appropriate unit of analysis is often meaningfully described as the utterance or repertoire (Hopper, 1998), or as Carter and McCarthy (2004) term it, units that are simply 'pragmatically adequate' for the action at hand. Language from this perspective is not about rule-governed a priori grammar systems that must be acquired before people can engage in communication, but is instead about communicative resources that are formed and reformed in the very activity in which they are used – concrete linguistically-mediated communicative and cognitive activity.

As this variety of psycholinguistic theory brings communicative activity to center stage, it requires a theory of language that is concerned with human communication rather than with more formal theories of language structure divorced from such activity. As we have described, formalist theories of language from Saussure to Chomsky have generally assumed a 'dichotomy between language and the extralinguistic world to which language refers' (Hanks, 1996: 118). The stance we argue for is one that calls into question both 'the ontological distinction between language and the world and the epistemological one between knowledge of language and knowledge of the world' (Hanks, 1996: 119). However, we recognize that this aspiration has not been fully realized within the cultural-historical tradition itself and in the sections to follow, we describe a critical (re)conception of language and communication that draws upon a wide range of historical and contemporary work.

Slab, Intersubjectivity, Prolepsis and the Interpretant

In his 1953 text *Philosophical Investigations*, Ludwig Wittgenstein introduced the idea of *language game* to underscore that language is 'inextricably bound up with the non-linguistic behaviour which constitutes its natural environment' (McGinn, 1997: 43). This is in opposition to 'the idea of language as a system of meaningful signs that can be considered in abstraction from its actual employment. Instead of approaching language as a system of signs with meaning, we are prompted to think about it *in situ*, embedded in the lives of those who speak it' (McGinn, 1997: 44). For Wittgenstein, in theoretical abstractions 'we turn our backs on everything that is essential to the actual functioning of language' and in doing this we turn language from something living into something dead. Our inability to explain how language is able to represent the world results precisely from the linguist's refusal to 'look at it where it actually functions' (McGinn, 1997: 44). Wittgenstein recognizes the biological substrate on which human consciousness is built, but like Vygotsky, he insists that human life is fundamentally cultural and as such is mediated by agreements (i.e. language- games) that are implicated in the non-linguistic activities of human agents (see also Malinowski, 1923).

To illustrate the idea of language game, we use Wittgenstein's oft-cited example of a stone mason and his assistant building a wall. The mason calls out to his assistant the utterance 'Slab!' To which the assistant responds by picking up the appropriate stone and passing it to the mason. At issue is how the assistant knows precisely how to respond to the mason's utterance. In a linguistics of a priori meanings and forms, a likely explanation would be that both the mason and his assistant understand the utterance 'Slab' to mean 'Bring me a slab'; hence, the single word utterance represents a reduction of the full underlying imperative sentence. Wittgenstein then asks how is it that when the stone mason produces 'Slab' he really means 'Bring me a slab'? Does the speaker say to himself the full sentence before uttering the shortened version, and does the assistant then expand the single-word utterance into the full imperative before fetching an appropriate piece of stone? For Wittgenstein, the answer to both questions is decidedly no. Furthermore, Wittgenstein asks, why can't things be the other way around – when someone says 'Bring me a slab' the person really means the shortened form of the sentence 'Slab?' Wittgenstein writes:

> Even if such an explanation [i.e. a full sentence underlying the single-word utterance] rather tempts us, we need only think for a moment of what actually happens in order to see that we are going astray here. We say that we use the command in contract with other sentences because *our language* contains the possibility of these other sentences. (Wittgenstein, 1953, paragraph 20)

But none of these other sentences, allowed by the grammatical possibilities of the particular language at issue, is present inside the speaker's mind when he utters 'Slab.' Thus, meaning is produced in the interplay between the utterance and the activity in which it plays a role. Similarly, if the mason produces the utterance 'Five slabs', says Wittgenstein, how does the assistant know to interpret this as a command to fetch five pieces of stone and not as a report on some state-of-affairs in the work site? For Wittgenstein, meaning does not reside in some abstract underlying sentence in the mind of the speaker and the listener but in the activity transpiring in the work site – that is, 'in the pattern of activity within which the use of language is embedded' (McGinn, 1997: 57). Meaning, in this sense, involves a process of 'attunement to the attunement of the other' (Rommetveit, 1992; see also Barwise & Perry, 1983), a formulation that is also supported and extended within ethnomethodology and conversation analysis. Heritage (1984), for example, makes the following observation: '[w]ith respect to the production of normatively appropriate conduct, all that is required is that the actors have, and attribute to one another, a reflexive awareness of the normative accountability of their actions' where 'normative accountability is the "grid" by reference to which *whatever* is done will become visible and accessible' (Heritage, 1984: 117; italics in the original).

Harold Garfinkel, the father of ethnomethodology, develops a characterization of communication that is heavily influenced by Wittgenstein. For Garfinkel:

> language is not to be regarded as a matter of 'cracking the code' which contains a set of pre-established descriptive terms combined, by the rules of grammar, to yield sentence meanings which express propositions about the world. Understanding language is not, in the first instance, a matter of understanding sentences but of understanding *actions* – utterances – which are constructively interpreted in relation to their contexts. This involves viewing an utterance against a background of *who* said it, *where* and *when*, *what* was being accomplished by saying it and in the light of what possible *considerations* and in virtue of what *motives* it was said. An utterance is thus the starting point for a complicated process of interpretive inference rather than something which can be treated as self-subsistently intelligible. (Heritage, 1984: 139–40; italics in original)

Garfinkel developed and supported this view with data from a creative series of 'breeching experiments' that were developed to illustrate that social scientific formulations of objectively rational action fall apart under local conditions. These experiments involved a researcher intentionally flouting the explicit rules of a game (chess, or tic-tac-toe) or the implicit norms of everyday conversation. The breeching experiments demonstrated that breakdowns in normative social action illustrate the mechanisms of social cohesion and trust that enable communicative interaction (see Garfinkel, 1967).

There is a certain irony in the view that argues for universal and prespecified meaning to reside in language. As the research of Rommetveit (1974), Vološinov (1973), Linell (1998) and Vygotsky (1987) shows, the greater the shared knowledge between interactants, the more likely they are to speak in fragments, leaving out meanings that would be redundant if explicitly expressed. Yet, the idealized 'view of common knowledge undergirds a theory of grammar based on full sentences' (Hanks, 1996: 147). If people did in fact share 'the identical homunculi of formalism, their language would surely be organized around incompleteness, not fully specified forms' (Hanks, 1996: 147–148). Understanding in concrete communicative activity does not rely on hitting on the correct underlying representation. There is no underlying sentence. There are only people engaged in the activity of communicating in concrete material circumstances with specific intentions. This, according to a linguistics of communicative activity, is how meaning is produced. Hence, as described by McCarthy (personal communication, February 9, 2004), possible 'underlying sentences' would only ever be likely to occur in 'displaced' communications such as writing – a poster advertising a product or offer, TV adspeak, or the analysis of a formal linguist. There is certainly room for the study of 'displaced' communications, but it is odd that so much of the edifice that is formal linguistics should have been built on intuitions of underlying form and grammaticality rather than evidence from non-displaced communicative events (see Tomasello, 2003).

Ragnar Rommetveit has directly challenged the conventional relations between ellipsis and presumed underlying representations in language, stating that:

> we may thus reverse the traditional linguistic approach to ellipsis: *ellipsis*, we may claim, *appears to be the prototype of verbal communication under ideal conditions of complete complementarity in an intersubjectively established, temporarily shared social world.* (Rommetveit, 1974: 29, italics in the original)

Intersubjective states are created and draw agents together toward a common focus, activity, process or goal (Rommetveit, 1974; Habermas, 1984). The dialogic exchange of ellipses and indexicals in both face-to-face and written exchanges makes possible participation frameworks which build socially distributed perceptions that are, so described by Goodwin (1996: 398) 'situated, context dependent ... and intensely local'. Rommetveit extends the uses of ellipsis beyond those of economy or the reduction of redundancy through the notion of prolepsis. Prolepsis describes what might be termed strategic social inclusion that might occur when one speaker underspecifies information that her or his interlocutor would not be presumed to know. The hearer is 'invited to step into an enlarged common space, and shared background knowledge is thereby created, rather than assumed' (van Lier, 1996: 161). Rommetveit describes prolepsis via the disclosure of a personal letter he received from his friend, Willem Hofstee, who originally proposed the term:

> ... Today I walked with one of the psychologists here past the Mayflower cinema in Eugene, where Bergman's latest film movie is being shown. He asked me whether I had seen it. I said no, and asked if he had. He said yes, he had. I asked him how he liked it, and he said 'I liked it very much, but Mary Ann did not'; without ever explicitly having 'made known' to me that he is married and that his wife's name is Mary Ann, that they went to see the film together, and a lot of other things – and (if I am correct) without assuming that I knew all this. His utterance was proleptic in that it triggered a search on my part for a shared social reality which in turn would provide a basis for understanding the sentence. Incidentally, it would have been barbaric and pedantic to say, 'Oh, Mary Ann is your wife'. To be precise, prolepsis here served to establish a relationship between his wife and me as persons who should at some time get together. My comment would have been a crude rejection of that implication. (Rommetveit 1974: 87–88)

As this example makes clear, minimally referencing presupposed knowledge is proleptic:

> precisely because that expanded social reality is taken for granted rather than explicitly spelled out. ... What is said serves on such occasions to induce presuppositions and trigger anticipatory comprehension, and what is made known will necessarily transcend what is said.
> (Rommetveit, 1974: 88)

In this sense, prolepsis can be seen as not only pragmatically adequate, but as pragmatically advantageous, by providing the interlocutor with the resources through which to imagine a shared referent.[2]

We find the semiotic philosophy of Charles Sanders Peirce (1897/1955) to also contribute to this discussion, particularly his notion of the 'interpretant.' Peirce elaborated relations between signs and grounds in the form of a speculative grammar, but not in the sense of syntax, rather toward the relations between sign and world (object) and sign and ideology. This latter relation, of linguistic sign to ideology, is the realm of the interpretant. In Peirce's model, interlocutors do not merely receive and interpret signs from one another. Rather, a sign is always met by a sign, meaning that understanding is constructed through the production of a sign by the receiver – the interpretant. In Peirce's model, the interpretant is evoked by the initial sign and may be more elaborate than, or semantically differentiated from, the catalyst sign. While the interpretant is not a copy of the original sign, it is semantically and pragmatically constrained by what Rommetveit (1992) as we discussed earlier, has termed 'the attunement to the attunement of the other'. This discussion has described numerous theorizations based on situated, real-time communicative activity. Their gist, taken together, is that 'ellipsis' is a deficiency-oriented construct that logically requires the existence of underlying representations.

We propose, building on Wittgenstein, Rommetveit and Peirce, that underlying representations are unnecessary in an account of the syntax of communicative interaction and its role in meaning making. Further, we suggest that a wide array of what are viewed as deficient language fragments, ellipsis and under-specification, are in fact pragmatically appropriate or even advantageous or necessary under conditions of everyday communicative activity.

Emergent Grammar

At this point the reader may be thinking – pragmatics and language- in-use is all well and good, but what is 'language' really? To address this question, we turn to the work of Paul Hopper (1998, 2002), who, like Vološinov, has argued that grammar is a consequence of communication, not a precondition. Of course systematicity of language use exists, but grammatical rules, such as they are, are argued to sediment out of the everyday activity of socially-organized communication. That is, grammar describes categories of observable repetition in discourse, no more and no less (see also Bybee & Hopper, 2002; MacWhinney, 2001). From this perspective, grammatical functions and units develop in the primordial, temporal environment of moment-to-moment verbal activity. Hopper proposes the concept of Emergent Grammar which he describes thus. Emergent Grammar

> proposes to bypass the problem of a fixed, prediscourse adult grammar, with its attendant problems of necessarily 'degenerate' input for both child acquisition and adult maintenance of language, by relocating structure, that is, 'grammar', from the center to the periphery of linguistic communication. Grammar, in this view, is not the source of

understanding and communication but a by-product of it. Grammar is, in other words, epiphenomenal.' (Hopper, 1998: 156)

Clarifying the often-confused terms 'emerging' and 'emergent', Hopper notes that 'emerging ... means 'in the course of development toward completion'. 'Emergent' by contrast suggests a perpetual process in which movement towards a complete structure of some kind is constant, but completion is always deferred. Linguistic structure is intrinsically incomplete, a work in progress, a site under construction' (Hopper, 2002: 6). Emergent Grammar offers a counterpoint to the 'fixed code' approach that argues for a stable linguistic system of form to meaning relations (for another critique of fixed code theory, see Harris, 1996). 'A language is not a painting-by-the-numbers canvas with a scheme laid out in advance ... rather it is put together fragment by fragment in scenes of social interaction, starting in infancy' (Hopper, 2002: 6). Communicative repertoires like human language are 'shared by speakers to the extent that speakers have common cultural experiences of communication, experiences that include not just speech but also the types of social action – the "scenes" – in which particular kinds of utterances figure' (Hopper, 2002: 6).

Using corpus linguistic methodology, Hopper illustrates language as an 'interactive phenomenon' through an analysis of pseudocleft utterances – sentences that begin with a WHAT word + (NP/subject if the WH is not the subject) + Verb + is/was + NP/object.

- What happened was that ...
- What they've done is ...
- What it is is that ...

Hopper shows that in the great majority of pseudoclefts occurring in spoken language corpora, only a small number of formulas are found. The verbs in the WH clause are predominantly 'do' and 'happen', or 'say' (less frequent), or another verb that is part of a fixed phrase such as 'what I suppose is' or 'what I mean is', etc. (Hopper, 2002: 9). It is pertinent that vernacular spoken pseudoclefts are 'fragmentary and – importantly – more formulaic' than the broad range of usages found in written discourse.

Using pseudoclefts as an example, Hopper describes the management of discourse, the ability to 'project future segments of talk and control the pace of delivery', as having two features:

- *Listener-centered:* creating a frame of reference for the upcoming portion of talk as action (using the verb do – 'what they've done is ... ') or event (with the verb happen – 'what happened was that ... ')

- *Speaker-centered:* using the pseudocleft as 'discourse junk' to gain a few seconds to organize the spate of talk to come. In such cases, attitudinal verbs can be used to accentuate affective stances.[3] Hopper illustrates other speaker-centered functions of the pseudocleft, such as using this repertoire to hold the floor while recasting ones argument ('what we're gonna do is, or what I'd like to do, I think, is to ... ') or to make one's comment seem authoritative (such as 'what you should do, though, is ... ').

So-called 'grammar' and the lexicon are bound up with one another as many corpus and non corpus-based studies have indicated.[4] Grammar, such as it is, is contingent upon, and in constant interplay with, its lexical environment. In this sense, 'grammar rules are only provisionally valid' (Hopper, 2002: 16) in that the greater the volume of language data analyzed, the fewer are the grammatical rules that hold up without recourse to hedge-categories such as exceptions, aberrations and special cases. Grammar is temporal and shifts from situation to situation, from generation to generation, and from modality to modality (see Thorne, 2000b, 2003, for a discussion of the variability of language use in Internet-mediated environments). In essence, 'grammar contracts as texts expand' (Hopper, 1998: 164).

Hopper concludes his 1998 article arguing that:

[w]hat adults know, and what children learn, is not an abstract system of units with meanings and rules for combining them, but ... integrated normative modes of interactive behavior and the accompanying social use of corporeal signs such as words and gestures, to which concepts like language and grammar are almost entirely secondary. (Hopper, 1998: 173)

This discussion raises a critical question – if grammar isn't preexisting, how is language learned? In response, we bring in recent work describing a usage-based model of language acquisition (Tomasello, 2003) that proposes mechanisms to account for the many important questions that Hopper's work, which is largely descriptive, leaves unaddressed.

Usage-Based Language Development

Tomasello's theory is based on the same understanding of language as a functional system that underlies the thinking of Hopper on emergent grammar and Rommetveit and Vološinov on language use. In this model, 'children begin to acquire language when they do because the learning process depends crucially on the more fundamental skills of joint attention, intention-reading and cultural learning – which emerge near the end of the first year of life' (Tomasello, 2003: 21). From this perspective, language is seen as a special and complex type of 'joint attentional skill' that people employ 'to influence and manipulate one another's attention' (Tomasello, 2003; see also Clark, 1996, for a discussion of language as joint action). Thus

> using linguistic symbols in utterances is a social act, and when this act is internalized in Vygotskian fashion the product is a unique kind of cognitive representation that is not only intersubjective (involving both self and other), but also perspectival in the sense that the child understands that the same referent could have been indicated in some other way – the speaker could have chosen another linguistic symbol to indicate a different aspect of this entity. (Tomasello, 2003: 28)

Although Tomasello's theory assigns a central role to culture, broadly construed, in the acquisition process, he does not overlook the importance of biological factors. However, Tomasello illustrates with examples from morphology, the lexicon, syntax and discourse that the representational innateness stance of Chomsky 'is a very unlikely theory' of language acquisition; for one thing, there has been no satisfactory way for this particular theory to account for the uneven and gradual nature of language development documented in children (Tomasello, 2003: 284). Thus for Tomasello (2003: 285) humans are 'biologically prepared for language,' but it does not follow that this requires 'specific linguistic structures'. He calls into serious question the standard arguments put forth to support representational innateness, including claims about a critical period, poverty of stimulus, a grammar gene and the ability of linguistic savants, all of which have been used to bolster the organ of language position proposed by generativists.[5]

Making reference to the research of Langacker, Hopper and others working within cognitive linguistics, Tomasello (2003: 170) points out that categories such as 'nouns' and 'verbs', for instance, do not refer to specific kinds of things 'but rather invite the listener to construe something in a particular way in a particular communicative context'. The difference between *an explosion* and something *exploding* can be understood as construing (i.e. bringing into discourse) the same experience either as a 'bounded entity' or as a process (Tomasello, 2003: 170). This is supported in the case of nouns by features such as determiners, which help listeners to 'locate a referent in actual or conceptual space' and for verbs by tense markers 'whose primary function is to help the listener to locate a process in actual or conceptual time' (Tomasello, 2003: 170–71). According to Tomasello, it seems clear that understanding the communicative function of words in utterances is crucial in determining such things as 'dual-category words' (e.g. *bite, kiss, drink, brush*, etc.). Importantly, although communicative function plays a central role in determining syntactic function and morphological processes, the attainment of the two types of knowledge is a piecemeal and locally-constrained phenomenon. Some children figure out morphological processes such as plural formation before they figure out syntactic function and for other children this developmental sequence is reversed (see Gopnik & Meltzoff, 1993; Thorne, 2000a, for a discussion of variability in linguistic environments and their effects on conceptual development). Children gradually develop from a local understanding of language to a more global and abstract level where what were once piecemeal bits of knowledge come together, but not in a full grammar in the sense understood in generative linguistics, but as a 'structured inventory of symbolic units' (Tomasello, 2003: 105; see also Halliday & Matthiessen, 2004). This system, similar in characteristics to Hopper's emergent grammar, contains 'multi-morphemic fluent units of speech that the child controls as single units.' This suggests that for both children and adults, competence incorporates not just individual words and morphemes but also 'larger chunks of language with relatively complex internal structures' that can be manipulated according to their communicative intentions (Tomasello, 2003: 105).

Summarizing his own work, Tomasello (2003: 325) highlights these key points of his usage-based theory of language acquisition. The model is thoroughly functionalist and 'based explicitly in the expression and comprehension of communicative intentions (intention-reading)'. Language is used primarily to 'direct people's attention to events and entities in the current joint attentional frame' (Tomasello, 2003: 325). The model is construction-based with a focus on whole utterances, not isolated words and morphemes, for utterances are 'the primary reality of language from a communicative point of view because they are the most direct embodiment of a speaker's communicative intentions' (Tomasello, 2003: 325–6). Tomasello (2003: 327) emphasizes that 'language structure emerges from language use, both historically and ontogenetically'. In conclusion, he argues that for language acquisition to advance, research should adopt:

> a view of human linguistic competence based less on an analogy to formal languages and more on empirical research in the cognitive sciences. ... How children become competent users of a natural language is not a logical problem but an empirical problem. (Tomasello, 2003: 328)

Linguistics of Communicative Activity and Vygotskian Theories of Development

For Vygotsky (1978), the key that links thinking to communicative activity resides in the double function of the sign, which simultaneously points in two directions – outwardly, 'as a unit of social interaction (i.e. a unit of *behavior*)', and inwardly, 'as a unit of thinking (i.e. as a unit of *mind*)' (Prawat, 1999: 268; italics in original). In this sense, signs, or more appropriately put, the significance and value of signs, possess reversibility in that they 'can act upon the agent in the same way they act upon the environment or others' (Lee, 1985: 81). Similar to Vološinov/Bakhtin, Rommetveit, Hanks, Wittgenstein and others we have drawn upon to construct the LCA framework, Vygotsky realized that the Saussurian sign, as a unit of communication and thinking, was too inflexible to the extent that it assumes stable meanings for all members of a speech community. In his later writings, Vygotsky argued for a dialectical tension between the stable meaning of linguistic signs, and an unstable, precarious element (Prawat, 1999: 269) that emerges as people engage in concrete, goal-directed communicative and psychological activity. Vygotsky characterized this distinction in a way that is similar to Rommetveit's notion of meaning potential: 'the word considered in isolation and in the lexicon has only one meaning. But this meaning is nothing more than a potential that is realized in living speech. In living speech this meaning is only a stone in the edifice of sense' (Vygotsky, 1987: 303). Later in the same text, Vygotsky remarks that 'in spoken language as a rule we go from the most stable and permanent element ... from its most constant zone, that is, the meaning of the word, to its more fluctuating zones, to its sense' (Vygotsky, 1987: 304–5). Vygotsky refers to the stable element of a sign as its meaning and to its emergent and contextually contingent element as its sense. This dual view of semiotic values – stable marco-cultural meaning and locally inscribed sense – was prescient in its time (more than 80 years ago). The works that we have reviewed here provide yet greater power for the project of understanding communicative processes as inherently cognitive processes, and cognitive processes as indivisible from humanistic issues of agency and construal of self and world.

Disinventing Language

The premise that unites much of this volume is that inherited linguistic typologies that arose under particular colonial and post-colonial conditions continue to invent language-culture taxonomies that may not provide a participant-relevant 'direction of fit' between words and the world – to borrow from Searle (1983). Indeed, Makoni has noted that there exist a large number of 'languages', constructed under conditions of colonial and post-colonial power-knowledge formations (often with good intentions, e.g. the South African constitution), that are de facto mere political-academic entities 'in search of speakers' (Makoni & Meinhof, 2003). According to Searle, what is special about culture, here seen as matrixes of power-knowledge, is:

> the collective assignment of functions to phenomena where the function cannot be performed solely by virtue of the sheer physical features of the phenomena. From dollar bills to cathedrals, football games to nation states, we are constantly encountering new social facts where the facts exceed the physical features of the underlying physical reality. (Searle, 1995: 228)

This is emphatically the case with the historical invention of language and language taxonomies (and by extension, models of language structure, use and development).

In conclusion, we wish to make a linkage to ideological and categorical problems that might be re-addressed through the disinvention lens and to connect the LCA framework to critical issues of meaning and disciplinary power. While cultural-historical approaches to language and development share a foundation with Marx and other traditions of critical scholarship, this element is sometimes missing in Vygotskian developmental research (for explicit treatments of this issue, see Sawchuk et al., 2005; Stetsenko & Arievitch, 2004b; Thorne, 2005). A legitimate question is whether, and how, Vygotskian theorizing might substantively contribute to the critical apparatus suggested by the disinvention theme.

We and others working within the tradition of cultural-historical activity theory argue that participation in the process ontology of everyday life is mediated by, and constrained by, symbolic and material artifacts that carry with them historically sedimented patterns of usage. Mediation in this sense involves explicit and implicit ideologies, folk beliefs, normative and expected conduct, as well as the institutionalization of dimensions of everyday practice that include the mundane (driving a motor vehicle), the divine (participation in religious services and rituals), and participation in work and learning environments that are governed by strictures such as accountability and epistemological prescriptivism. While this 'grid of discipline' – to paraphrase Foucault (1979) – is inherently porous and unstable in many respects, we would emphasize the importance of seeing human agency as the culturally-mediated capacity to act (Ahearn, 2001). This capacity is both enabled and constrained, on the one hand, by cultural-institutional factors developed over time and, on the other hand, by the dynamic of a particular interaction happening at a given moment in time. And this is precisely the point at which cultural-historical activity theory can make a difference as it does not separate understanding (research) from transformation (concrete action). Modern activity theory in particular, though also used descriptively and analytically as a diagnostic framework, is fundamentally an applied methodology. That is, it encourages engaged critical inquiry wherein an investigation would lead to the development of material and symbolic-conceptual tools capable of enacting positive interventions. Engeström (1999) expresses this potential through the idea of 'radical localism,' the notion that the capacity for change is alive in the details of everyday practices which, en masse, make up society. Sharing a common intellectual and activist lineage that also informs critical pedagogy and structurationist sociology, the hope is to collaboratively develop an increasingly critical research and activist apparatus for use in developmentally focused research. From this perspective, cultural-historical and poststructuralist approaches share aspirations for political engagement, while also offering distinctive contributions to the project of critical scholarship.

In summary, with this chapter, we have tried to show some of the attributes of erasing the Saussurian-Bloomfieldian circle around language with the goal of recovering the organic connection between language, communicative activity, cognition, culture and the consequential nature of theoretical formulations. In application to language representations, the imposition of language as a 'natural object' entails the relegation of speakers to mere instances of bio-physical categories of reference (Foucault, 2003). Our counter-narrative, or disinventing *tactic* (per de Certeau, 1984), is to put forward a linguistics of communicative activity that is based on a view of language as a historically contingent emergent system, one that provides a repertoire of semiotic devices that people can use to realize their communicative intentions, to interpret the communicative intentions of others and, perhaps most importantly, to foster the conditions of possibility for transforming self and community. Thus, the fundamental challenge for progressive language theorists does not involve language in the abstract, but rather the semiotic inscription of communicative practice and its rendering into visible representations that are ecologically inclusive of speaker-relevant points of view and actionable as resources for personal and societal transformation.

Acknowledgements

Portions of this text were inspired by prior texts on Vygotskian cultural historical theory and second language development by Lantolf and Thorne (2006) and Thorne (forthcoming).

Notes

1. In a recent book examining technologies as they are used in everyday human activity, Bonnie Nardi and Vicky O'Day address the elusiveness of perception. The example they discuss references research on 'inattentional blindness' (Mack & Rock, 1998), a claim made by visual perception researchers which suggests that processing visual information is a conscious act that requires focused attention to the visual field. Routine and repeated activities are susceptible to inattentional blindness, and inattentional blindness may also occur when or if one is unready to pay attention to certain objects in the visual field (Nardi & O'Day, 1999: 15).
2. Other language theorists have described related concepts, such as Roland Barthe's 'readerly' (a text that stabilizes the reader through meeting expectations) versus more connotative writerly texts (requiring interpretation from the recipient, destabilizing expectations) (see Barthe, 1975).
3. For example, 'what worries me is that ... ', 'what he is concerned about is that ... ', 'what scares her is that ... ' and 'what amazes me is that ... ', and so on.
4. For a pedagogical example of corpus-based approaches to grammar, see Carter *et al.* (2000).
5. Tomasello proposes four psycholinguistic processes in his model of language acquisition: (1) *intention-reading* and *cultural learning*; (2) *schematization* and *analogy*; (3) *entrenchment* and *preemption*; and (4) *functionally-based distributional analysis*. We will not discuss these in detail here, but interested readers can consult Tomasello's 2003 volume.

References

Agar, M. (1994) *Language Shock: Understanding the Culture of Conversation*. New York: Quill.
Ahearn, L. (2001) Language and agency. *Annual Review of Anthropology* 30, 109–37.
Anderson, P. (1984) *In the Tracks of Historical Materialism*. Chicago: University of Chicago Press.
Bakhtin, M. (1986) *Speech Genres and Other Late Essays* (M. Holquist, ed. and C. Emerson, trans.). Austin: University of Texas Press.
Bakhurst, D. (1997) Activity, consciousness and communication. In M. Cole, Y. Engeström and O. Vasquez (eds) *Mind, Culture and Activity: Seminal Papers from the Laboratory of Comparative Human Cognition*. Cambridge: Cambridge University Press.
Barthe, R. (1975) *The Pleasure of Texts*. New York: Hill and Wang.
Barwise, J. and Perry, J. (1983) *Situations and Attitudes*. Cambridge: MIT Press.
Becker, A.L. (1982) Beyond translation: Esthetics and language description. In H. Byrnes (ed.) *Contemporary Perceptions of Language: Interdisciplinary Dimensions*. Georgetown Roundtable on Languages and Linguistics. Washington, DC: Georgetown University Press.

Boas, F. (1983/1911) *The Mind of Primitive Man* (revd edn). Westport, CT: Greenwood Press.
Bourdieu, P. (1988) *Homo Academicus*. Stanford: Stanford University Press.
Bowerman, M. and Choi, S. (2003) Space under construction: Language-specific spatial categorization in first language acquisition. In D. Gentner and S. Goldin-Meadow (eds) *Language in Mind* (pp. 387–428). Cambridge, MA. The MIT Press.
Bright, W. (ed.) (1990) *The Collected Works of Edward Sapir*. Berlin: Mouton de Gruyter, 1990.
Bybee, J. and Hopper, P. (2002) Introduction to frequency and emergence in linguistic structure. In J. Bybee and P. Hopper (eds) *Frequency and Emergence in Linguistic Structure*. Philadelphia: John Benjamins.
Carter, R. and McCarthy, M. (1995) Grammar and the spoken language. *Applied Linguistics* 16 (2), 141–58.
Carter, R., Hughes, R. and McCarthy, M. (2000) *Exploring Grammar in Context*. Cambridge: Cambridge University Press.
Carter, R. and McCarthy, M. (2004) 'There's millions of them': Hyperbole in everyday conversation. *Journal of Pragmatics* 36 (2), 149–184.
Chaiklin, S. (2001) The institutionalization of cultural-historical psychology as a multinational practice. In S. Chaiklin (ed.) *The Theory and Practice of Cultural-Historical Psychology* (pp. 15–34). Aarhus: Aarhus University Press.
Chomsky, N. (1957) *Syntactic Structures*. The Hague: Mouton.
Chomsky, N. (1965) *Cartesian Linguistics*. New York: Harper and Row.
Chomsky, N. (1992) *Knowledge of Language: Its Nature, Origin and Use*. New York: Praeger.
Chomsky, N. (2000) *New Horizons in the Study of Language and Mind*. Cambridge: Cambridge University Press.
Chomsky, N. (2002) *On Nature and Language*. Cambridge: Cambridge University Press.
Clark, H. (1996) *Using Language*. Cambridge: Cambridge University Press.
Cole, M. (1996) *Cultural Psychology: A Once and Future Discipline*. Cambridge, MA: Belknapp Press.
Collins, C. (1999) *Discourse, Social Change and the CHAT Tradition*. Aldershot: Ashgate.
Crowley, T. (1996) *Language in History: Theories and Texts*. London: Routledge.
Davydov, V. (1999) The content and unsolved problems of activity theory. In Y. Engeström (ed.) *Perspectives on Activity Theory* (pp. 39–52). Cambridge: Cambridge University Press.
de Certeau, M. (1984) *The Practice of Everyday Life*. Berkeley: University of California Press.
Engeström, Y. (ed.) (1999) *Perspectives on Activity Theory*. Cambridge: Cambridge University Press.
Foucault, M. (1972) *Archaeology of Knowledge & the Discourse on Language*. New York: Pantheon Books.
Foucault, M. (1979) *Discipline and Punish: The Birth of Prisons*. New York: Vintage Books.
Foucault, M. (2003) *Society Must be Defended: Lectures at the College de France, 1975–1976* (D. Macey, trans.). New York: Picador.
Fauconnier, G. and Turner, M. (2002) *The Way We Think: Conceptual Blending and the Mind's Hidden Complexities*. New York: Basic Books.

Frawley, W. (1997) *Vygotsky and Cognitive Science: Language and the Unification of the Social and Computational Mind*. Cambridge: Harvard University Press.
Garfinkel, H. (1967) *Studies in Ethnomethodology*. Englewood Cliffs, NJ: Prentice Hall.
Gentner, D. and Goldin-Meadow, S. (eds) *Language in Mind*. Cambridge, MA: MIT Press.
Goodwin, C. (1996) Transparent vision. In E. Ochs, E. Schegloff and S. Thomas (eds) *Interaction and Grammar*. Cambridge: Cambridge University Press.
Gopnik, A. and Meltzoff, A.N. (1993) Words and thoughts in infancy: The specificity hypothesis and the development of categorization and naming. In C. Rovee-Collier and L.P. Lipsett (eds) *Advances in Infancy Research* (Vol. 8: pp. 217–249). New Jersey: Ablex.
Gumperz, J. and Levinson, S. (1996) *Rethinking Linguistic Relativity*. Cambridge: Cambridge University Press.
Habermas, J. (1984) *The Theory of Communicative Action* (Vol. 1). Boston: Beacon Press.
Halliday, M.A.K. and Matthiesen, C. (2004) *An Introduction to Functional Grammar*. London: Arnold.
Hanks, W. (1996) *Language and Communicative Practice*. Boulder, CO: Westview Press.
Harris, R. (1996) *The Language Connection: Philosophy and Linguistics*. Bristol: Thoemmes.
Heritage, J. (1984) *Garfinkel and Ethnomethodology*. Cambridge: Polity Press.
Hopper, P. (1998) Emergent grammar. In M. Tomasello (ed.) *The New Psychology of Language: Cognitive and Functional Approaches to Language Study*. London: Lawrence Erlbaum Associates.
Hopper, P. (2002) Emergent grammar: Gathering together the fragments. Paper delivered as the Plenary Address, Pennsylvania State University Summer Institute of Applied Linguistics, July 10.
Jones, P. (1999) The ideal in cultural-historical activity theory: Issues and perspectives. In S. Chaiklin (ed.) *The Theory and Practice of Cultural-Historical Psychology*. Aarhus: Aarhus University Press.
Joseph, J. and Taylor, T. (eds) (1990) *Ideologies of Language*. London: Routledge.
Joseph, J., Love, N. and Taylor, T. (2001) *Landmarks in Linguistic Thought II: The Western Tradition in the Twentieth Century*. New York: Routledge.
Lantolf, J.P. (2000) Second language learning as a mediated process. *Language Teaching* 33, 79–96.
Lantolf, J. and Thorne, S.L. (2006) *Sociocultural Theory and the Genesis of Second Language Development*. Oxford: Oxford University Press.
Latour, B. (1999) *Pandora's Hope. Essays on the Reality of Science Studies*. Cambridge, MA: Harvard University Press.
Lee, B. (1985) Intellectual origins of Vygotsky's semiotic analysis. In J.V. Wertsch (ed.) *Culture, Communication and Cognition: Vygotskian Perspectives*. Cambridge: Cambridge University Press.
Leontiev, A.A. (1981) *Psychology and the Language Learning Process*. London: Pergamon.
Levinson, S. (2003) *Space in Language and Cognition*. New York: Cambridge.
Levinson, S. (2003) Language and mind. In D. Gentner and S. Goldin-Meadow (eds) *Language in Mind* (pp. 25–46). Cambridge, MA: The MIT Press.

Lévi-Strauss, C. (1979) *Myth and Meaning.* New York: Schocken Books.
Lévi-Strauss, C. (1987) *Anthropology and Myth.* New York: Blackwell.
Linell, P. (1998) *Approaching Dialogue: Talk, Interaction and Contexts in Dialogical Perspectives.* Amsterdam: John Benjamins.
Lucy, J.A. (1996) The scope of linguistic relativity: An analysis and review of empirical research. In J. Gumperz and S. Levinson (eds) *Rethinking Linguistic Relativity* (pp. 37–69). New York: Cambridge.
Luria, A.R. (1976) *Cognitive Development.* Cambridge, MA: Harvard University Press.
McGinn, M. (1997) *Wittgenstein and the Philosophical Investigations.* London: Routledge.
Mack, A. and Rock, I. (1998) *Inattentional Blindness.* Cambridge, MA: MIT Press.
MacWhinney, B. (2001) Emergentist approaches to language. In J. Bybee and P. Hopper (eds) *Frequency and Emergence in Linguistic Structure* (pp. 449–470). Philadelphia: John Benjamins.
Makoni, S. and Meinhof, U. (2003) Introducing applied linguistics in Africa. *Africa and Applied Linguistics. AILA Review* 16, 1–13.
Makoni, S. and Pennycook, A. (2005) Disinventing and (re)constituting languages. *Critical Inquiry in Language Studies: An International Journal* 2 (3), 137–156.
Malinowski, B. (1923) *Argonauts of the Western Pacific: An Account of Native Enterprise and Adventure in the Archipelagoes of Melanesian New Guinea.* Prospect Heights, IL: Waveland Press.
Miller, G.A. (1951) *Language and Communication.* New York: McGraw Hill.
Miller, G.A. (1962) Some psychological studies of grammar. *American Psychologist* 17, 748–62.
Nardi, B. and O'Day, V. (1999) *Information Ecologies: Using Technology with Heart.* Cambridge, MA: MIT Press.
Peirce, C. S. (1897/1955) *Philosophical Writings of Peirce* (J. Buchler, ed.). New York: Dover Publications.
Pinker, S. (1991) Rules of language. *Science* 253, 530–535.
Prawat, R.S. (1999) Social constructivism and the process-content distinction as viewed by Vygotsky and the pragmatists. *Mind, Culture and Activity: An International Journal* 6, 255–73.
Rommetveit, R. (1974) *On Message Structure: A Framework for the Study of Language and Communication.* London: John Wiley & Sons.
Rommetveit, R. (1992) Outlines of a dialogically based social-cognitive approach to human cognition and communication. In A.H. Wold (ed.) *The Dialogical Alternative: Towards a Theory of Language and Mind.* Oslo: Scandinavian University Press.
Saussure, F. de. (1959) *Course in General Linguistics.* New York: McGraw Hill.
Sawchuk, P., Duarte, N. and Elhammoumi, M. (in press) *Critical Perspectives on Activity.* New York: Cambridge.
Schegloff, E. (1996) Turn organization: One intersection of grammar and interaction. In E. Ochs, E. Schegloff and S. Thomas (eds) *Interaction and Grammar.* Cambridge: Cambridge University Press.
Scribner, S. (1985) Vygotsky's uses of history. In J.V. Wertsch (ed.) *Culture, Communication and Cognition. Vygotskian Perspectives.* Cambridge: Cambridge University Press.
Searle, J. (1983) *Intentionality: An Essay in the Philosophy of Mind.* Cambridge: Cambridge University Press.

Searle, J. (1995) *The Construction of Social Reality*. New York: Free Press.
Stetsenko, A. and Arievitch, I.M. (2004a) The self in cultural-historical activity theory: Reclaiming the unity of social and individual dimensions of human development. *Theory & Psychology* 14 (4), 475–503.
Stetsenko, A. and Arievitch, I.M. (2004b) Vygotskian collaborative project of social transformation: History, politics and practice in knowledge construction. *Critical Psychology* 12.
Swain, M. (2000) The output hypothesis and beyond: Mediating acquisition through collaborative dialogue. In J. Lantolf (ed.) *Sociocultural Theory and Second Language Acquisition* (pp. 97–114). Oxford: Oxford University Press
Thorne, S. L. (2000a) Second language acquisition and the truths about relativity. In J. Lantolf (ed.) *Sociocultural Theory and Second Language Acquisition* (pp. 219–244). Oxford: Oxford University Press
Thorne, S. L. (2000b) Beyond bounded activity systems: Heterogeneous cultures in instructional uses of persistent conversation. *Proceedings of the Thirty-Third Annual Hawaii International Conference on System Sciences*. Los Alamitos, CA: IEEE Computer Society,
Thorne, S.L. (2003) Artifacts and cultures-of-use in intercultural communication. *Language Learning & Technology* 7 (2), 38–67.
Thorne, S.L. (2005) Epistemology, politics and ethics in sociocultural theory. *Modern Language Journal* 89, 393–409.
Thorne, S.L. (forthcoming) Fragments and repertoires as language development: From Nativism(s) to cultural historical mediation. *Applied Linguistics*.
Timpanaro, S. (1975) *On Materialism*. London: Verso.
Tomasello, M. (1999) *The Cultural Origins of Human Cognition*. Cambridge: Harvard University Press.
Tomasello, M. (2003) *Constructing a Language: A Usage-Based Theory of Language Acquisition*. Harvard University Press: Cambridge.
van Lier, L. (1996) *Interaction in the Language Curriculum: Awareness, Autonomy and Authenticity*. New York: Longman.
van Lier, L. (2004) *The Ecology and Semiotics of Language Learning: A Sociocultural Perspective*. New York: Kluwer.
Vološinov, V.N. (1973) *Marxism and the Philosophy of Language*. New York: Seminar Press.
Vygotsky, L.S. (1978) *Mind in Society: The Development of Higher Psychological Processes* (M. Cole, V. John-Steiner, S. Scribner and E. Souberman, eds). Cambridge, MA: Harvard University Press.
Vygotsky, L.S. (1986) *Thought and Language*. Cambridge, MA: The MIT Press.
Vygotsky, L.S. (1987) *The Collected Works of L.S. Vygotsky* (Vol. 1) *Problems of General Psychology: Including the Volume Thinking and Speech* (R.W. Reiber and A.S. Carton, eds). New York: Plenum Press.
Vygotsky, L.S. (1997) *The Collected Works of L.S. Vygotsky* (Vol. 4): *The History of the Development of Higher Mental Functions*. New York: Plenum.
Vygotsky, L.S. (1998) *The Collected Works of L.S. Vygotsky* (Vol. 5): *Child Psychology*. New York: Plenum.
Wells, G. (2002) The role of dialogue in activity theory. *Mind, Culture and Activity: An International Journal* 9, 43–66.

Whorf, B. (1956) The relation of habitual thought and behavior to language. In J.B. Carroll (ed.) *Language, Thought and Reality: Selected Writings of Benjamin Lee Whorf* (pp. 134–59). Cambridge, MA: MIT Press.
Williams, R. (1977) *Marxism and Literature*. New York: Oxford University Press.
Wittgenstein, L. (1953) *Philosophical Investigations*. New York: Macmillan.

Chapter 8
(Dis)inventing Discourse: Examples from Black Culture and Hiphop Rap/Discourse

ELAINE RICHARDSON

Introduction

Although rap music and Hiphop elements have been adopted and adapted by many cultures around the world,[1] this chapter focuses on Hiphop discourse as a subgenre and discourse system within the universe of Black discourse which includes African American Vernacular English (AAVE) and African American Music (AAM) among other diasporic expressions. The central question that guides this analysis is how rappers on the one hand display an orientation to their situated, public role as performing products and, on the other, connect their performance to discourses of authenticity and resistance.

An aspect of my project is to shed light on the connection between the discursive (dis)invention of identity and the (dis)invention of language. In attempting to do this, I bring together issues and concepts that are explored in disciplines of *folklore, ethnomusicology, sociolinguistics* and *discourse studies*. I begin by defining African American Vernacular Discourse (AAVD) as a genre system within Black diasporic discourses and in a selected sample of its various idioms, with a brief overview of the sociocultural, political and economic contexts for selected genres. I then turn to an exploration of the function and use of Hiphop/rap discourse, using the example of a rap performance by the African American Southern rap group Outkast. The analysis is informed by principles of Critical Discourse Analysis (CDA). Discourse is central to social practices and questions of power and can benefit from CDA which foregrounds the hierarchy of social structure, social inequality and unequal power arrangements. CDA illuminates the expression of such in its examination of the multiple and contradictory nature of signs and discourses. The semiosis of symbols, signs and visual imagery are also analyzed as part of discourse as they too reflect these social practices (Halliday, 1978; Fairclough & Chouliaraki, 1999; Sebeok, 2001; van Dyke, 2001).

Black and African American Vernacular Discourses

The concept and practice of Black discourse refers to the collective consciousness and expression of people of Black African descent. This consciousness reflects (unconscious and conscious) ancestral and everyday knowledge. Broadly speaking, the designation, the Diaspora of Black Discourse(s) allows us to group a range of African, Neo-African and Afro-American language varieties, expressive forms and linguistic ideologies for comparative analysis of specific historical, political, socio-cultural and sociolinguistic features. Via slavery, colonization, neo-imperialism, migration, wars, global technological processes and diasporic crossing, Continental Africans and their descendents participate in the (dis)invention and global flow of Black discourse. Black discourses are not fixed and static. They are dynamic and reflexive systems of:

> behaving, interacting, valuing, thinking, believing, speaking and often reading and writing that are accepted as instantiations of particular roles ... by specific groups of ... people. ... [Black] Discourses are ways of being ['an African descendant']. They are 'ways of being in the world'; they are 'forms of life'. They are, thus, always and everywhere *social* and products of social histories. (Adapted from Gee, 1996: viii)

It is important to draw attention to the inclusion of reading and writing or Africanized literacy in the definition of Black discourse, as literacy is informed by discourse and is an ideologically-charged social construction (Richardson, 2003).

In the North American context, we can identify African American Vernacular Discourse(s) (AAVD) by manifestations of its many signature themes and forms. It includes the various socio-cultural forms and institutions developed by African Americans to express their distinctive existence. From this perspective, there are African American ways of being and communicating that derive from particular histories, geographies and social locations. Some of these ways of being were developed during slavery and are influenced by two crucial factors: (1) the demand from dominant whites that all manner of behavior and communication of African people display their compliance with domination and supposed inferiority, and (2) African people's resistance to this demand 'through the use of existing African [communication] systems of indirectness' (Morgan, 2002: 24). As Morgan (2002: 24) explains ' ... indirectness includes an analysis of discourses of power ... .' Once the phenomenology of indirectness operated both within white supremacist encounters and African American culture and social encounters, interactions, words or phrases could have contradictory or multiple meanings beyond traditional English interpretations. The grammatical and pronunciation patterns of African American Vernacular English (AAVE) are often analyzed as apart from its ideological-discursive aspects for purposes of structural analysis. In this chapter, the emphasis is on AAVE and African American music (AAM) as part and parcel of AAVD, as all of these are inextricably linked systems and are a direct result of African–European contact on the shores of West Africa and in what became the New World. In the present work, AAVE includes the broad repertoire of themes and cultural practices as well as narrowly conceived verbal surface features used by many historic and contemporary African Americans, which indicate an alternate worldview. In other words, AAVE represents the totality of Vernacular expression. AAVE should be understood as African American survival culture. On the level of language, although the majority of the words are English in origin, their meanings are historically and contextually situated relevant to the experiences of African Americans. Further, a point that is often overlooked is that there is a Standard AAVE. Scholars of AAVE argue for an expanded conception of AAVE, whereby many speakers command a wide range of forms on the continuum from more creole-like to more standardized forms. In this sense, 'an educated, middle-class [B]lack person may express his or her identification with African American culture, free of the stigma attached to nonstandard speech [/grammar] ...' (Morgan, 2002; and see Debose, 1992; Rickford, 1987,1999).

To put it another way, African American Standard and Vernacular discourses are in dialectical and dialogic relation to other diasporic discourses, American discourses, as well as other global discourses. By extending the definition of African-American language usage beyond syntax, phonology and vocabulary to include speech acts, non-verbal behavior and cultural production, the role of language as a major influence in reality construction and symbolic action is emphasized. This makes the multi-ethnicity of symbols more apparent (Asante, 1974) and suggests that standard metalinguistic descriptions cannot capture the complexity of what is going on here. Yet it is not only linguistic metalanguages that are challenged here but also the ways in which languages are tied to identity. Everyday experiences of African Americans require heightened attention to language use and ritual performance. Uniquely Black usages of language occur in most domains of life including Street Life, Church Life and Politics. Thus, theorizing about African-American language use requires emphasis on rhetorical context, the language users, their history, values, social-cultural, political and economic position (Debose, 2001).

It is helpful to think of the linguistic continuum construct as part and parcel of the the socio-cultural continuum. From the enslavement era through the present, African American beliefs and practices are informed by those of various African cultures and respond to, borrow from and negotiate the practices of the dominant culture. The social location of the performer and the audience determine how meaning is interpreted. Social actors can manipulate various elements of the continuum in line with their rhetorical goals. When we think of African American language as inseparable from African American Discourse, we keep in mind the cultural frames, performance traditions, idioms etc that inform the expressive forms, the senses and sounds of real people conveying meaning to each other within the context of a shared (or not, depending on one's social location) set of assumptions about the nature of the world.

Residing on the upper most part of the Black Diaspora discourse continua are diverse West and Central African beliefs and practices, communication patterns and musical roots. In general, across each of these domains respectively, we can identify an African ethos that extended to the so-called New World context, beginning in the 17th-century, encompassing both sacred and secular speech, expressions and musical idioms. Though Smitherman is focusing on American Black Talk, her sentiments relate on the level of the African Diaspora. She writes: 'Black Talk crosses boundaries of age, gender, region, religion and social class because it all comes from the same source: the [Black] Experience and the [African] oral tradition embedded in that experience' (Smitherman, 2000a).

In the enslavement era in the North American context, the speech was more creole-like. The work songs employed African-oriented vocal shadings and polyrhythm to transform everyday experience into sound; the field hollers imitated sounds in the natural environment; folktales invoked African values, proverbs and characters; protest songs included Africanized indirection, signifying and critique; the spirituals employed African-derived melodies, harmonics, call and response and promoted African-influenced understandings of spirit possession. Let me, briefly, give two historical examples of the African performance tradition: corn shucking and Juba. In one sense, the performances involved in 'corn shucking' helped the enslaved to organize and endure the work of harvest time. They used songs and games to make the work bearable. The lyrics and the sound creation fed their inner and outer needs for spiritual and self-upliftment. Inwardly, the music through its use of call–response and improvization provided an individual and communal soul liberating experience. Outwardly, the occasion of the corn shucking and its accompanying festivity was an opportunity for the enslaved to be served by the house servants or sometimes even Ole Missus and Master, and to lyrically comment on life as they saw it. The lyrics below demonstrate such commentary:

Shuck corn, shell corn,
Carry corn to mill.
Grind de meal, gimme de husk;
Bake de bread, gimme de crus';
Fry de meat, gimme de skin';
And dat's de way to bring 'em in. (Perrow, 1915: 139)

I believe the verbal art of 'shuckin and jivin' evolved from this survival strategy of performing the 'corn shucking' during the 1800s. Clarence Major (1970/1994) defines 'shuckin and jivin' as 'originally, southern "Negro" expression for clowning, lying, pretense,' the term originating around the 1870s (Major, 1994). Similarly, juba – the eating of unwanted food – was sung, danced and patted out polyrhythmically to endure the harsh conditions under which these people labored. As explained by Beverly Robinson 'to prepare psychologically to eat what was usually labeled slop, [the enslaved people] made up a song that sounded like merriment but carried a double message.' Plantation owners would invite their friends over to have the song performed for them for their enjoyment. The owners were never aware of the meanings signified through the song (Robinson, 1990: 216) as seen in a brief excerpt below, comprising lyrics side by side with a translation:

| Juba this and Juba that | Means giblet this [a little of this] and giblet that [a little of that] |
| Juba killed a yella' cat | Because they couldn't say mixed-up Food might kill the white folks. They was afraid to say that because white folks'd kill them. |

(Bessie Jones, direct descendant of enslaved people as cited in Robinson (1990)

Stereotyping is a dynamic phenomenon, historically shaped by the actions of both enslavers who sought to control the enslaved, and by the enslaved to thwart the imposition. During the early 19th century, White blackface minstrelsy became the most popular form of entertainment. This phenomenon had the further effect of 'divest[ing] [B]lack people of control over elements of their culture and over their own cultural representation generally.' (Lott, 1996: 6) Ironically, by the end of the 19th century, the only performance opportunities open to Black performers was via minstrel houses, where they had to compete with the counterfeit representations of blackness provided by the White minstrels. The minstrel example provides us with a microcosmic look at the tensions embedded within discourse in society. Discourses are affected by societal phenomena and represent competing worldviews. This is not to suggest that the foundation of Black discourse is opposition to white discourse. As Smitherman (1977/1986: 42) explained, 'many aspects of black ... behavior are Africanized adaptations which can be seen as logical cultural consequences rather than as strictly racially based [sociocultural forms] reflecting black reactions to whiteness.' Thus, in our analyses of each era and domain of the African-American experience, we must bring to bear the contexts that influence African-American expression. To put it crudely these are: Slavery/rural-agrarian, Reconstruction/rural-sharecropping, Harlem Renaissance/rural-urban-industrial, Civil Rights/Black Power/post-industrial and now Post Civil Rights/informational, global digital and technological/service oriented. In this age of global information and digitization of knowledge, those with the means of global distribution control dominant definitions and representations of certain discourses through commerce. This is also true from an historical perspective. Black cultural producers had no control over outside interpretation of their work.

A Working Definition of African-American Rap/Hiphop Discourse

Why study Hiphop discourse? Hiphop is a rich site of cultural production that has pervaded and been pervaded by almost every American institution and has made an extensive global impact. Hiphop discourse, no matter how commodified or 'blaxploited', offers an interesting view of the human freedom struggle and aspects of the knowledge that people have about the world. As discussed most eloquently by Houston Baker (1984) in *Blues, Ideology, and Afro-American Literature: A Vernacular Theory.* All Afro-American narrative can be traced (in part) to an 'economics of slavery' and is tied to a bill of sale. Thus, like 'traditional' African American language data, Hiphop discourse tells us a lot about socioeconomic stratification and the struggle between culture and capital. Hiphop discourse, like previous Afro-American expressive forms is a Black creative response to absence and desire and a site of epistemological development. Though it is often seen as mere corporate orchestration, Hiphop is a site of identity negotiation, and a site that therefore challenges many common assumptions about language and identity. Unlike 'traditional' African-American language data, commercial Hiphop discourse is wholly centered within the new capitalism. The aspect of the new capitalism that pertains to this study is 'knowledge work.' That is, the insider's knowledge, business and industry are used to design products to tap certain values and create consumer identities by manipulating symbols and markets. This knowledge is recontextualized and recycled in the space of commercial Hiphop performances promoting stereotypical 'common sense' ideas about African Americans and deflecting attention away from the poor social conditions that make certain occupations or preoccupations a welcome alternative. As such, Hiphop is both associated with ethnic (Black consciousness) and national (general American) consciousness.

This being the case, many would argue that there is no authentic culture to study in rap music or Hiphop discourse for mass consumption, since rap has long become a global industry removed from its primary audience. However, study of folk culture is not constrained to isolated groups untouched by contemporary post-industrial society. Folk are 'the people who know,' who have a special knowledge from their vantage point of the world, from their routine social experiences. The discourses in which they participate are always already hybrid. From this perspective, any group can be a folk group. The study of folk groups in the contemporary world involves studying their hybridity, an aspect of which can be examined through studying the impact of technologies on the interaction of discourses, between audience, performer and the making of meaning. (Kelley, 1992)

Hiphop discourse is a genre system of AAVE/Black discourse. I prefer AAVE to encompass the other genres within the African American discourse communities because in relation to dominant discourse the total genre system is Vernacular or counterlinguistic. I want to emphasize here that this counter reality is reflective of constant engagement with dominant notions of reality. As a starting point, we may see Hiphop discourse as a subsystem in relation to African American and other discourses.

Hiphop language can be defined as influenced by African Oral Traditions of rhythmic 'talk-singing, [signifying], blending reality and fiction,' and [in the mainstream] it has come to mean any kind of strong talk or rap (Smitherman, 1994: 190). Additional African language practices employed in rap lyrics are *call–response, tonal semantics, semantic inversion/flippin' the script, mimicry, narrativizing, toasting, boasting/braggadocio, image-making* and *punning*.

Call–response is used to draw the listener into the performance. A performer uses some lyrical hook or refrain that can be easily repeated by the listener. For example, an emcee (preferred term for a skilled lyricist) shouts, 'Where the real Hiphop at?' The proper response from engaged participants is: 'Over here,' thus showing participation. Tonal semantics refers to the use of vocal inflection and vocal rhythm to convey meaning. Semantic inversion or flippin the script refers to turning a meaning into its opposite or divesting a concept of its received meaning to inscribe one reflective of the speaker's experience. Mimicry, the imitation of sounds, has the effect of critique in many cases and is used in signifying, which refers to the employment of indirection to make a point or to poke fun. Narrativizing is the story-telling mode consisting of re-living and dramatization of what went on or what is imagined to happen in the future. Toasting refers to folk poetics, while boasting and braggadocio are narrative traditions wherein the speaker/rapper asserts his or her superb and many times exaggerated characteristics or abilities. Image-making is the use of metaphorical language, tending toward the graphic, the concrete, and, for its effect, punning depends on witty use of signifiers/terms with multiple referents (see Smitherman, 1977; for fuller definitions with extended examples; see also Smitherman, 2000b: 268–283 for a discussion of the Communicative Practices of the Hiphop Nation).

Hiphop language is graphic and brash, 'and it adheres to the pronunciation and grammar of [AAVE] ...' (Smitherman, 1994: 18). Hiphop lexicon is largely provided by AAVE speakers, with some words donated from Spanish, Caribbean Englishes and from graffiti vocabulary (argot):

> 'Hiphop's language ideology is consciously and often defiantly based on urban African American norms, values and popular culture constructed against dominant cultural and linguistic norms. It thus relies on the study, knowledge and use of [AAVE] and General American Vernacular English [GAVE] linguistic features and principles of grammaticalization. (Morgan, 2001: 188)

As such, AAVE discourses, in any of their genres, are highly reflexive systems of communication. By reflexive I mean that certain linguistic/semiotic/discourse/literacy practices are used in certain contexts precisely because of the situation of use. Historically, African-American language and people have been represented in society as coming from a debased culture, and that's the best case scenario. The worse is that Blacks have no culture, no language. This rhetorical situation should draw attention to the ways in which Hiphop discourse, like other Black discourse, is masked inside English as lingua franca. Black discourses are survival francas, since their use is tied to capital, which one needs to survive in this world, and as such they unsettle the centrality and conception of language in lingua franca. The notion of linguistic market seems particularly appropriate here.

'the linguistic market, in fact, is part of a broader symbolic market, and one can see the self as the commodity that is being produced for value in the market. Thus one is both agent and commodity' (Eckert, 2000: 13). From this vantage point, the sounds, visual images, identities, labels, names etc. associated with Afro-American language, discourses and people are largely a heterogeneous set established historically, institutionally and economically by those with power to assign meaning, worth and value.

This presents a dilemma for rap performers, since their narratives are commodified in the global economy of rap music and Hiphop culture, leaving them in the popular imagination as agentless narrators compliant in their own oppression. The mantra of Hiphoppers, 'keep it real,' reflects their preoccupation with authenticity, which is often popularly understood as emphasis on surviving a hostile society, variously interpreted as the hood, the streets, the system, 'the real.' The ability to survive, 'to make a way outta no way,' and to rhythmically narrate this experience in such a way that it resonates with the primary audience is what is at stake in evaluation of rappers' performance, delivery, style, as authentic. Given that rap music and rappers are seen as commodities globally marketed largely by exploitation of stereotypical language and images of 'niggas,' 'pimps,' 'gangstas,' 'militants,' 'hos,' 'bitches' and 'bucks,' how do they on the one hand display an orientation to their situated, public role as performing products and on the other create a performance that is connected to discourses of authenticity and resistance? This chapter takes up these aspects of communication together with the social, cultural and political positioning of social actors. In the few examples I discuss here, I focus on the relationship between linguistic and social stereotypes. These stereotypes are realized both on the levels of surface features and discourse. I employ the term stereotype in two senses. In one sense, it is used to refer to a generic cultural model, the way that we understand and organize the world, storylines, connected images, informal theories, received symbolic forms, 'shared by people belonging to specific social or cultural groups' (Gee, 1999: 81). The other sense in which I use stereotype is as it refers to dominant discourse practices concerning African Americans, including 'common sense' prejudiced statements, discriminatory behavior, that often go uncontested as normal and acceptable. What I hope to demonstrate is rappers' exploitation of linguistic stereotypes to upset and redefine social reality from meanings rooted in their everyday experiences, thereby (dis)inventing identity and language. In what follows, I will offer examples of rappers' (dis)invention of dominant and socially constructed stereotypes.

'OutKast' of the Whole World

To reiterate, the communicative styles and ways of knowing of the performers can be traced to Black Vernacular expressive arts developed by African Americans as resistance and survival strategies. Many of the experiences such as racism, police brutality, miseducation and identity imposition are issues that are fundamental to the African-American struggle and are dealt with in various cultural expressions. Thus, rap performances, like all expressive forms, must be considered in relation to beliefs, values, mores and complex ideologies that underlie the street apparel, hard body imagery and the sometimes seeming celebration of misogyny, thuggishness, and larger-than-life personas narrated in the music. One way to look at the celebration of gangsta practices, thuggishness, rampant materialism and apparent disrespect for law and mainstream values in hiphop is in relation to Black vernacular folk epic story and song tradition. In African American culture, there are two character types in particular that appear in rap music – the 'bad nigger' and the badman or badwoman. The 'bad nigger' is a type of trickster that defies dominant mainstream values and sometimes those of traditional Afro-American culture. He 'threatens the solidarity and harmony of the group' and may bring potential harm to everyone (Roberts, 1989: 199). Conversely, the badman/badwoman is an amalgamation of the trickster and the conjurer and is associated with a secular lifestyle that appeals to some segments of the Black community for 'badmanism' offered an alternate route to success through gambling or some other illegal activities (Roberts, 1989: 206). The badman often resorted to gun violence in an act of self-defense or victimization. Imani Perry's discussion of the outlaw aesthetic in Afro-American culture is very instructive:

> The outlaw image appears in very obvious symbols and metaphors in the music, but it also exists on a more esoteric level in the intellectual world of hiphop. The name of the rap duo OutKast is brilliant for its concise articulation and celebration of the life behind the Du Boisian veil. The ease with which African Americans can accept conspiracy theories as truth lends evidence to this distinct outcast epistemological framework. Given the inconsistency between the constitutional and symbolic meanings of Americanness and the experiences of African Americans, we are left with a healthy suspicion and curiosity. Outkast centralizes the position of Otherness as a site of privileged knowledge and potential. (Perry, 2004: 107)

The performance embodied in the recording and video of the song 'the Whole World' by the rap duo, Outkast, seems highly reflexive and explicitly conscious of the rhetorical situation. It employs several contentious stereotypes and is careful to connect itself to the blues and jazz traditions. The performance isn't easily dismissed as wholesale corporate orchestration.

The music, lyrics and visuals invoke meanings through sounds, images and ideographs that underscore the discursive dialectic of dominant and vernacular discourses. In the examples that follow, it is helpful to keep in mind that southern stereotypes associated with the south, also affected rappers who were seen as 'country' and backward until 'Dirty South' rap caught on. Although we can cite numerous Southern rap songs that invoke angst, aggression and opposition to the status quo, Southern rap can still be identified by some industry powerbrokers as happy music.[2] Rapper, David Banner, explains, 'Many labels look at Southern rap as happy black music because there is so much emotion in it. But because we're not time-traveling through the pyramids doesn't mean we can't be deep.'[3]

'The Whole World' video is set in the Big Top, the circus. Both the setting and the title suggest a major theme of the song: the whole world is a stage, life is a play and everyone is cast in supported roles. Though the lead actors are expected to bring their own knowledge of the world into their characters, the roles are scripted. One has to be very creative to manipulate meaning inside this structure. The circus decontextualizes and exploits performances by trained animals, people, or clowns, for example, and (re)presents them as strange, spectacular or exotic. Similarly, the apparatuses of the global world power reduce culture to decontextualized commodities and cultural workers to panderers. These themes are demonstrated throughout the performance.

One of the rappers, Andre, wears a White face, clownish, voodoo-styled make up and a blondish-white wig, which invokes a host of associations (Figure 8.1).

In its popular digital representation, the painted Black male is presented as spectacle, invoking as his make up suggests a clownish-voodooish image. The Black man as clown reinscribes the mocking image of a 'backward' people – not to be taken seriously. But upon further inspection we know that the clown's surface movements and expressions of hilarity reflect solemn observations about the human condition. Similarly, Voodoo as a cultural practice and way of understanding the world became taboo among most Americans and reduced to a commodity, thriving in dominant discourse as witchcraft, fortune-telling, 'mumbo-jumbo.' In the popular imagination voodoo is cheap entertainment, something that can be bought for $1.99 per minute from actors like 'Miss Cleo.' In the North American South, Voodoo was a total belief system that included ancestral religious traditions, herbal and medical care for the oppressed community unavailable to them by any other means.

Concomitantly, the Black male wearing white face-image troubles the central concepts of minstrelsy: (1) the presentation of authentic blackness by Whites, alternatively termed, the White stereotype of blackness; and (2) the White stereotype of whiteness. The white paint and the blonde wig on a Black body symbolize Whites' view of blackness through whiteness, and Blacks' distortion of 'superior' whiteness. Conversely, Blacks' struggle against this imposed worldview creates authenticity within Black culture.

Not only do visual images in the video represent these contesting discourses, AAVE phonological and lexical systems are also employed by the rappers to (dis)invent or reinscribe and upset stereotypes, such as that

Figure 8.1 Representation of rapper in clownish White face/voodoo styled make up

of the Ignorant N—. Historically, racist discourse embued the southern Black person (and lower class whites) with qualities such as slow, dim witted.[4] Their speech supposedly reflected their limitations. However, many African American speech patterns are remnants of African heritage, or reinterpretations of English. In either case, they are part of African-American culture. Conscious use of such speech patterns then on the part of African-American rappers signals their refusal of a negative evaluation of their Black heritage.

The Black speech pattern, vocalized intersyllabic /r/ is used in the first lyrical phrase of the song: 'Yeah I'm afraid like I'm sca'ed as a dog.' Conscious inscription of Black Southern identity linguistically ushers forth both Black and dominant interpretations of the meaning of this phrase. This pattern of employing southern Black speech is continued throughout and realized in the rapper's use of lexical items such as 'sing' and 'along' as [saNg] and [ŭlooNg], where the medial vowel sound, the open 'o' is prolonged to produce a stereotypical 'southern drawl.' This elongated open 'o' occurs four times in the opening verse of the song. Inventing and then rupturing the symbols of Black southern ignorance underscores the synthetic nature of language.

AAVE verbs such as 'git down' (in the line – 'the whole worl loves it when you don't git down, ohwn') are employed in a way that defies unequivocal interpretation. 'Git down' means 'to do something enthusiastically' or to make progress. However, in this context it is preceded by the negator 'don't.' As such, the phrase could mean 'don't git up,' the opposite of 'git down' (or to make no progress). This coupled with the AAVE phonological marker [I] in 'git' where more mainstream varieties of English use /E/ invokes multiple and competing discourses. In this sense, 'don't git down' is an example of signifying, where signifying is 'a way of encoding messages or meanings which involves, in most cases, an element of indirection' (Mitchell-Kernan quoted in Gates, 1988: 80). A mainstream American English interpretation of 'don't git down' is 'don't feel sad.' Historically, this stereotype invokes the happy darky. Recall that Black social cultural forms such as Juba were interpreted by outsiders to represent the enslaved populations' contentment with their condition as represented by their singing and dancing. This interpretation becomes more apparent when examined within the context of the chorus, where the phrase occurs, which I take to represent the thematic significance of the song. The chorus phrase 'Cause the whole worl loves it when you don't git down' is functioning as a cohesive device. The chorus begins with the discourse connector 'cause.' This suggests support or evidence for the views expressed in the lines that precede it. One reading of the phrase is, the whole world knows about

Blacks, in this case the stereotype presented, The Ignorant N/Ignorant Southern N.

Another discourse marker used to (re)invent or (re)present and contest the Ignorant N Stereotype is onomatopoeia, as it is used to represent nonsense syllables, though of course they make sense to the utterer. In recurring lines of the chorus, the *onomatopoeic phrase*, sung in a jazz scat style, *'Bah bah da, bah bah bah da da'* symbolizes dissonance between dominant and Black culture and their differences in the consumption of Black sociocultural forms. Onomatopoeia is a sign whose phonetic shape resembles its referent in some sense. In this context, then, the non-sense syllables are representative of the decontextualized and digitally diffused Black sound. For the primary audience, ultimately, Black sounds function to sustain life, but as we move away from the primary rap audience, or from the origins of Black culture, Black sounds are not fully understood as core culture but appreciated as popular sources of revenue, entertainment and Black Noise. Metaphorical variation also indexes the Ignorant N/Southern Black identity stereotype. The phrase 'Yeah I'm afraid like I'm sca'ed as a dog,' already mentioned, invokes the stereotype of the unreasonably- afraid unmanly subhuman coward that was made popular at the height of White American minstrelsy. Similarly, another metaphor employed in the lyrics 'raining inside' (as in 'this is the way that we walk on a sunny day when it's raining inside and you're all aloo-own ... ') signifies a dark and dreary existence or a blues mood. As I've already indicated the metaphor 'don't git down' invokes the 'happy darky.'

The next example employs metaphorical variation and /r/ variation, signaled in zero postvocalic 'r' as in the following: 'Whateva floats yo boat or finds yo lost remote.' The interpretations of the metaphor 'whateva floats yo boat' in the context of this performance signal floating as the ability to go with the tide, 'life preservance,' 'being suspended near the surface' and 'fluctuating freely in relationship to other currencies, as determined by supply and demand: said of a currency (*Webster's New World College Dictionary*: 517). Certainly these possible meanings implicate the commodification of Black performance but they also raise the issue of a certain agency within that commodification. Similarly, 'Finds yo lost remote' indicates movement away in time or in space as a method of agency. Taken together, the metaphors in these lines point to the continuity of the struggle whether survival strategies are interpreted as superficial and contemporary or distant and historical, they are deeply rooted, interconnected and linked to the interlocking systems of racism, patriarchy and capitalism.

The stereotype of the Bad N— is invoked, inscribed and upset by several African-American communication practices among them /r/ vocalization, the dozens, braggadocio and homonymy. Most of the uses of intersyllabic and postvocalic /r/ occur in words or phrases which signal the Bad Man language tradition in Afro-American folklore. The Bad Man's roots are in the African trickster. In the North American context, he surfaces in animal tales. As previously mentioned, the Bad Man also represents defiance of White authority from slavery through freedom:

> He is disdainful of social conventions ... breaks rules, violates taboos and ... is not intimidated by the law, the police, or even the devil ... . Despite the fact that his exploits are self-serving and sometimes at the expense of his community members (including African American women, who are often sexually objectified), this figure continues to endure, some folklorists conjecture, because he suggests a defiance to racial oppression and submission. (Gilyard, 2004)

For intersyllabic /r/ vocalization in AAVE lexicon, we have a number of terms: 'quarter' [kwatə], 'shorts' [shawtz] and 'sports' [spawtz]. Postvocalic /r/ can be noted in terms like 'hater' [heðə], 'sucker' [suckə], 'quarter' [kwatə], 'daughter' [dawtə], nigga [niggə], 'meter' [mɪtə], 'neither' [nɪðə], 'weather' [wɛə], 'brother' [bruðə], 'sever' [sɛvə], 'whatever' [wutɛvə] and 'your' [yo].

The commanding phrase, 'Take a little trip hata pack up your mind,' where the Hiphop lexical item 'hater' is a shortened version of 'player hater,' indicates an envious person, one who expresses extreme dislike for another's success in any life endeavor, especially envious of a man who has multiple relationships. It is also used in response to negative criticism. The persona in this verse could be understood as speaking to an oppositional audience, perhaps one which does not like or understand the rapper's performance. One of the song's lines, 'I caught a sucka dyin cause he thought he could rhyme,' employs 'sucka' a general AAVE term for an unhip person. It can be interpreted here as a dis, an example of signifying in the sense of witty put down (Smitherman 1977).

The zero 'r' in the phrases 'th'ow the porsche at you' and 'th'ow a shell in it' evinces AAVE Bad Man braggadocio and alludes to Black struggle. Both literally and figuratively, the Black social actor manipulates words, materials and identities to survive rhetorically and physically: 'th'ow the porsche at you' refers to ways in which Black sociocultural forms serve to colonize new markets and yet offer some semblance of freedom to cultural workers. In particular, the phrase points to the rappers as sellers of American and global products and representatives of the so-called American dream. The rapper is used as a tool of oppression yet symbolizes freedom to those similarly situated in the global ranks of the dispossessed.

Homonymy is another process whereby Hiphop discourse wreaks lexical havoc against the establishment. In the lyrics of this song, several referents function as homonyms. In its technical sense, a word would have to appear more than once and used to indicate different referents in order to be classified as a homonym. Here, however, certain words are only used once creating a black hole, if you will, in the sense of highly condensed energy, that pack multiple meanings into one signifier. The signifiers 'stage' and 'battle' in the context of this song could be read as underscoring the topos of role playing in the historical Black struggle, as 'stage' refers multiply to 'stage' as platform, 'stage' as movement in time, stage as to represent or present. Battle can also be interpreted multiply as 'verbal dual' or 'struggle/conflict.' Similarly, the term 'crack' is invoked. The foremost stereotypic role that it invokes is Blacks as drug-dealers of crack, that 'highly purified cocaine in small chips used illicitly usually for smoking [or for selling]' (*Meriam Webster's Online*). 'Crack' also refers to violence as in 'a sharp resounding blow.' Dominant discourse has encoded the negative aspects of these stereotypes into the language and foisted them more heavily onto Blacks than other social groups. Cleverly, as he is wont to do, the rapper seeks to break this chain with his own 'crack' as in 'a witty remark,' with language, as another pertinent sense of 'crack' reveals. 'Shell' referred to in the phrase 'th'ow a shell in it' also functions as a homonym. It has four relevant and distinct meanings. First, shell conjures a symbol of ancient Africa, the cowry shell, which has been used as money, jewelry and as a charm among other things. The second meaning of shell – outside covering – refers to the 'masks' that people are required to wear for various rhetorical purposes. Another possible meaning of shell refers to inside covering – not letting the world know one's true identity or feelings. And still another meaning of shell is explosive. All of these senses of 'shell' draw attention to the topos of the performance of identities.

Finally, 'shades' also functions homonymically. In the phrase: 'I take my shades off,' 'shades' reinforces the topic of identity performance, as 'shade' indicates 'darkness' 'gradation of color' and 'difference of variation.' 'Shades' also references the Black way of being and knowing known as cool, since sunglasses or shades are a symbol of cool. As such, *taking one's shades off* indexes that burdensome social practice of multiplying oneself, but also the yearning toward a more unified self or unmasked self. To reiterate, these surface features represent stereotypes that are connected to discourses.

The emphasis here is on the multiplicity of meanings and their reception in a crossover context – that is – who one is, in relation to the performer determines the meanings that will be selected as authentic. The job of the Black performer is to manipulate and (dis)invent Black discourses as is rhetorically convenient, to open the semantic field so that there is a wider space for meaning-making potential, while simultaneously indicating privileged Black meanings that resonate within specific contexts of production and reception. The use of stereotypes confirms an awareness of self-representation among the performers, how Black people are represented to themselves within society. Rappers constantly re-create, reshape and reinvent these forms to reaffirm Black humanity. What is often overlooked and perhaps should be restated here is that Black discourse is reflexive and reflective of the context from which it emanates: tied to capital, tied to a bill of sale but also struggling to define self. This is true of hiphop as a subgenre within Black discourse as well.

Societal values are embedded within hiphop, as Black discourses struggle for self-definition in the face and space of languages and systems of domination that would annihilate them. Although Hiphop reinvents and recycles African diasporic performance traditions and ways of knowing, it is naive to think that [Black people] have:

> somehow lived in American society for hundreds of years and yet have remained untouched, uninfluenced by the world around us. It is this romanticized notion of our blackness (the myth of the noble savage) that allows many people to refuse to see that the social orders of black [discourses are themselves stratified to the core]. (adapted from hooks, 1981: 116)

Paying serious attention to these forms may help us to understand cultural change in this current phase of global imperialism.

OutKast's performance in the 'Whole World' is richly complex and clearly not exhausted in this brief explication. My point, however, is to show that the best rap performances reflect the tensions apparent between dominant and subordinate discourses. In the tradition of Black discourse, Black social actors reject imposed definitions and seek to reinscribe their own versions of reality from their perspectives. In using these trickster discourses to survive hostile conditions, rappers exploit linguistic stereotypes to upset and redefine social reality from meanings rooted in their everyday experience, thereby (dis)inventing relationships between identity and language. Where conventional Anglo-American discourses attempt to ascribe certain language forms to certain identities, or particular identities to language forms, Hiphop discourses cross African American, General American English, Caribbean English and Spanish among other language backgrounds to move the crowds and shift the framing of identities tied to those languages. Through African-American oral traditions, they recall African language histories from before the European invention of languages and imposition of metadiscursive regimes, drawing on language possibilities that can cross, challenge and unravel hostile conditions. They are constantly inventing, (dis)inventing, redefining and reconstructing language to meet their needs and goals and thus constantly engaged in the discursive (dis)invention of identity and the (dis)invention of language.

Notes

1. Japan, New Zealand, Bosnia, Italy, Spain, France, Germany, South Africa, Canada and Hawaii are examples. For more see Tony Mitchell (2001).
2. Some examples would be Lil John & the East Side Boyz 'Don't Fuck Wit Me' (Kings of Crunk), Gangsta Boo 'Life in the Metro' (Enquiring Minds), Slim Thug's 'Click Clack' (Already Platinum) and David Banner 'Ain't Got Nuthin' (Certified).
3. On WWW at http://www.rapnewsdirect.com/News/0-202-257306-00.html#.

References

Alim, H.S. (2003) We are the streets: African-American language and the strategic construction of a street conscious identity. In S. Makoni, G. Smitherman, A. Ball and A. Spears (eds) *Black Linguistics: Language, Society and Politics in Africa and the Americas*. London: Routledge.

Alleyne, M. (1980) *Comparative Afro-American: An Historical-Comparative Study of English-Based Afro-American Dialects of The New World*. Ann Arbor: Karoma.

American Tongues (1987) Videorecording. New York: Center for New American Media.

Asante, M. (1974) A metatheory for Black communication. Paper presented at the Annual Meeting of the New York State Speech Association, Loch Sheldrake, April. ERIC Document ED 099945.

Baker, H. (1984) *Blues, Ideology and Afro-American Literature: A Vernacular Theory*. Chicago: The University of Chicago Press.

Chude-Sokei, L. (1997) Dread discourse and Jamaican sound systems. In J.K. Adjaye and A.R. Andrews (eds) *Language, Rhythm and Sound: Black Popular Cultures into the Twenty-First Century* (pp. 185–202). Pittsburgh, PA: University of Pittsburgh Press.

Debose, C. (1992) Codeswitching: Black English and Standard English in the African-American linguistic repertoire. *Journal of Multilingual and Multicultural Development* 13 (1&2), 157–167.

Debose, C. (2001) The status of Variety X in the African American linguistic repertoire. Paper given at the New Ways of Analyzing Variation in English (NWAVE) Conference, October.

Eckert, P. (2000) *Linguistic Variation as Social Practice*. Oxford: Blackwell Publishers.

Fairclough, N. and Chouliaraki, L. (1999) *Discourse in Late Modernity*. Edinburgh University Press.

Fishman, J. (1997) Language, ethnicity, and racism. In N. Coupland and A. Jaworski (eds) *Sociolinguistics: A Reader* (pp. 329–340) New York: St Martin's Press.

Gates, H.L. Jr (1988) *The Signifying Monkey: A Theory of Afro American Literary Criticism*. New York: Harvard University Press.

Gee, J. (1996) *Social Linguistics and Literacies: Ideology in Discourses*. London & Bristol, PA: Taylor & Francis.
Gee, J. (1999) *An Introduction to Discourse Analysis: Theory and Method*. New York: Routledge.
Gilyard, K. and Wardi, A. (2004) African American folklore. In *African American Literature*. New York: Longman.
Halliday, M.A.K. (1978) *Language as a Social Semiotic*. Baltimore, MD: University Park Press.
hooks, b. (1981) *Ain't I a Woman: Black Women and Feminism*. Boston: South End Press.
Kelley, R. (1992) Notes on deconstructing the 'Folk.' *The American Historical Review* 97 (5), Research Library Core, 1400–1408.
Lott, E. (1996) Blackface and blackness: The minstrel show in American culture. In A. Bean, J. Hatch and B. McNamara (eds) *Inside the Minstrel Mask: Readings in Nineteenth-Century Blackface Minstrelsy* (pp. 3–32). Hanover: Wesleyan University Press.
Major, C. (1994) *Juba to Jive: A Dictionary of African-American Slang*. Penguin Books.
Maultsby, P. (1991) Africanisms in African American music. In J. Holloway (ed.) *Africanisms in American Culture*. Vloomington, IN: Indiana University Press
Meriam Webster's Online Dictionary. On WWW at http://www.m-w.com.
Mitchell, T. (2001) Introduction: Another root, Hip Hop outside the USA. In T. Mitchell (ed.) *Global Noise: Rap and Hip-Hop Outside the USA*. Middletown, CT: Wesleyan University Press.
Mitchell-Kernan, C. (1988) Signifying. In H.L. Gates Jr *The Signifying Monkey: A Theory of Afro American Literary Criticism*. New York: Harvard University Press.
Morgan, M. (1994) The African American speech community: Reality and sociolinguistics. In M. Morgan (ed.) *Language and the Social Construction of Identity in Creole Situations* (pp. 251–281). Los Angeles: UCLS Center for Afro-American Studies.
Morgan, M. (2001) 'Nuthin But a G Thang': Grammar and language ideology in hiphop identity. In S. Lanehart (ed.) *Sociocultural and Historical Contexts of African American English* (pp. 187–209). Philadelphia: John Benjamins Publishing Company.
Morgan, M. (2002) *Language, Discourse and Power in African American Culture*. Cambridge: Cambridge University Press.
Perrow, E.C. (1915) Shuck corn. *The Journal of American Folk-lore* 28, 139.
Perry, I. (2004) *Prophets of the Hood: Politics and Poetrics in Hip Hop*. Durham, NC: Duke University Press.
Rickford, J. (1987) *Dimensions of a Creole Continuum*. Stanford: Stanford University Press.
Rickford, J. (1999) *African American Vernacular English: Features, Evolution, Educational Implications*. Oxford: Blackwell.
Richardson, E. (2003) *African American Literacies*. New York: Routledge.
Roberts, J.W. (1989) *From Trickster to Badman: The Black Folk Hero in Slavery and Freedom*. Philadelphia, PA: University of Pennsylvania Press.
Robinson, B. (1990) Africanisms in the study of folklore. In J. Holloway (ed.) *Africanisms in American Culture*. Bloomington, IN: Indiana University Press.
Sebeok, T. (2001) *Global Semiotics*. Bloomington, IN: Indiana University Press.

Smitherman, G. (1977/1986) *Talkin and Testifyin: The Language of Black America* (reissued with revisions). Boston: Hougton Mifflin, and Detroit: Wayne State University Press.
Smitherman, G. (1994) *Black Talk: Words and Phrases from the Hood to the Amen Corner.* Boston: Houghton Mifflin.
Smitherman, G. (2000a) *Black Talk: Words and Phrases from the Hood to the Amen Corner* (revd edn). Boston: Houghton Mifflin.
Smitherman, G. (2000b) *Talkin that Talk: Language, Culture and Education in African America.* New York: Routledge.
Southern Rap. On WWW at http://www.rapnewsdirect.com/News/0-202- 257306-00.html#.
van Dyke, T. (2001) Critical discourse analysis. In D. Schriffin, D. Tannen and H. Hamilton (eds) *The Handbook of Discourse Analysis* (pp. 352–371). Malden, MA: Blackwell Publishers.
Webster's New World College Dictionary (1997) 3rd edn. New York: Simon & Schuster Macmillan Company.

Chapter 9
Educational Materials Reflecting Heteroglossia: Disinventing Ethnolinguistic Differences in Bosnia-Herzegovina

BRIGITTA BUSCH and JÜRGEN SCHICK

Introduction

Heteroglossic situations in classrooms are rather the rule than the exception, not only in urban spaces where the issue of the multilingual school is debated widely in academics and in politics, but also in situations that might correspond at first sight to what for a long time has been considered the norm, the monolingual classroom. This then becomes especially visible when, in the context of wider political changes, sudden shifts in language policy orientations also occur. Although processes of globalization and regionalization as well as the formation of larger political units beyond the level of nation state have de-centred the role of the nation state in many domains, language policies and education policies are still firmly rooted within the nation state paradigm. As educational materials for school usage are usually centrally produced and commissioned by national authorities, they not only reflect and shape national identities on the discursive level, but are also considered as a means of promoting a single unified standard as the national language or one of the national languages. In their strictly normative orientation, they not only often fail to build on the learners' own language resources, but can also accentuate processes of exclusion as they do not allow for deviation and variation, and emphasise the symbolic bond between national/ethnic identity and language.

In this chapter we focus on the development of the school manual *Pogledi* ('*Views*') (2000) designed for primary schools throughout Bosnia-Herzegovina (BiH) where in the present post-conflict situation language policies tend to emphasise national/ethnic differences by promoting the use of distinct 'pure' standard forms. The manual is based on a radically new approach, consisting mainly of authentic texts, i.e. texts with no didactic or linguistic intervention. Literary texts, newspaper articles, advertisements and so on used in the book were left in their original form. The texts in the book thus represent a wide range of language in use: they mirror the heteroglossia (Bakhtin, 1981) of the Bosnian society. The manual allows pupils and teachers to recognize themselves and their linguistic practices in at least some of the texts, and relieves them from the pressure of a single prescribed standard. In the first section we will focus on recent language developments in the space[1] of former Yugoslavia. In the second[2] we will give an overview of recent political developments in Bosnia-Herzegovina and particularly the ethnic divisions that still characterize the school system. The final section reflects our experiences during the development of the manual *Pogledi*.

Unification vs. Division: Language Policies in the Space of former Yugoslavia

The history of the Socialist Federal Republic of Yugoslavia (SFRJ) can be characterized as a sensitive, sometimes fragile equilibrium between centralistic and federalistic forces. Centrifugal and centripetal tendencies expressed themselves also in the debates around language and language policies. The South Slav space is usually described as a language continuum beginning at the Alpine mountain range in the north and stretching right to the shores of the Black Sea. Segmentation into different languages was determined by extralinguistic factors and depended on the respective political centres (Neweklowsky 2000). The number of officially recognized languages in the area varied. Until World War II there were three: Slovenian, Serbocroatian and Bulgarian. In 1944, when the Federal Yugoslav Republic of Macedonia was founded, the number rose to four. To regroup the varieties spoken in the area of the member republic into an official standard language and to name it Macedonian was a compromise between the Serbian side, which claimed the Macedonian dialects as Serbian, and the Bulgarian side, which insisted on them being Bulgarian (Bugarksi 2004).

In 1954 an agreement was signed concerning language use in the Bosnian, Croatian, Montenegroan and Serbian member republics. It confirmed that Serbo-Croatian/Croato-Serbian was the official language in all four member republics, and allowed variation at the levels of lexikon, syntax and phonetics as, for example, the parallel and equal use of the ekavian and jekavian[3] variant. Within the logic of imagining the South Slavic space as a language continuum, ekavian is usually attributed to the eastern parts (mainly Serbia) and jekavian to the western areas (Croatia, Bosnia, Montenegro). That the notion of the language continuum was an idealized construct to promote the idea of unity in diversity became clear in the course of the more recent Yugoslav history when the 'Croatian spring' movement in the 1970s stipulated the recognition of a separate Croat language and based this claim on emphasizing a centuries-long tradition of a distinct Croat literary language. Škiljan (2001: 96) in his historic account of the linguistic situation in the South Slavic space draws attention to the fact that the notion of a dialect continuum is only a partial representation because historically there were also simultaneously different idioms present: the languages of changing state administrations (e.g. the Ottoman Empire, the Austro-Hungarian Monarchy, the Kingdom of Serbs, Croats and Slovenes), different liturgical languages (e.g. Latin, Old Church Slavonic), idioms used in literary production with supra-dialectical or supra-vernacular systemic features, each with its own linguistic community (and with individuals participating in more than one community), with its own communicative efficiency and with its own symbolic power. Škiljan's examples mainly refer to pre-nation state periods when the use of a particular idiom had a social rather than a territorial connotation.

In the middle of the 1980s the first indications of the disintegration of the Yugoslav state became apparent, as, on the political level, the centres in the member republics gained in importance over the central state authorities. The Communist party split into six ethnonational parties that were eager to control the public sphere in their relative territories (Puhovski, 2000: 42). Borders became a central topic in political and media discourses, and Dragičević-Šešić (2001: 72) speaks of an 'obsession with maps' which 'flooded the cultural space'. There were different kinds of maps, 'ethnic' maps, 'historical' maps – showing the picture of the inner borders as quite different to what then were the actual borders between the Yugoslav member republics. Later these 'simple lines on maps became true borders, obstacles to human communication' (Dragičević-Šešić, 2001: 75), 'people have gone, been killed, expelled or forcibly settled on all sides, and mostly out of zones the maps prescribed' (Dragičević-Šešić, 2001: 84). Borders were reified and constructed as 'natural' dividing lines and had an external dimension – as a separation line between the successor states, and as an internal dimension excluding 'others' from the national consensus (Hodžić, 2000: 24).

Referring to ethnic conflicts, Bourdieu makes the point (1982: 138) that borders are not to be considered as a 'natural' category, but as social and political constructs. He emphasizes that the drawing of borders is linked to constructing, deconstructing and re-constructing social groups. This is linked, as he states, with a particular vision of the world affirmed by demarcation from other world visions, and there is a dialectic relationship between these world visions and social practices. Pushing Bourdieu's argument a little further, the drawing of borders encompasses also a dimension of discursive constructedness, since discursive acts are one form of social practice through which social actors constitute objects of knowledge, situations and social roles as well as identities. Discursive acts are socially constitutive in a variety of ways being largely responsible for the production, the maintenance as well as the transformation of social conditions. Or as Wodak *et al*. (1999: 8) put it '... through linguistic representation in various dialogic contexts, discursive practices may influence the formation of groups.' Similarly it can be argued that language boundaries are social, political and discursive constructs. In this context metalinguistic discourses need particular attention (Busch, Kelly-Holmes, 2004).

In the process of the disintegration of the former Yugoslavia in the 1990s, language played a crucial role in political and media discourses that aimed at affirming state boundaries between the newly-founded nation states. Whereas Serbo-Croatian/Croato-Serbian had been the official state language in the Federal Republic of Yugoslavia, the newly founded nation states declared Croatian (1990) and Serbian (1992) as the official languages in the respective states and Bosnian/Croatian/Serbian (1993) in Bosnia-Herzegovina. With these steps, the Serbo-Croatian/Croato-Serbian language ceased to exist on the political and on the legal level. Or as the well known writer Rada Iveković puts it:

> In the name of the (national) ideal – defined as an aim to achieve – language was seen as a means to materialize what had not actually come into being. ... Linguistic reform promoted by the state aimed at transforming society ... These transformations should extinguish the preceding system and wipe out memories linked to this time as well as denominate the new concept and the social and political context. (Rada Iveković, 2001, translation by B. Busch)

Constructing and Affirming Language Boundaries

Linguistic activities in the different states tended to emphasize differences, and a range of standard language reference works – dictionaries, grammars, orthographies – appeared. In Serbia 'difference' was mainly labelled through promoting the Cyrillic script as the Serbian national script. In public the idea of the Cyrillic script being imperilled by the current practice of the equal use of both Cyrillic and Latin scripts was launched and the defence of the Cyrillic seen as national duty. The constitutional amendments adopted in 1989 still allowed the Latin script for ethnically mixed regions, but prescribed that the official script in Serbia is Cyrillic. Consequently Latin inscriptions disappeared from public spaces, state-controlled media and school manuals. Latin script was pushed into the background and reduced more or less to the private domain. The defence of the Cyrillic was a topic not only in the media but also in intellectual circles. For example, at the university of Belgrade a society for the protection of the Cyrillic was founded with the aim to 'prevent the annihilation of the Cyrillic script as the first step in the annihilation of the Serbian national identity' (cf. Jakšić, 2001: 14).

In 1993, when the war in Bosnia-Herzegovina was raging, the potentates in Republika Srpska, the Serbian part of Bosnia-Herzegovina, aligned their efforts of 'language cleansing' to the 'motherland' by adopting not only the Cyrillic script but also by prescribing in 1993 the ekavian variant for public use. In fact the authorities were well aware that the ekavian variant which is widely spread in Serbia was not used in the Serbian part of Bosnia in daily practice. The idea was that the 'ekavica should be given back to the people to which it belongs ... in order to liberate it from foreign influences.'[4] All media were compelled by law to the exclusive employment of the ekavica and the Cyrillic script. In schools the manuals produced in Belgrade (in the Cyrillic script and in ekavian) were in use. The forced ekavization ended in a fiasco, and in 1998 the Republica Srpska authorities had to revise their decision and to re-allow the use of the jekavian variant in the public domain.

In Croatia a number of linguistic advice handbooks for a large general public appeared and were circulated among journalists and school teachers. Differential dictionaries that listed words labelled as Serbian and gave their Croatian equivalents were published in cheap pocket editions. It is interesting to note that there are considerable differences between these dictionaries, not only in the number of lexical items they list, but also in general orientation. Some represent an extreme attempt at purism, drawing on lexical items which stem from the language reform introduced by the totalitarian NDH[5] state during World War II, others are more 'moderate' (Okuka, 1998: 88; Langston, 1999: 186f). The aim of such dictionaries and handbooks was, as formulated by certain authors, 'to bear witness to the existence of a separate Croat language' (Brodnjak, 1991; cf. Langston, 1999: 187) and to assist people who are 'striving to speak good Croatian in daily life to demonstrate their national consciousness also by means of language' (Pavuna, 1993; cf. Langston, 1999: 180). The authorities in the Croatian part of Bosnia aligned their language policy with the Croatian 'motherland'. Official documents and media appearing in the Croatian part of Bosnia followed the linguistic guidelines produced in Zagreb.

While in the Serbian part of Bosnia-Herzegovina language policies endeavoured to fortify the links with the respective 'motherlands', in the Bosnian/Bosniak part, authorities were eager to affirm their independence by promoting another standard which emphasized turcisms[6] as inherently Bosnian and stressed differences in orthography. In the Bosnian language handbook, which also lists 'correct' and 'incorrect' words, language is coupled with national duty and loyalty as expressed in the foreword: 'we expect from you that you know your language and care for it' (Halilović, 1996: 7). In the state of Bosnia-Herzegovina there are now three emotionally loaded standards in use in the public domain. Although differences are being accentuated – especially on the level of lexicon and script – these differences do not exclude mutual comprehension.

State-controlled media and the school system were seen in the newly-founded states as a means of implementing the national languages, not only by using the new emerging standards but even more by transporting and amplifying metalinguistic discourses that linked 'correct' language use to national loyalty, and stigmatized 'wrong' language use as 'yugos-nostalgic'. Metalinguistic discourses that amalgamated political statements, philological positions and folk beliefs about language were also spread through advice columns which flourished in the media and created a policing environment. School authorities immediately started to implement new curricula and to publish new school manuals. In Bosnia-Herzegovina Serbian and Croatian authorities mainly drew on material published in the 'motherlands' and only partly developed their own materials. Bosnian authorities produced manuals for their sphere of influence.

In the national euphoria language boundaries had to be drawn, the unitary languages had to be brought into existence and needed to be policed. The unitary language, as Bakhtin (1934/1981: 270) formulates it, 'is not something given (*dan*) but is always in essence posited (*zadan*) – and at every moment of its life it is opposed to the realities of heteroglossia' and 'gives expression to forces working toward concrete verbal and ideological unification and centralization, which develop in vital connection with the process of sociopolitical and cultural centralization.' Despite the considerable pressure and the centralizing efforts even in public language use, the 'reality of heteroglossia' could not be wiped out. Even during the war, oppositional and independent media like Feral Tribune in Croatia or Oslobodjenje in Bosnia-Herzegovina allowed a plurality of voices and styles and took part in metalinguistic discourses with a critical and often sarcastic tone (Busch, 2004). Still, within the institutional context of the school environment a monolingual habitus is prevailing and 'wrong' language use can be sanctioned by social exclusion and school failure. In an expert discussion, we organized during the development of the school manual *Pogledi* the linguist Milan Šipka summarized: 'The problem is not that there are differences, but how these differences are experienced and how people identify with respect to these differences. The problem is not communication, but the symbolization of language.'

There are very few empirical studies on the change of language use in the space of former Yugoslavia and it is difficult to say how much the efforts to promote unitary languages have actually resulted in changes in daily language practices in the public sphere. Langston (1999) presents a study based on a corpus he obtained from text samples taken in 1996/97 from different Croatian media, which he compares to samples taken in 1985. He concludes: 'Noticeable changes in lexical usage in the Croatian media have indeed taken place since the break-up of the Yugoslav state, but on the whole they are relatively minor' (Langston, 1999: 188 f). It seems that even the state media that had been principal actors in spreading metalinguistic discourses in their daily practice differ from the proclaimed principles. As far as school manuals are concerned, there are analyses available that focus on discriminatory discursive practices and on stereotypes present in texts but they do not systematically draw attention to exclusive practices in language use which are equally discriminatory.[7] As school manuals have to pass revision and approbation procedures by school authorities it can be expected that often they not only comply with dominant and unitary discourses but also represent the unitary language proclaimed as the standard. In the manual *Pogledi*, designed for the whole of Bosnia-Herzegovina, we attempted to avoid this less visible form of exclusion by drawing as much as possible on original texts that represent the multi-voicedness of society.

Separatist Educational Policies in Post-war Bosnia-Herzegovina

Bosnia and Herzegovina (BiH) has yet to come to terms with its recent armed conflict. The effects of the conflict – which, at the time of writing, ended nine years ago – were devastating for the people of BiH. It is estimated that up to 250,000 were killed or were reported missing. Approximately half of the population were forced to leave their homes, either seeking refuge in another country or being displaced internally. Today's political situation in BiH is the result of the system upon which nationalist politicians agreed in the Dayton peace negotiations. Dayton was a means to end the war and one of the incentives to sign the agreement was to at least partly reward nationalist politicians and politics. Not surprisingly, nationalist politicians are still in control at several levels of government today. The

Dayton Peace Accords of 1995 left BiH with a rather complex structure. The agreement divides the state into two areas known as 'Entities' – the Federation of Bosnia and Herzegovina (FBiH) and the Serb Republic (Republika Srpska, RS). The BiH Constitution assigns to the central state legislative power over only a few areas, leaving all areas not expressively granted to the state level, including education, within the responsibilities of the two Entities. The result of this framework is a division of public authority on occasionally more than three levels (the central state, the Entities and several local levels) and makes BiH both an over- and under-governed state where 'too many layers of government accomplish too little' (Democratization Policy Institute, 2002: 2).

The structure of authority in FBiH is organized quite differently from that in RS. In FBiH, power is widely decentralized and devolved to 10 Cantons and the municipalities within these federal units. The situation in RS could not be more different. With the municipality and Entity levels, the RS constitution knows only two functional levels of authority. De facto, power is concentrated at the Entity level. This complex power structure in BiH is augmented even more by the too-many international actors, who often lack coordination and joint planning. Furthermore, the international community (IC) lacks its own policing mechanism, and seems to have insufficient oversight over local policing structures (see Democratization Policy Institute, 2002: 3). Domination of nationalist rhetoric in BiH politics has made the IC believe that inter-ethnic conflicts are the main obstacle in the peace process. However, inter-ethnic reconciliation is but one axis of the peace-building process. The other one concerns the transition from a one-party system to a multi-party system, from a socialist to a market economy (European Stability Initiative, 1999). The main nationalist parties, the Bosnian Croat HDZ, the Bosnian Serb SDS and the Bosniak SDA are struggling to keep their authoritarian powers, wealth and influence they had acquired during the war. As a result, eight years of international efforts of pushing the peace process forward have so far been only partly successful.

Within the existing political and social context, it is not surprising that BiH youth seek to leave the country, if given the opportunity to do so (United Nations in Bosnia and Herzegovina, 2003: 25). The enormous brain drain brought by the armed conflict between 1992 and 1995 could easily continue until prospects for a more prosperous future appear. School children and teachers, having been severely affected by the conflict, are still facing a variety of post-war problems today. These relate to poverty and a high unemployment rate (of parents or other care givers) amongst those returning after having been refugees, internal displacement, a weak infrastructure and a state of political and economic transition in general and within the education system more specifically. The state of the education system reflects the overall situation of fragmentation and uncertainty. The constitutional framework of BiH does not install any coordinating body or institution for education issues at state level. While a Ministry of Education and Science continues to exist at the level of the Federation, education policy and related legislative powers are primarily vested with the cantons. By contrast, education in RS is solely on the Entity level under the responsibility of a central Ministry of Education. Apart from the meetings of Education Ministers hosted by the Office of the High Representative (OHR) and recently by the Organization for Security and Cooperation in Europe (OSCE), there is very limited coordination between the Entities or among the cantons in the Federation.

Since Dayton did not set out any clearer or harmonizing regulations, education remained in the hands of nationalist politicians, who see education as a means of establishing three separate languages, cultures and histories (OECD, 2001: 7). Within these structures, three different curricula and sets of textbooks are in use in the territory of BiH. In particular, the so-called 'national subjects' like language and literature, history, arts, and even geography continue to be a matter of political debate. Despite several attempts of the international community to revise textbooks in terms of intolerance and offensive passages (partly by blacking-out words and sentences), textbooks still contain problematic passages and texts. The fact that the constitution recognises three official languages – Bosnian, Croatian and Serbian – has become a vehicle for a nationalistic agenda of separation of the education system. In practice, the language issue is often used as an argument that joint teaching of children with different national backgrounds is not viable (Council of Europe, 1999: 3f).

In RS, Serbian is prescribed as the medium of instruction. In the Federation, either Bosnian or Croatian is the official language of instruction, depending on the majority population in the respective area. While 'minority'[8] children may generally attend classes in the curriculum and language of the local majority with all its nationalistic elements (OECD, 2001: 16), in practice the politics of separation have led to two wide-spread phenomena in BiH education: the bussing of children to 'mono-ethnic' schools outside of their area of residence and the 'two-schools-under-one-roof' system. According to a working paper distributed by the OSCE entitled 'Education reform agenda: An update,' by June 2003 there were still 26 school buildings housing 52 schools. In these schools, separate Bosniak and Croat curricula were in use and separate administrative structures existed. Children (as well as teachers) had no mutual contact, used separate school entrances and had separate breaks and teachers did not share the same teacher's room.

The increasing numbers of returnees over the years raises further the issue of adequate education for minority children, including related questions of curriculum, textbooks and language of instruction. In March 2002, the international community urged the Entity education ministers to sign an 'Interim Agreement on Accommodation of Specific Needs and Rights of Returnee Children in Education'. The agreement stipulates that all children in both Entities shall be instructed in subjects of general education on the basis of the curriculum where they are presently living or in areas to which where they and their families return. Despite positive developments in certain areas, political obstruction has hampered wider-scale education reform in BiH over recent years. Since summer 2002, education reform in BiH has been coordinated by the OSCE. Under the authority of the Education Issue Set Steering Group (EISSG), made up of the heads of the major international organizations involved in education, working groups comprising local and international education experts are developing strategy papers, implementation plans or simply sharing information on ongoing reform projects.

As a first result of these coordinated activities, the BiH education authorities presented an Education Reform Agenda in November 2002, listing various goals for reform of the education system and proposed actions for the realization of these goals. Shortly before the end of the 2002/03 school year, the state parliament adopted a state-level framework Law on Primary and General Secondary Education. The law stipulates general education principles, which for the first time are to be applied in both Entities. In particular, the law contains provisions concerning human rights standards, horizontal and vertical mobility of students, country-wide recognition of diplomas, autonomy of schools and rights of parents and students within the school community. Since, as mentioned above, no specific education institution exists at the level of the state, the Ministry of Civic Affairs is in charge of the implementation of the framework law. In the future, Entity and canton education laws shall be harmonised with the framework law. In August 2003, the IC urged the twelve Entity and Canton Ministers of Education to sign an Agreement on a Common Core Curriculum for primary and general secondary education. According to the agreement, all students in BiH shall be taught in accordance with the Common Core Curriculum in the future.

Whether the new framework law, the common core curriculum and all related activities can bring about the hoped positive results still remains to be seen. Given the record so far, a certain skepticism prevails. Nevertheless, education reform in BiH seems to be slowly moving ahead. However, in its above-mentioned working paper the OSCE also recognizes a legitimate doubt that any positive momentum of change would not stagnate, if the international community does not push and significantly finance the reform agenda. Reform initiatives are hardly forthcoming from local authorities, which leaves the international community still as the main driving force behind the process.

Pogedi: A School Manual Based on Multi-Perspectivity and Multi-Voicedness

Within the described framework of three parallel education systems, and textbooks often providing biased information on the other nationalities, the NGO KulturKontakt Austria started in 1998/99 with a project aiming at the 'Development of Supplementary Teaching Material for Civic Education in BiH'. The project had the objective of counteracting the existing situation by making available integrative and multi-perspective teaching materials based on innovative didactics and methodology as well as contributing to inter-ethnic cooperation and tolerance. The result and final product of the project was a manual entitled *Pogledi: Open Teaching and Intercultural Learning*, which can be used in interdisciplinary lessons of language and literature, geography, history, arts, music and other subjects. Topics, methodological and didactic approaches of the book were defined and elaborated by a project team consisting of some 25 teachers, teacher trainers, principals, members of the pedagogic institute and NGO representatives in a series of workshops between 1998 and 2000. The development work of the local team was coordinated, advised and moderated by three Austrian experts[9] in the field of teacher training, intercultural and civic education and project work. Draft versions of the teaching units were tested in eight primary schools in Sarajevo and other towns, both in RS and the Federation. Consultations between the editorial team and the teachers involved in implementing the draft units ensured that valuable feedback from practice could still be considered for the final version of the book. Choosing the time consuming and intensive bottom-up approach offered the possibility of finding a viable compromise between what is desirable in terms of school-book development in a polarised post-conflict situation and what is feasible in terms of day-to-day practice.

The manual *Pogledi* consists of six teaching units dealing with the life of students between 13 and 15 years. Although each teaching unit is separate, there are some didactic and structural principles common to all six. The role of the student is conceived as active and creative, the teacher in this process is not only a mediator, but also an advisor and guide to the student on his or her way to greater independence. Consequently dialogic forms such as open learning or project-oriented learning dominate. Topics focus on supplementary information and skills development not contained in the existing textbooks, especially with regards to the facilitation of inter-ethnic understanding and cooperation. What makes *Pogledi* unique even in today's context, and different from other teaching material developed by or with the support of international organizations, is that the book exists in only one single form. Whereas other materials are/were printed in three different versions, namely in Bosnian, Croatian and Serbian, there is only a single *Pogledi* version for upper primary and secondary schools throughout the whole of Bosnia-Herzegovina, the Federation as well as the Republika Srpska. This was not achieved by inventing an 'interlanguage' or by reverting to the language in use in textbooks in the region before the outbreak of the war, but by representing a wide range of language actually in use in BiH today.

Following the principle of an open-learning curriculum, each of the six units contains a collection of material offered to the learners as a resource. The texts and other materials are reproduced in their original form; that is to say, no didactic or linguistic interventions were made. Literary texts form different periods of time are present as well as contemporary texts stemming from diverse sources such as the media, advertisements, leaflets and official publications. Generational differences in language use are as much apparent as differences in language use due to the rural–urban divide, to political orientation or to geographic location. Some texts, like the one taken from the *Official Bulletin of the Federation of BiH* or texts announcing jobs in more official settings, conform to the new standard. Media texts show considerable variation, and this is even the case for articles reprinted from papers that have appeared over the past few years. Whereas media close to the ruling party strive to employ a 'correct' and uniform standard, others (like the Sarajevo-based daily *Oslobođenje*) have a quite different editorial policy and leave it up to the authors to choose their own style (Busch, 2004). Texts written for commercial purposes frequently draw on elements from youth codes or on borrowings from other linguistic environments.

Although differences are visible, it becomes obvious that they are not a major obstacle to communication. Care was taken that every single unit itself comprises a very wide range of texts. Texts in German and English were also included in the *Pogledi* text collection, as many of the learners have connections with these languages, not only through school and the media, but also through their personal biography. Some have themselves spent some time in exile during the war years; most have family members living and working abroad. As far as the introductory essays are concerned and the description of goals and the didactic guidelines of the six teaching units, two of these were written in the Bosnian standard, two in the Croatian and two in the Serbian (one of which is written in Cyrillic). The *Pogledi* manual was officially presented in February 2001, was very well received throughout almost the whole BiH and was granted the status of approved teaching material. Between April and June 2001, more than 4500 copies of *Pogledi* were distributed to primary and secondary schools throughout BiH via the 12 Ministries of Education. Up to the end of 2002, 25 introductory workshops on how to use *Pogledi* had been held by members of the local project team in 20 towns in BiH, reaching approximately 600 teachers. Between May and September 2002, experiences with *Pogledi* and its achieved impact were evaluated among the participants of the introductory workshops.

Although the evaluation confirmed fears that the local authorities did not distribute the books to all schools in BiH, 86% of the teachers seem to have had access to *Pogledi*. In bigger towns the distribution density is somewhat higher than in rural areas. Teachers, students and parents widely welcomed the new teaching material and its innovative approaches. Practice has shown that interdisciplinary teaching is possible in accordance with the existing curricula, despite certain difficulties. In the classrooms, the main focus was on small learning projects, and the various teaching methods proposed in the book. Especially when implementing these 'active learning' projects, teachers reported highly positive experiences with the students. In cases where teachers faced obstacles to using *Pogledi* in the teaching process, the problems mostly related to reluctant principals and school inspectors, poor cooperation of teacher colleagues, necessary adjustments of timetables and – despite their low-budget concept – to financing of the learning projects. Given the relatively short time between the circulation of the book and the evaluation, these figures are quite impressive.

Conclusions

Whether *Pogledi* has been successful in initiating a 'new learning culture' in BiH schools cannot be answered yet, and definitely varies from school to school. Overall, it can be argued that *Pogledi* has stood the test of practice. The teaching material developed and produced locally facilitates not only the introduction of new methods and didactics, but also the development of a new learning culture in those schools where it is used. Probably its biggest achievement lies in its contribution to fostering understanding in classrooms that have been under the influence of separatist politics for too long.

The basic principle that guided the development of *Pogledi* is that of a learner-centred approach. It aims at developing the ability to compare, evaluate, criticise and formulate one's own position. Neither as far as content is concerned nor on the level of language use was a normative approach taken. The idea was to make the multi-voicedness of society visible in all three dimensions which Bakhtin (Todorov, 1984: 56) described: heterology (*raznorečie*), i.e. the diversity of discourses, heteroglossia (*raznojazyčnie*), i.e. the diversity of language(s) and heterophony (*raznoglossie*), i.e. the diversity of individual voices. The idea is linked to the aspiration of counterbalancing mechanisms of exclusion and division. On the one hand, the individual learner will find him- or herself and their linguistic practices represented in at least some of the texts. On the other hand, they can find out for themselves that variation and difference is not necessarily a question of ethnicity or nationality, but depends on a range of other factors and does not necessarily hinder communication and understanding. Therefore *Pogledi* should be understood not as a manual that simply celebrates the colourful brightness of difference, but as a manual that has an emancipatory approach.

The manual *Pogledi* was designed for the specific post-conflict situation of Bosnia-Herzegovina, for a situation in which (national) language policies became a means of affirming national identities and of accentuating differences. In this process of disinventing and reconstructing standard languages according to new power aspirations and geometries, the intimate link between standard language and the nation state paradigm becomes evident. Reconfiguring borders and boundaries on a territorial and on a symbolic level also creates new minority-majority relations. In spite of the efforts of implementing a language policy that fosters a unitary national language via the education system and via the media, working with contemporary texts produced and used in everyday contexts shows that the *Lebenswelten* (life worlds) are heteroglossic. This is not only due to the processes of migration but also because information and communication flows have become more multi-directional.

The higher visibility of heteroglossia in some parts of the public domain is a phenomenon that can be observed in many countries. It coincides with a widely observed de-centring of the nation-state paradigm as the organizing principle in society. Some of the core functions that the nation state fulfilled in the past are now being delegated to other bodies on a supranational or a sub-national level or to the private sector. This can be observed especially in the field of media. Whereas in the past in Europe the idea of a national public sphere dominated, and media decisively contributed to the implementation and spread of national languages, in transnational, regional and private media increasingly 'impure' linguistic practices can be seen (Busch, 2004). Within the education system a monolingual habitus (Gogolin, 1994) still prevails, although teachers are confronted with classes in which children from heterogeneous language backgrounds learn together. This is not only the case in urban centres with their specific histories of migration, but also in areas such as border regions.

Concepts of language awareness, of the development of meta-linguistic skills – such as translation, transfer and the development of strategies of comprehension – are increasingly being recognised as interesting learning strategies. The development of learning materials which allow for difference and variation in an emancipatory sense could be especially fruitful in situations with a complex linguistic setting:

- for situations where language use (in spoken and/or written from) differs significantly from codified standard languages (as for example with Romany or the Nguni languages in South Africa);
- for so-called mother-tongue teaching in urban centres where children from larger language spaces than the national are taught in a common course (as in the case of Bosnia, Croatia and Serbia, or from the Maghreb and the Middle East);
- for border regions (such as Alsace) where the regional dialect is spread in a cross-border dimension, whereas the two standard languages when taught as isolated subjects do not seem to have much in common.

Overcoming the monolingual habitus in education is decisive when it comes to questions of school success or failure, of social inclusion or exclusion.

Notes

1. In the context of language, it is more appropriate to use the term 'space' than 'territory' of former Yugoslavia.
2. The second section was written by J. Schick in 2003, and refers to the situation in Boznia-Herzogovina at that time.
3. Ekavian and jekavian relates to the reproduction of the old Slavonic sound 'Jat', which can be reproduced as 'e' or 'je' – as in the word for river 'rijeka' (jekavian) or 'reka' (ekavian).
4. *Alternativna informativna mreža* (AIM), 13 Sept 1993. This example is also discussed in Bugarski (1995).
5. The fascist NDH state (Nezavisna Država Hrvatska/Independent Croatian State) introduced a language reform that aimed at marking the difference between a Serbian and a Croatian language. In the course of this reform, an

etymological orthography was propagated and internationalisms were labelled as serbisms.
6. Turcisms are terms from Turkish that have been incorporated into the language
7. R. Rosandić and V. Pesić (1994). A dossier on school books and stereotyping was compiled by the AIM network in July 1995 under the title 'rat knjigama' (see: http:www.aimpress.org).
8. Where the term 'minority' is used in the rest of this chapter, it does not refer to the concept of national minorites, but only to illustrate the relation in numerical terms of two (or more) national groups within a certain area. Bosniaks, Croats and Serbs are all constituent peoples of BiH and cannot be considered as national minorities in any part of BiH.
9. The following long-standing experts were involved in the project: Margarethe Anzengruber, teacher for history and German in Vienna; Brigitta Busch, then director of the Arbeitsstelle für Interkulturelle Studien of the Council of Europe in Klagenfurt; Dietmar Larcher, then Professor for Intercultural Studies at the University of Klagenfurt and head of the Boltzmann-Institute for Intercultural Education Research in Klagenfurt.

References

Bakhtin, M. (1934/1981) *The Dialogic Imagination* (M. Holquist, ed.). Austin, TX: University of Texas Press.

Bourdieu, P. (1982) *Ce que parler veut dire: L'économie des échanges linguistiques*. Paris: Fayard.

Brodnjak, V. (1993) *Razlikovni rjeènik srpskog i hrvatskog jezika*. Zagreb: Hrvatska sveuèilišna naklada.

Bugarski, R. (1995) *Jezik od mira do rata*. Beograd: Slovograph.

Bugarski, R. (2004) Language and boundaries in the Yugoslav context. In B. Busch and H. Kelly-Holmes (eds) *Language Discourse and Borders in the Yugoslav Successor States* (pp. 21–38). Clevedon: Multilingual Matters.

Busch, B. (2004) *Sprachen im Disput: Medien und Öffentlichkeit in mutlilingualen Gesellschaften*. Klagenfurt: Drava.

Busch, B. and Kelly-Holmes, H. (2004) Language boundaries as social, political and discursive constructs. In B. Busch and H. Kelly-Holmes (eds) *Language Discourse and Borders in the Yugoslav Successor States* (pp. 1–13). Clevedon: Multilingual Matters.

Council of Europe (1999) *Education in Bosnia and Herzegovina: Governance, Finance and Administration*. Strasbourg: Council of Europe.

Democratization Policy Institute (2002) *An Agenda for Bosnia's Next High Representative*. On WWW at http://www.anonime.com/dpinstitute/europe/balkans/bosnia_and_hercegovina/20020501_bosnia_agenda.pdf. Accessed 01.12.03.

Dragičević-Šešić, M. (2001) Borders and maps in contemporary Yugoslav art. In N. Švob-Đokić (ed.) *Redefining Cultural Identities* (pp. 71–87). Zagreb: Institute for International relations.

European Stability Initiative (1999) Reshaping international priorities in Bosnia and Herzegovina: Part I, Bosnian Power Structures. On WWW at http://www.esiweb.org/reports/bosnia/showdocument.php?document_ID=4. Accessed 1.12.03.

Gogolin, I. (1994) *Der monolinguale Habitus der multilingualen Schule*. Münster: Waxmann.

Halilović, S. (1996) *Gnijezdo lijepih reci: Pravilno – nepravilno u bosanskome jeziku*. Sarajevo: Bastina.

Hodžić, A. (2000) Preoccupation with the 'other'. In N. Skopljanac Brunner, S. Gredelj, A. Hodžić and B. Krištofi? (eds) *Media & War* (pp. 19–41). Zagreb and Belgrade: Centre for Transition and Civil Society Research, Agency Argument.

Iveković, R. (2001) *Autopsie des Balkans: Ein psychohistorischer Essay*. Graz, Wien: Literaturverlag Droschl.

Jakšić, B. (2001) The disintegration of Yugoslavia and the division of language. Unpublished paper presented at the International Conference Slanugae-Society-History: The Balkans. Thessaloniki, 11–12 November.

Langston, K. (1999) Linguistic cleansing: Language purism in Croatia after the Yugoslav break-up. *International Politics* 36, 179–201.

Neweklowsky, G. (2000) Serbisch, Kroatisch, Bosnisch, Montenegrinisch: Perspektiven. In L. Zybatov (ed.) *Sprachwandel in der Slavia: Die slavischen Sprachen an der Schwelle zum 21. Jahrhundert* (pp. 543–559). Frankfurt/Main: Peter Lang Verlag.

OECD (Organization for Economic Co-operation and Development) (2001) *Thematic Review of National Policies for Education – Bosnia and Herzegovina, Stability Pact for South Eastern Europe*. CCNM/DEELSA/ED 3.

Okuka, M. (1998) *Eine Sprache, viele Erben. Sprachenpolitik als Nationalisierungsinstrument in Ex-Jugoslawien*. Klagenfurt: Wieser.

Pavuna, S. (1993) *Govorimo li ispravno hrvatski? Mali razlikovni rjeènik*. Zagreb: Integra.

Pogledi (2000) *Pogledi: Otvorena nastava i interkultuuralno ucenje. Materijal i upute*. (2000) Sarajevo: Kulturkontakt.

Puhovski, Ž. (2000) Hate silence. In N. Skopljanac Brunner, S. Gredelj, A. Hodžić and B. Krištofić (eds) *Media & War* (pp. 41–53). Zagreb and Belgrade: Centre for Transition and Civil Society Research, Agency Argument.

Rosandić, R. and Pesić, V. (1994) *Ratništvo, Patriotizem, Patrijarhalnost*. Beograd: most.

Škiljan, D. (2001) Languages with(out) frontiers. In N. Švob-Ðokić (ed.) *Redefining Cultural Identities* (pp. 87–101). Zagreb: Institute for International relations.

Todorov, T. (1984) *Mikhail Bakhtin: The Dialogic Principle*. Manchester: Manchester University Press.

United Nations in Bosnia and Herzegovina (2003) *Youth in Bosnia and Herzegovina 2003. Are You Part of the Problem or Part of the Solution?* On WWW at http://www.undp.ba/publications/Youth%20in%20BiH.pdf.

Wodak, R., de Cillia, R., Reisigl, M. and Liebhart, K. (1999) *The Discursive Construction of National Identity*. Edinburgh: Edinburgh University Press.

Chapter 10
After Disinvention: Possibilities for Communication, Community and Competence

SURESH CANAGARAJAH

So where do we go from here? Once we acknowledge that languages are inherently hybrid, grammars are emergent and communication is fluid, we are left with the problem of redefining some of the most basic constructs that have dominated the field of linguistics. It appears that matters like linguistic identity, speech community, language competence and even language teaching are based on constructs of homogeneity and uniformity that we have invented over time. Once these closed systems are taken away, we are confused as to how we can practice language communication.

In a move that will sound paradoxical, I want to argue that in order to find answers for the new questions that emerge after disinvention we have to return to precolonial/premodern societies and the ways language communication was practiced then. In some senses, this is not surprising. It is modernism (and the related movements of colonization and nationalism) that inspired the movement for inventing languages. These movements considered the fluidity and hybridity in precolonial forms of communication a problem and strove to move toward codification, classification and categorization that mark the field of linguistics today. Though post-modernism and post-colonialism have generated a healthy critique of these movements of disciplinary invention (see Hall, 1997; Mignolo, 2000), there is a lot to learn from precolonial communities on how to move forward in addressing the new forms of communication and community that are evolving in contemporary society.

Borrowing from this tradition doesn't mean that we can adopt premodern linguistic practices wholesale. We have to adapt those values and practices to contemporary social conditions. In fact, we have additional resources in the postmodern world to practice these values in more creative and complex ways. So, for example, while premodern societies in my own locale in South Asia interacted with a few communities living in physical proximity – those speaking Tamil, Sinhala, Malay, Pali and Sanskrit, for example – we can interact with more diverse communities now. In addition to the fact that migration and relocation have thrown distant communities into close proximity, we enjoy the resources of the digital and electronic media to force multilingual interaction. Furthermore, the new technologies also provide expanded modes for mixing our semiotic resources to make communication more efficient (see Cope and Kalantzis, 2000; Gee, 2000). Therefore, we have to imaginatively apply the linguistic values and practices of the past to present day conditions.

Before I outline some of the possibilities for communication, competence and community after disinvention, it is important to state where I am drawing my inspiration from. Many Asian, African and Latin American scholars are rediscovering the ways communication took place in pre-colonial times in their locality. Consider what Khubchandani lists as the dominant traits of indigenous communication in the South Asian context – 'the essence of Indian plurality:

(1) fuzziness of language boundaries;
(2) fluidity in language identity;
(3) identity claims versus language communication; and
(4) complementarity of intra-group and inter-group communication.'

(Khubchandani, 1997: 87)

The implications are profound. Local people are so multilingual, interacting with many language groups in the neighboring villages, that it is difficult to say where one language/group begins and the other ends. In fact, there is so much rampant code switching and mixing that western scholars like John Gumperz developed these constructs of multilingual communication from early fieldwork in India. Kubchandani (1997: 84) argues elsewhere that 'community' for local people was based not on unitary languages, but a shared space where many languages live together. In other words, community was conceived in spatial terms, not in linguistic or cultural terms. Therefore, people in India still have difficulties identifying themselves in terms of one language (see Singh, 1998). In each successive census they declare their first languages differently. Moving on to items (3) and (4) in the list, Kubchandani implies that local people managed to keep in tension and to dynamically negotiate competing claims such as identity/communication and inter/intra-group communication without letting them become a source of conflict and disharmony. Their language practices were based on negotiation rather than on fidelity to unitary constructs.

I would like to discuss the options ahead for communicating in English as an International Language. We have made much headway in recognizing English as a 'family of languages' (Crystal, 2004: 40). Linguists now acknowledge that all the varieties of English are equally functional in the postmodern world, jostling against/with each other in complex ways. In fact, the very demography of English is changing, proving that postcolonial speakers of English are more in number and that the language is used more in non-native contexts (see Graddol, 1999). The new models of English posited by scholars like MacArthur (1987) and Modiano (1999) show traditionally dominant varieties such as British or American English sharing the same status as newer varieties such as Chinese English or Bangladeshi English. There are already projections by applied linguists that 'It may not be many years before an international standard will be the starting-point, with British, American and other varieties all seen as optional localizations' (Crystal, 2004: 40). The problem, however, is that scholars still see a need for a new common system to enable communication between the different English-speaking communities. There are research undertakings for discovering a lingua franca English (LFE), made up of common elements in the emergent varieties, with traditional native varieties treated as the standard for comparison. Scholars such as Seidlhofer (2004) conceive of LFE as a common dialect that speakers of World Englishes can use to facilitate communication among each other. However, this activity smacks of another form of invention with the traditionally dominant varieties continuing to enjoy power. Can we move towards a radical pluralism, whereby speakers of all local varieties can negotiate their differences for effective communication (and compare Pennycook in Chapter 4)?

To move toward this ideal, we have to first conceive of an English-speaking community that is not based on commonalties. For a long time speech communities have been formed around shared features. The first obvious candidate for this commonality was a shared language or at least a shared grammar system. Needless to say, these communities have been linguistic utopias (Pratt, 1991), positing a commonality that is non-existent. Some may say that linguistic utopias are oblivious to differences and may even suppress differences. But the formation of post-modern multilingual communities has inspired other ways of conceiving community. As people from diverse locations now share the same geographical space, scholars are asking themselves:

> Can there be communities without the guarantees of stability? Is the essence of a common language and shared history the only guarantee for a collective identity? ... Communities overlap, abut and adjoin to each

other. What holds them together can rarely be identified by unique values or an exclusive set of characteristics. (Papastergiadis, 2000: 196–197)

This scholar's answer sounds mystical as he posits:

We need to explode the myth of pure and autonomous communities, reject the earlier mechanistic and territorial models of community and present new perspectives on the concepts of space and time which can address the dynamic flows that make community life. There is a need to take a more processual view of power and agency, to note that communities are not just dominated by rigid structures and fixed boundaries but are like a 'happening'. (Papastergiadis, 2000: 200)

This model is not so idealistic when we think of present-day diaspora communities and precolonial multilingual communities. In precolonial times, when Tamils, Sinhalese, Moors and Veddhas lived side by side, this is how they formed communities. They enjoyed overlapping communities, often constructed temporarily for pragmatic immediate purposes. So, for example, there are 'communities' in markets, schools and worship places where speakers of different languages would gather to accomplish common objectives. We have to now imagine how speakers of different varieties of English may form such communities in the postmodern world. Different domains of activity may bring speakers of different varieties of English together to accomplish their purposes.

But how do these speakers communicate efficiently, even for temporary periods, if a common grammatical system is not shared? Here we can learn from the notion of *communities of practice* that enables us to posit shared pragmatic strategies without having to invent common centralized codes (Hensel, 1996; Wenger, 1998). From this perspective, what speakers need are ways of negotiating difference rather than codes that are shared with others. Here, again, these are the ways in which multilingual communities (who came with codes that were widely disparate, compared to the varieties of English we are considering here) interacted with each other in precolonial South Asia. Some pragmatic strategies are as follows: varieties:

- code-switching, crossing (Rampton, 1995);
- speech accommodation (Giles, 1984);
- interpersonal strategies: i.e. repair, rephrasing, clarification, gestures, topic change, consensus-oriented, mutually supportive (Gumperz, 1982; Seidlhofer, 2004);
- attitudinal resources: i.e. patience, tolerance and humility to negotiate differences (see Higgins, 2003).

Consider how these pragmatic strategies would help communication between people with different varieties of English or even different languages. As we all know, through code-switching people may strategically deploy even a few tokens from another language to enable communication. Multilingual people come with the communicative competence to interpret these acts of code alternation without being confused by them. Speech accommodation is another strategy that enables multilingual people to inch closer to one another, making modifications in their speech in deference to the other, even as they stretch themselves to understand the difference of their interlocutors. Moving beyond language-based practices, we can even consider social interactional strategies that help communicate through difference. As we can see from the list above, these strategies are not related to the use of codes as in the previous strategies. These are largely extra-linguistic practices that multilingual people use to communicate with each other. In the same vein, we can consider psychological resources that help communicate through difference. Higgins (2003) reports on an interesting research with small groups of native and non-native students, negotiating differences in English language varieties. She finds that non-native students are more successful in interpreting the meanings of words from diverse varieties as they bring attitudinal resources that help them do so. I would argue that these attitudes are the cultural capital of multilingual people, developed through history. Monolinguals fail to develop these resources as they assume the need for similarity in order to enable communication. Certainly, in postmodern communication, such practices are widely in use as speakers from diverse cultures and languages are compelled to interact with one another and achieve common objectives even if they don't share common languages.

If this is the evolving shape of communities and communication in a world of disinvented languages, how do we proceed with language teaching? How do we develop competence in new languages or varieties of English? As is evident in the previous paragraph, we have to develop negotiation strategies among our students. We have to train them to assume difference in communication and orientate them to sociolinguistic and psychological resources that will enable them to negotiate difference. This means that we have to move away from an obsession with correctness. Correctness usually assumes the existence of a common/legitimate core of grammar that can only come about through the practices of invention discussed in this book. This also means that, rather than focusing on rules and conventions, we have to focus on strategies of communication. This shift will enable our students to be prepared for engagement in communities of practice and collaboratively achieve communication through the use of pragmatic strategies. Our pedagogical objective is not to develop mastery of a 'target language' (that cliché in our field), but to develop a repertoire of codes among our students. We have to develop the sensitivity to decode differences in dialects as students engage with a range of speakers and communities. What would help in this venture is the focus on developing a metalinguistic awareness. For this purpose, we have to shift our attention from mastery of grammar rules, which is the traditional focus of language classrooms. Developing the sensitivity to an intuitive understanding of the way linguistic communication works would help students better in the postmodern world to work through/with the fluidity in codes that they see around them. Through all this, we are helping students shuttle *between* communities, and not to think of only joining *a* community. The latter was the focus in all language teaching. We created the expectation that by learning another language the students would ideally become insiders to a community. We now know that communities don't work that way. There are no permanent insiders or outsiders anymore. All of us are engaged with each other for specific objectives and then disband and form new communities for other needs.

To develop this pluralistic orientation to community, communication and competence, we need to encourage a greater flow of local knowledge from different localities (see Holliday, in press). The wisdom of language practices in precolonial communities shouldn't be ignored. We have to learn how communication worked in contexts of rampant multilingualism and inveterate hybridity in traditional communities, before European modernity suppressed this knowledge in order to develop systems of commonality based on categorization, classification and codification.

References

Cope, B. and Kalantzis, M. (eds) (2000) *Multiliteracies: Literacy Learning and the Design of Social Futures*. London: Routledge.
Crystal, D. (2004) *The Language Revolution*. Cambridge: Polity.
Gee, J.P. (2000) New people in new worlds: Networks, the new capitalism and schools. In B. Cope and M. Kalantzis (eds) *Multiliteracies: Literacy Learning and the Design of Social Futures* (pp. 43–68). New York: Routledge.
Giles, H. (ed.) (1984) The dynamics of speech accommodation. *International Journal of the Sociology of Language* 46 (Special topic issue).
Graddol, D. (1999) The decline of the native speaker. *AILA Review* 13, 57–68.
Gumperz, J.J. (1982) *Discourse Strategies. Interactional Sociolinguistics* 1. Cambridge: Cambridge University Press.
Hall, S. (1997) The local and the global: Globalization and ethnicity. In A.D. King (ed.) *Culture, Globalization and the World System* (pp. 19–40). Minneapolis, MN: University of Minnesota Press.

Hensel, C. (1996) *Telling Our Selves: Ethnicity and Discourse in Southwestern Alaska*. New York: OUP.
Higgins, C. (2003) 'Ownership' of English in the Outer Circle: An alternative to the NS/NNS dichotomy. *TESOL Quarterly* 34/3, 615–644.
Holliday, A. (in press) *The Struggle to Teach English as an International Language*. Oxford: Oxford University Press.
Khubchandani, L.M. (1997) *Revisualizing Boundaries: A Plurilingual Ethos*. New Delhi: Sage.
McArthur, A. (1987) The English languages? *English Today* 11, 9–13.
Mignolo, W.D. (2000) *Local Histories/Global Designs: Coloniality, Subaltern Knowledges, and Border Thinking*. Princeton: Princeton University Press.
Modiano, M. (1999) Standard English(es) and educational practices for the world's lingua franca. *English Today* 15 (4), 3–13.
Papastergiadis, N. (2000) *The Turbulence of Migration*. Cambridge: Polity Press.
Pratt, M.L. (1991) Arts of the contact zone. *Profession 91*, 33–40. New York: Modern Language Association.
Rampton, B. (1995) *Crossing: Language and Ethnicity among Adolescents*. London: Longman.
Seidlhofer, B. (2004) Research perspectives on teaching English as a lingua franca. *Annual Review of Applied Linguistics* 24, 209–239.
Singh, R. (ed.) (1998) *The Native Speaker: Multilingual Perspectives*. New Delhi: Sage.
Wenger, E. (1998) *Communities of Practice*. Cambridge: Cambridge University Press.

Index

Authors

Aaby, 16, 149
Agar, 173-4
Ahearn, 188
Albert, 158
Alexander, 80-1
Alisjahbana, 48, 52-4, 56-7
Anderson B., 7-8, 11, 15, 18, 50-1, 57, 98, 105
Anderson, P., 174
Anwar, 48, 56-7
Appadurai, 11, 99, 101
Arievitch, 175, 188
Armstrong, 122-3, 125
Auroux, 142, 146, 148, 153

Badudu, 57
Bailey, 100
Baker, C., xiii
Baker, H., 201
Bakhtin, 171, 187, 217, 221, 229
Bakhurst, 171
Barros, 141, 143-4, 147, 149, 152,
Barthes, 95-6, 109
Barton, 154
Barwise, 179
Bauman, 2, 17-8, 22, 25, 27, 140, 147, 149-50, 156
Becker, 51, 55-7, 171, 173
Beier, 159
Benjamin, 54
Benson, 76
Bernstein, 72
Bhabha, 136-9, 141, 145, 156-7, 163, 165
Blommaert, 3, 6, 18, 22, 27, 94
Boas, 135, 147-50, 156, 173
Bourdieu, 116-7, 121, 126-7, 129-32, 161, 172, 218-9
Bouvet, 123
Bowerman, 176
Branson, 20, 124, 126, 129, 131, 132 (fns 2, 4, 6, 7)
Breckenridge, 73
Breton, 71

Briggs, 2, 17-8, 22, 25, 27, 140, 147, 149-50, 156
Brodnjak, 220
Brown, 13
Bruner, 160-1
Bruthiaux, 102, 105
Brutt-Griffler, 28
Bugarksi, 217
Burde, 4, 104-5
Busch, 219, 221, 227, 230
Butler, 110, 112
Bybee, 182

Camargo, 153
Canagarajah, xiii, 18, 27, 108
Canguilhem,
Carneiro, 155
Carter, 79, 174, 177
Castro, 158
Cavalcanti, 164
Chaiklin, 175
Chakrabarty, 135-6, 138-9, 165
Chimhundu, 1, 13, 70, 76
Choi, 176
Chomsky, 92, 170-1, 173-5, 177, 185
Clastres, 160
Cohn, 5-6, 12, 66, 68-9
Cole, 173
Collins, 171
Comaroff & Comaroff, 16
Cook, 73, 81-82, 84
Cope, 234, 238
Coquery-Vidrovitch, 82-3
Crowley, 68, 173
Crystal, 26, 64, 100-1, 235
Cunha, 155

Dalby, 64
D'Angelis, 153-4
Danziger, 27, 63, 70
Dasgupta, 105
Davydov, 171
de Beaugrande, 75-6, 79

240

de Saussure, 121, 173
Debose, 198-9
Degraff, 20, 31, 106
Derrida, 155, 158
Dirlik, 136-7, 166
Dixon, 94-5, 98
Djite, 65-7, 70
Doke, 73
Dragičević-Šešić, 218
Dwyer, 74

Eckert, 204
Eco, 122
Ehret, 28
Elkins, 157
Engeström, 175, 189
Errington, 15-6, 44, 68, 83

Fabian, 12, 16, 28, 30, 66, 74, 136
Falola, 82
Fanon, 24, 75
Fauconnier, 173-4
Fausto, 161
Ferreira da Silva, 140
Foucault, 17, 77, 112, 116, 131, 172, 188-9
Frawley, 176
Freire, 141

Gal, 1-2, 69
Gardner-Chloros, 83, 85
Garfinkel, 172, 179-80
Gates, 208
Gee, 197, 204, 234
Geertz, 18
Gentner, 176
Giles, 236
Gilyard, 210
Goldin-Meadow, 176
Goldsworthy, 55
Goodwin, 181
Goody, 154
Gopnik, 186
Grace, 2, 16, 31, 35, 79-80
Graddol, 235
Greenberg, 64
Greenblatt, 140, 149
Grierson, 9-10
Grin, 102
Gumperz, 84, 176, 234, 236
Guss, 158
Guthrie, 68

Habermas, 180
Halilović, 221

Halim, 54
Hall, 29, 233
Halliday, 170, 186, 197
Hanks, 171-2, 177, 180, 187
Hardt, 6, 101
Harries, 1, 73-4
Harris, 3, 18-9, 35, 80, 93, 108, 120, 154, 183
Herbert, 70
Heritage, 179
Higgins, 236-7
Hill, 11
Hobsbawm, 5-6
Hodžić, 218
Holborow, 105
Hopper, xi, 34, 109-10, 172, 177, 182-4, 185-6
Hornberger, 28
Hvalkof, 16, 149
Hyden, 77

Illich, 46, 53, 57
Inoue, 1, 28
Irvine, 1, 2, 20, 69, 74-5
Iveković, 219

Jacquemet, 30, 85
Jaffe, 2, 9
Jakšić, 220
Janks, 103
Jeater, 24, 78
Jones, 171
Joseph, 2, 7-8, 111, 172

Kachru, 100, 104-5, 108
Kalantzis, 234
Kandiah, 109
Kant, 92
Kartodirdjo, 48
Keifenheim, 158
Kelley, 202
Kembo-Sure, 69
Kress, 155
Krishnaswamy, 4, 104-5
Kroskrity, 3, 18-20, 94
Kuzar, 1, 13, 23
Kyeyune, 17

Lagrou, 158
Langston, 220, 222
Lantolf, 175, 190
Latour, 17, 172
Le Page, 110
Lee, 187
Leeman, 11

Leite, 145
Lelyveld, 10
Leontiev, 175
Levinson, 176
Levi-Strauss, 174
Linell, 180
Lopes da Silva, 156
Lott, 200
Lucy, 176
Ludden, 10
Luria, 176
Lysandrou & Lysandrou, 102

MacGonagle, 73
MacWhinney, 182
Major, 200
Makoni, 4, 13, 15, 24, 27-8, 29, 63, 66, 69, 73, 77, 107, 172, 188
Malinowski, 99, 178
Mamdani, 8, 15, 24
Mann, 64
Mannheim, 1
Masagara, 67
Mashiri, 78
Masolo, 85
Matthiesen, 170
Mawadza, 78
Mazrui A., 4, 78
Mazrui, A.M., 78
McCarthy, 79, 174, 177
McGinn, 178-9
McMahon, 124-5
Meinhof, 15, 24, 27, 68, 79, 188
Meltzoff, 186
Menezes de Souza, 154
Mignolo, 16, 101, 135-6, 138-40, 145, 156, 165, 233
Miller, D., 20, 124, 126, 129, 131, 132, fns 2, 4, 6, 7
Miller, G., 175
Milroy, 97
Modiano, 235
Moedjanto, 48
Moeliono, 48, 57
Monserrat, 145-6
Morgan, 197-8, 203
Mudimbe, 4, 71
Mufwene, 81, 106-7, 109
Mühlhäusler, 3, 11, 18-9, 65, 92, 106, 129-31
Mvula, 67

Ndebele, 90
Negri, 6, 101
Nettle, 26

Neweklowsky, 217
Ngom, 81-2, 84
Njoroge, 65

Okuka, 220
Ong, 119, 121, 154

Papastergiadis, 236
Parakrama, 104-5, 107-8
Paranjape, 136
Pattanayak, 12
Peirce, 172, 181, 182
Pennycook, 15, 25, 30, 100-1, 104, 172
Perrow, 200
Perry, I., 205
Perry, J., 179
Phillipson, 66, 90, 101
Pike, 15, 149-50, 156, 165-6
Pinker, 170
Poedjosoedarmo, 44, 54
Povinelli, 3, 23, 31
Prah, 75, 81
Pratt, 235
Prawat, 187
Pringgodigdo, 47-8
Prinsloo, 76, 79
Puhovski, 218

Rafael, 14-5, 26
Rajagopalan, 23
Ramanathan, 103
Rampton, 236
Ranger, 4-7, 25, 70, 73, 75, 77
Razack, 162
Reagan, 30, 91
Renault-Lescure, 158
Richardson, 197
Rickford, 198
Rigg, 50, 55
Roberts, 205
Robinson, 200
Romaine, 11-2, 26
Rommetveit, 172, 179-82
Rosa, 141

Said, 2, 7, 74-5
Salanova, 153
Salm, 82
Samarin, 14
Saussure, de, 121, 173-4
Sawchuk, 188
Schegloff, 171
Schieffelin, 26
Schryver, 76, 79

Searle, 188
Sebba, 106
Seidlhofer, 235-6
Shadily, 47-8
Siegel, 45, 55
Silva, 153
Simatupang, 48
Sinclair, 79
Škiljan, 218
Skutnabb-Kangas, 11, 26
Smitherman, 199, 201-3, 210
Sonntag, 22-3
Spear, 6-7, 24
Spivak, 117, 128
Springer, 67
Santoso, 48
Stetsenko, 175, 188
Stokoe, 121, 123, 127
Street, 154
Stroud, xiv, 63, 70-1, 84
Summers, 63
Swain, 175

Tabouret-Keller, 110
Taylor, 172
Thomas, 2, 15, 23-4
Thorne, 171, 175, 184, 186, 188
Timpanaro, 173-4, 176
Toer, 45
Tollefson, 102-3
Tomasello, 172, 180, 184-6
Toolan, 19
Truddell, 63
Trudgill, 96
Turner, M., 173-4

Turner, T., 155

van der Veer, 73
van Lier, 174-5, 181
Vansina, 6
Vološinov, 171-3, 175, 180, 182, 185, 187
Vygotsky, 171, 175-6, 178, 180, 187

Wallerstein, 5, 46
Warmelo, 70
Wasik, 62-3
Watts, 97
Webb, 69-70
Weber, 9
Wells, 171
Whiteley, 65
Whorf, 172-3, 176
Widdowson, 79
Wiener, 129
Wilkinson, 45
Williams, C., xiii
Williams, G., 65, 83-5
Williams, R., 44, 51, 170
Willinsky, 93
Winchester, 92-3
Wittgenstein, 172, 177-9, 182, 187
Wolff, 44
Woolard, 8, 19, 99

Yngve, xi, 3, 17-9, 27, 62-4, 71, 81-2, 84

Zeleza, 4
Žižek, 98-9
Zoetmulder, 44
Zurbuchen, 53

Subject index

Abbé de l'Epée, 119
Aboriginal Australians, 4
– Aboriginal English, 107
activity theory, 189
– mediation, 188
Australia, 23
Africa, 1, 4, 14
– beliefs and practices, 199
– detribalized'/'trousered' Africans 24
– historiography, 6
– languages
  disinventing discourses of, 64
  English discourses on, 79
  as hermetically sealed units, 69
– linguistic map, 66
– linguistics & applied linguistics, 65, 76

– sociolinguistics, 71-2
– hybridity, 24
– *The Invention of Africa* (Mudimbe), 4, 71
– *The Invention of Tradition in Colonial Africa* (Ranger), 4-7
– literacy, 197
African American 34
– Black discourse, 197, 203
– music (AAM), 196-7
– Vernacular English (AAVE), 107, 197
Afrikaans, 1, 13, 84–
Alsace, 230
Anda, 52
anthropology,
– linguistic, 19
– and scientific methodology, 148

– and sociolinguistcs, 131
applied linguistics, 31, 37, 153
– and colonialism, 67, 75
– critical, 28
assessores, 146-7, 164
Auslan (Australian Sign Language), 124

bahasa, 42-3
Bahasa Indonesia, 13, 31, 45, 57
Bahasa Malay, 1, 45
Balinese sign language (Kata Kolok), 124
bangsa, 43
Bantu, 69
– proto-Bantu, 68
– ur-Bantu, 68
banyan tree, xi, 69
bilingual education, xii, 151
bilingualism, 77
– additive, 28
– transitional, 143
biological metaphors, 25
Bloomfield, 174
Boas, Franz, 147-50
Bosnian, 221, 224, 227-8
Brazil, 33, 135-169
Bulgarian, 217
Burundi, 67

Cartesian mind/body dualism, 121, 174
census ideology, 11-2, 16, 65
– countability, 10
Chibaba, 7
ChiChewa, 67, 72
ChiNyanja, 1
ChiShona, 67, 72-3, 75-6, 78
Chomsky, 92, 173, 185
– nativism, 174
Christianity, 14, 76
– Bible, 75
– civilization, 141
– conversion to, 141
– cosmology, 143
– *see also* missionaries
classifiers, 124
code-switching, xiii, 237
coevalness, 147
– denial of, 136, 138-43
collateral damage, 16, 31, 35-6
colonialism, 1
– British, 5, 72
– cultural constructs, 100
– European 8, 43
– images, 78
– imperialist tendencies, 117

– inventories, 66
– coloniality, 135
– *see also* missionaries
communicative
– action, 129
– activity, 171
– function, 186
– linguistics of communicative activity (LCA), 171
– repertoires, 183
– resources, 177
communities of practice, 236
community
– imagined 7-9
– spatial, 234
constructionism,
– discursive, 99
– historical, 98-9
– ontological, 98
– social 97-8
Côte d'Ivoire, 65
Creoles, 13, 20-1, 68, 106-7, 109
– creole exceptionalism, 20, 106
Croatian, 218-9, 224, 227-8
– media, 222
crossing, 236
Cyrillic script, 219, 220
cultural capital, 237
culture, 42, 44
– embodiment, 155
– enactment, 155
– non-normative, 160
– preservation, 151
– Deaf, 119

Descartes, 92, 121, 127, 174
development, 43, 50-1, 53-4
dialectic process, xi, 7-8
dialects, 9, 20
– continuum, 218
dictionaries, 92-3
– bilingual, 76
– as discourse, 75
– *Oxford English Dictionary*, 92-3
difference, 123, 165
discovery attitude, 6
discrimination, 106, 119, 120, 130, 204, 211
– stereotypes, 204, 211
disinvention, 111, 166, 188, 233
– of identity, 196
– invention, 6, 172
– language, xi, 64, 171, 187, 196, 237
– and reconstructon, 229
– tactics of, 139, 156, 165, 189

education, 126
- multilingual, 216
- school, xiv
- state-sponsored, 51
emergent grammar, xi, 110, 182-3
English, xiv, 63, 72, 90, 227, 234-5
- access to, 103
- and alleviation of poverty, 102
- and class, 102
- collusionary, delusionary and exclusionary effects of, 101
- construction of, 96
- counts of English speakers/users, 100
- as a delusionary language, 101-2
- as discursive field, 112
- as a divisive language, 103
- English medium, 103
- Englishing, xiv, 111
- as an exclusionary language, 103
- and global flows of culture and knowledge, 101
- as globalisation, 112
- hegemony of, 23
- heterogeny position, 104
- as human capital, 112
- as an imperial project, 93
- as an International Language (EIL), 32
  myth of, 104, 109
- as language of international communication, 100
- lingua franca English (LFE), 235
- mobilisations, 112
- as natural, neutral and beneficial, 100
- as neoliberalism, 112
- other Englishes, 107, 109
- pluralisation of English(es), 90, 104, 107
- putting into discourse, 104
- as a second language, 36
- standard English, xii, 96-7
  myth of, 97
- Test of English as a Foreign Language (TOEFL), 35
- World Englishes, 104-5, 235
  concentric circle model, 105
enumeration of languages, xiii, 2, 12, 64
- enumerative strategies, 11, 16
- enumerative modality, 66
epilinguistics, 142, 146, 148, 153
Ethnologue, 11
ethnomethodology, 179
Eurocentrism, 130, 135
- epistemology, 74, 77-8
- linguistics, 160
- phonocentrism, 155, 157-8

- traditions of grammatization, 162, 166
- Western cosmologies, 56, 117
- *see also* colonialism, linguistics

Fijian, 1, 14
fingerspelling, 121, 125
French, 9, 63

gamelan, 46
Garfinkel, 179
gender differences, 125
Germany, 227
gesture, 119, 123, 125
globalisation, 43, 52-3, 100-1, 216
glossematics, 121
governmentality, 2
grammar, 110
- as contingent upon its lexical environment, 184
- ellipsis and prolepsis 180-1
- emergent, xi, 110, 182-3
- epiphenomenal, 183
- fixed-code approach, 183
- grammaticality, 180
- grammatization, 162
- linguistic descriptions, 142
- nouns, and verbs 185
- power/knowledge relationship, 141
- as product of communication, 34
- pseudoclefts, 183
- strategic possibilities of the ungrammatical, 127
Guere, 67

Hallidayan tradition, 170
Hebrew, 1, 13
Herder, 24
heteroglossia, 216, 217, 221, 229
heterology, 229
heterophony, 229
hiphop, 34
- discourse, 196, 201
- as genre system, 202
- rap, 34
- semantic inversion, 203
history, 172
- critical historiography, 1, 28
- historical quality, 96
homogeneity, 101, 233
homonymy, 211
hybridity, 138, 233

iconicity, 118, 121
identity, acts of 110, 112

– Asian values, 53
– racial, 106
India, 12, 103
– invention of languages, 10
– *Survey of India* (Grierson), 9-10
indigeneity, 3
indigenous cultures, 149
– education, 139
– languages, xii, 15, 63, 68, 72, 78, 80, 83, 145
    shift away from, 82
    preservation of, 144, 151, 163
– literacy, 152
– oral tradition and orality, 139, 144, 147
– people, 23
    prenational selves, 23
    assimilation of, 142
– perspectivism, 158, 163
– turn, 157
Indonesian, 129
Inkha, 1
interdisciplinarity, 228
Israel, 1

Javanese, 44, 55

Kali'na, 158
Kaluli, 26
Kashinawa, 33, 158-9
Kata Kolok, 124-5, 127-8
– sociolinguistics of, 129
Kenya, 65
kinship networks, 124
Kitchen Kaffir, 67

language(s)
– abstract concepts, 125
– agentive acts, 110, 138
– as autonomous/separate, 10, 17-9, 35, 91, 94
– boundaries, 219, 221
    fuzziness of, 234
– cognitive and cultural connections, 176
– as culture, 118
– code-switching, xiii, 237
– contextualised understanding, 112
– desire, 103
– effects of, 22, 104, 109, 112
– endangerment of, 26
– enumerability of, xiii, 2, 12
– enumerative strategies, 11, 16
– as epistemic violence, 21, 35, 117, 127
– erasure, 1
– exceptionalism, 31
– family trees, 57, 68-9

– fictions, 17
– fluidity, 233-4
– fractal recursivity, 2
– heritage, 28
– heteroglossic nature of, 34, 216-7
– hierarchies within, 57
– iconization, 2
– ideal languages, 73
– ideologies of, 18, 35
– industrialised definitions of, 51, 57
– the institution of, 111
– as interlinguistic descriptions, 7
– in isolation, 62
– kidnapping of, 140
– langue & parole, 173
– linguistic descriptions of, 81, 144
– as locally derived, 112
– maintenance of, 3
– maps, 218
– materialisation, 22, 111- 112
– mobilisations, 109
– as a natural object, 171
– as negotiation, 34
– as an object of contemplation, 121
– performance, 173
– as practice, 123, 126
– pragmatics of, 35
– preservation, 11
– as a real object, 63
– reconstitution, xi, 3, 27-31
– reconstruction, 3
– reification of, 83
– relational-contextual tradition, 170
– repertoire of codes, xiii, 238
– as a resource, 80
– rights of, 22, 35
– sedimentation of forms, xi
– as a socially bound practice, 47
– and speech, 173
– spoken languages, 118
    multi-dimensional nature of, 119
– standard language ideologies, 97
– standardisation, 52-3
    normatization, 160
– status of, 64
– symbolization of, 222
– systematicity, 110
– target language, xiii
– translatability of, 57
– Western, 51
languageness, 32
languaging, xi, xiv
language acquisition, 186
– second, 36

language cleansing, 220
language continuum, 217-8
language games, 177-8
language-free communities, 14, 32, 35
language planning, 62, 64, 216
– nations, 45, 105, 216
– state-centric perspective of, 83
language testing, 35
– washback, 36
Latin, 15, 140, 145
Latin America, xii
Leibnitz, 92
lexicography, 76
– magna vocabulary, 79
linguanyms, 66
linguistic
– anthropology, 19
– borders, 218
– citizenship, xiv, 71
– communities, 131
– continuum, 199
– description 141
   impossibility of 94
– ecology, 129
– habitus, 130, 132 n8
– human rights, 71
– imperialism, xiii, 120
   research as, 128
– imposition, 74
– inventories, 74
– legitimacy, 119
– market, 204
– oppression, 117, 131
– pluralism, 235
– positivism, 94
– prescriptivism, 108
– purism, 220
– uniformity, 233
– utopias, 235
linguistics, 116
– Americanist tradition, 147, 149, 152
– analytic contradictions, 171
– applied 31, 37, 153
– *assessores*, 145
– autonomous texts, xii, 2, 79
– collateral damage of, 16, 31, 35-6
– of communicative activity (LCA), 171
– comparative method, 68-9
– conventional, 123, 126, 130
– corpus, 79
– formalist 170, 180
– grammatic descriptions, *see* grammar
– historical, 28
– human, 19, 62-3

– integrational, 18-9, 35
– intellectualist philosophy, 121
– material effects of, 2
– objectivism, 68-9, 74, 150, 152
– oppression of minorities, 117, 130
– orthodoxy, 108
– paradox, 33
– phoneme, 141, 146, 152
– phonocentrism, 139, 155
– reallinguistik, 29
– scientism and rationalism, 131 , 144, 147, 173-4
– segregational, 11, 18
– sound-based, 128
– structuralism, 94-5, 174
– twentieth century, 172
– universalism, 42
– Western categories, 55, 122
literacy , 14, 33, 127-8, 151
– and citizenship, 151
– graphic, 175
– print, 75
– phonocentric concepts of, 166
– *see also* orality, writing
local knowledge, 20, 136-7, 160, 238
– community as spatial, 234
– contextualization, 159
– critical localism, 18, 137
– cultures of vision, 158
– localisation, 53
– predation and domestication, 161, 163
– production of locality, 99
– radical localism, 189
– Third World knowledges, 135
– truth-value as social, 159
Locke, 18
locus of enunciation, 16, 33, 136-8, 145

Macedonian, 217
Malawi, 65, 67, 72
Malay, 45
Marxism, 171, 176, 188
metadiscursive regime, 2, 16
metalanguage, 1, 55, 97-8, 166, 198
metalinguistics, 80, 142, 146, 148, 153, 219
– awareness, 238
– discourses, 221-2
– skills, 230
mime, 122
– mimesis, 118
– mimicry, 203
minstrelsy, 200
missionaries, 7, 26, 78, 140, 150, 153
– Jesuit, 139

– Swiss, 73
modernity, 18, 49, 136
– logic of, 140
– modernist move, 147, 150, 156
– and tradition, 49
monolingualism, 11, 77, 101
– habitus, 222, 230
– mono-ethnic schools 224
– pluralization, xii-xiii
mother tongue, xii, 12, 29, 164
– essentializing, 30
– education, 14, 22
multilingualism, xiii, 16, 22, 35, 80-1, 107, 234
– as pluralization of monolingualism, 22, 29, 80
– movement, 84
– networks, 71
multimodality, 157
multi-voicedness, 229
mutual comprehensibility, 107
myth, 95, 159
– Malinowskian charter, 99
– of origin, 98

naming,
– arbitrary relationship, 49
– *bobot*, weight of name, 49
– as descriptive and constitutive, 70
narrative, 154-5, 159-161
– narrativizing, 203
native speakers, 105
negotiation strategies, 237
neo-liberalism, 53, 90
New Order, 42
Nguni, 230
Niger-Congo, 69
Northern Sotho, 70

onomatopoeia, 209
ontology, 90-1, 116
– rational ontological arguments, 91
– St Anselm's ontological argument, 91
orality, 121, 149, 154
– performative and synaesthetic, 155
– verbal repertoire, 84
– and writing, 139, 149
orthography, 74, 153

Panopticon, 77
Papua New Guinea, 11, 26
performativity 110
phenomenology, 95
– of indirectness, 198

Philippines, 26
Pike, Kenneth, 149-50
pluralisation, 22
– pluricentricity, 104
– radical pluralism, 235
– strategies of, 108
Pogledi, 216, 222, 226-8
Portuguese, 152, 154, 159, 162
postcolonialism, 15, 24, 31, 105, 139, 165, 188, 235
– creolistics, 31
– precolonialism, 233, 236
– provincializing the West, 136
poststructuralism, 97, 112
– critical scholarship, 189
psycholinguistics, 175

Romany, 230
Runyakitara, 1
Rwanda, 67

Saussure, 33, 116, 121-2, 127, 173-4, 187
scientificity, 17, 19, 94, 116, 141
– empiricism 92
Scots, 5
sedimentation, 110, 182
semiotic reconstruction, 110, 112
Senegalese, 2
Serbian/ Croatian, 217, 219, 224, 227-8
– ekavian and jekavian variant, 220
SeTswana, 84
Shona, 1, 7, 24, 32
signs, 187
– arbitrariness 78, 118, 122-3, 127
– interpretant, 182
– Saussurian, 187
– signifier, megalomania of, 174
sign language, 13, 20-1, 32-33, 117-129
– devaluation of, 121
– fingerspelling, 121, 125
– radical linguistics of, 123
– and symbolic violence, 123
SiNdebele, 76
Slovenia, 217
sociolinguistics, 35, 47-8, 96, 109, 131
Soeharto, General, 48
South Africa, 27, 29, 66-7, 70, 73, 77
– constitution, 188
South Asia, 234
Soyinka, Wole, 4
Sapir-Whorf hypothesis, 176
Spanish, xii
– Spanglish, xiii
– standard, xii

speech accommodation, 236-7
style, 126
stylistic commons, 14
  inventories, 14
  marked discourses, 129
Summer Institute of Linguistics (SIL), 15, 141-3, 147, 149-50

Tagalog, 15-6
Tamil, 234
time and space
  – community as spatial, 234
  – concept of, 136
  – narrative of transition, 135-6, 141-4, 149, 155, 163
  – spatiality, 50, 138, 234
  – time and clocks, 50
Tsonga, 1, 24, 32, 73-5
Tsotsitaal, 84
Tswana, 24, 70
translinguistic practices, xiii,
  – translingual activism, 36
  – transidiomatic practices, 30, 36, 85
  – translation, 36
Tupi, 140, 145

Uganda, 72

vernacular, 46, 53
  – activity, 47
  – education, 103
  – literacy, 14
  – urban, xii, 26, 81-3, 85
Vološinov, 176
voodoo, 206
Vygotsky, 176
  – cultural-historical psychology, 175
  – cultural-historical tradition, 171
  – psycholinguistics, 177

Wittgenstein, 177-8
Wobe, 67
writing, 56, 118, 139, 152, 157, 164
  – as disembodied sound, 121
  – reducing languages to, 92
  – *see also* literacy, orality

Xhosa, 84

Yoruba, 14, 16, 24
Yugoslavia, 34, 217-9, 222

Zambia, 65
Zimbabwe, 7, 25, 70
Zulu, 84

For Product Safety Concerns and Information please contact our EU Authorised Representative:

Easy Access System Europe

Mustamäe tee 50

10621 Tallinn

Estonia

gpsr.requests@easproject.com

www.ingramcontent.com/pod-product-compliance
Ingram Content Group UK Ltd.
Pitfield, Milton Keynes, MK11 3LW, UK
UKHW022217250326

4937IPUK00005B/36